Something Better Than The Best

Vandergrift
Pennsylvania

Something Better Than The Best

The Story of America's First Successful, Worker-owned, Planned Community

Limited Edition ISBN 0-9652242-2-8
Hardcover ISBN 0-9652242-0-1
Softcover ISBN 0-9652242-1-X

The 1995 Vandergrift Centennial Committee, Inc., and
The Victorian Vandergrift Museum and Historical Society
Vandergrift, Pennsylvania USA
Published 1996.

804

Apollo Iron & Steel Company

GEORGE G. McMURTRY, President.
WILLIAM B. RHODES, Secretary.
WALLACE E. BACHE, Treasurer.

Represented in New York by
CHARLES D. FULLER,
139 GREENWICH STREET.

Pittsburgh, April 25th, 1895

OLMSTED, OLMSTED & ELIOT
REC'D. APR 27 1895
ACK'D. 27 telegram
ANS'D. 27th by
READ BY

Mr. Frederick L. Olmstead,

Brookline, Mass.

Dear Sir:

Our Company proposes to build a new town on a tract of land located a mile and a half below our present works (at Apollo, Pa.), comprising 640 acres of farm property. We desire to have a town that in many features will be unique, and in all respects more attractive than the average manufacturing town of the present day. In fact, we want something better than the best. We want to know - first, if you can undertake the laying out of this town for us, and in the second place, what are your terms for getting up the plans for a town of this character? Also, please say if you can come out here and look over the ground with us, and when you could do this. That is to say, how soon can you come out here? We are anxious to get this work started, and, of course, the quicker we could begin operations the better. We might say that we propose building a new works in this new town that will probably employ in the beginning fifteen hundred men. The property lies on the Kiskiminitas River, in Westmoreland County, Pa., and is considered one of the most available sites for a town lying within forty miles of Pittsburgh.

Awaiting your prompt reply, we remain,

Yours very truly,
Apollo Iron & Steel Co.
Wallace Bache Treasurer

OVER

Digitally Enhanced Image of Original Letter Sent to F. L. Olmsted by McMurtry's Company. Note McMurtry's Name (upper left) and the Company's Expectations of Olmsted.

Table of Contents

1995 Vandergrift Centennial Committee, Inc.

The Committee extends its thanks to the Mayor and Borough Council, which it served under, for its cooperation, financial assistance and support for the 1995 Centennial celebration Founded at the request of the Vandergrift Council President and Borough Secretary in late 1992, the 1995 Vandergrift Centennial Committee began public proceedings in January of 1993 and was officially designated the Borough's Centennial Committee in April, 1993. It completed its commission in Spring, 1996, with the publication of *Something Better Than The Best*, Vandergrift's history.

Borough of Vandergrift

County of Westmoreland

Commonwealth of Pennsylvania

Alan Mikula
Mayor

Jack Jewart
Council President

Council Members

Richard Arduino

Kathy Chvala

Janice Kamada

Vernon Sciullo

Lorelie Whaley

Guido Chierici

Jim Dunmire

Eugene Raschiatore

Taylor Troiano

Christine Wilson

Jeffrey Zinchini

Stephen DelleDonne
Borough Secretary

1995 VANDERGRIFT CENTENNIAL COMMITTEE
Board of Directors

In Memory Of
Honorable Joseph A. Petrarca
Honorary Chairman

Deann L. Cline
President
Mary Jane Slicker
Vice President

Alan Mikula
Secretary
Elizabeth Caporali
Treasurer

Board Members

Jack Jewart
Joanne Batiz
Richard Cowan

Robert H. Mills
Bernice McCutcheon
Stephen J. Myers, Jr.

Diana Barger and Janice Allman, previous Board Members

Larry Loperfito
Legal Counsel, Advisory Board Member

Centennial Sub-Committees

Children's Activities	Janice Kingirski
	Kim Stover
Community Picnic	Lorraine Poleski
Costume Ball	Jane Barger
Education	Sandra J. Shuster
	Jeffrey S. Garrett
Formal Ball	Barbara Ferrante
Fund Raising	Deann Cline
Hospitality	Ann Krafick
	Adeline Maraffi
Independence Day	Deann Cline
	Lenny Collini
Parade	Deann Cline
	Betsy Horvat
Physical Arrangements	Beth Caporali
Promotional Items	Dan Albert
	Dick Cowan
Public Relations	Stephen J. Myers, Jr
Religious Heritage	Robert H. Mills
Sports Organization	Jay Santora

Acknowledgments

Something Better Than The Best is a work of the Education Sub-Committee of the 1995 Vandergrift Centennial Committee, co-chaired by Sandra J. Shuster and Jeffrey S. Garrett. In the spirit of George McMurtry's Vandergrift, this book represents the work of many who joined together in an unselfish labor of love. Community members contributed untold hours to make it a reality. We acknowledge those who contributed and should any be omitted in this account, we beg their forgiveness.

We are deeply thankful to ***Kenneth M. Blose,***
the main author of this history book,
who labored diligently and tirelessly

Reverend James E. Laero
Bethel Family Church
Style Editor

Elizabeth Mitchell
Copy Editor

Judy Laurinatis
Editor

Debi A. Shupe
Writer and Research

John Owens
Wrote and coordinated
Vandergrift's 75th Anniversary History
Historical Consultant

Eugene Iagnemma
Historical Consultant

Harold Doutt
Primary Photographic Resource

Dorothy Mikula
Typist

Marilyn Henley
Typist, Proofreader

Christopher B. Myers
Technical Advisor/Computer Support

Sidebar Writers

Diana Barger
Ken Blose
Heather Bothel
Andrea Bracken
Beth Caporali
Jenette Elliot
Cynthia Gadola
Jeffrey Garrett
Fran Grimes
Lisa Hinkleman
Leslie Imm
James Laero
John Linkes
Bernice McCutcheon
John Owens
Marie Pugliese
Martha Serwinski
Cora Lee Scott
Debi Shupe
Lorelie Whaley
Jolie Williamson

Dr. Carl Meyerhuber
Consultant

Greg Bothel
Architectural Consultant

Stephen J. Myers, Jr.
Project Manager/Marketing Consultant

Robert and Carol Mills
Consultants/Interviewers

Dr. Jay Start
Liason, Indiana University of Pennsylvania

Regina Heilman
Editing Assistance

Daniel G. Shorthouse
Interviewer/Writer

Mary Canzano
Layout Consultant

Jennifer Laurinatis
Layout/Design Consultant

Amy S. Myers
Photographer

Cliff McGuire
Technical Advice, Layout

Bonnie McGuire
Technical Advice, Layout

William Sullivan
Technical Advice/Software Support

Tim Henley
Graphics/Cover Design

Cheryl Carrico
Typist/Resource

Ron Ankeny
Picture Resource

Assistance

Judy Tweten
Nancy Zornow
Carol Ceschin
Garry Humphrey

Resource

Richard Hunger
John Jenks
James Kerr
John Millberger
Joseph Petrarca
Steve DelleDonne
William Hays
Tim Polka
Lillian Pugliese

Pictures

Gertrude Keirn
Darlene Doutt Leda
CoraBelle Walter

Research

Mary Alice Adams
Kathy Fennell
Cynthia Gadola
Carmella Giunta
Melissa Holmes
Joan Iagnemma
Leslie Imm
Jason Kennerdale
James Laero
Cora Lee Scott
Terry Tometsko
ZoeAnna Shorthouse
Lorelie Whaley

Research Assistance
Special thanks to Kiski Area High School

Dr. John Meighn
Administrative Assistant
for Secondary Education

Dr. John M. Shaner
Principal

Mr. Ted Kulas
Librarian

Introduction

Something Better Than The Best

It was in my second day of heavy weeding and pruning that I came across the scraggly little tree. I was working up hill through an overgrown orchard, wrestling with what seemed an endless tangle of vines and underbrush. The orchard had been left unattended for more than a decade. The task was daunting, but my father and I had hopes of rescuing his surviving fruit trees.

By the time we reached the little tree we had already chopped down and hauled away a small forest of fast growing saplings that had inundated the orchard. We were weary and in no mood to debate the value of one small, unidentifiable tree. The tree resembled none of the other apple or pear trees in the orchard. After a brief discussion we decided that it must be part of the undergrowth and prepared to set the ax to it. But a last minute change of heart by my father saved the tree. Wiping his brow, he instructed me to *"Leave it until summer. Three months from now it will show us what kind of tree it is."* With that, the little tree was saved and we went on to finish the remainder of the orchard.

Three months later, the orchard was bursting with hundreds of green and red baking apples, and right in the center of the orchard was that little tree—loaded with the biggest yellow delicious apples I had ever tasted. The tree proved itself in time by its fruit.

It is a simple principle to every tree, every man and every dream. All things prove themselves in time by what they produce. History is a tree, spreading its branches through time, showing the fruit of men's dreams into the lives of future generations. Good men and women leave a legacy of character and integrity to be seen in their children. Great men and women produce fruit which drops to the lives of many generations. At various times a generation will pause to recognize the impact such fruits have had upon their own lives. Such is the occasion for this book.

A little more than a century ago, a man of character and vision planted the seeds of his dream in a valley near a small river in southwestern Pennsylvania. The man himself died in 1915, but he is known and honored to this day by the legacy of his own character. The fruit of his dreams still proclaim his name from every corner of "the Workingman's Paradise." The investments which he made, not only in the town's industry but in the townspeople themselves, live on in a unique spirit of excellence, unity and community pride.

George G. McMurtry was an industrialist with a revolutionary dream. His dream produced a unique marriage between two very traditionally separate forces in society, industry and labor. He believed that investment in both would bring higher productivity and greater profit. His was not a dream of a welfare state, but rather a dream of producing a contented work force through social and economic opportunity. McMurtry dreamed of a town where his steel workers could govern themselves, own their own homes, teach their own children and worship in their own churches. In a time when most steel towns were nothing more than a cluster of ramshackle homes along muddy streets, McMurtry was planning a monument to Victorian architecture and modern landscaping ideals.

George McMurtry's dream became reality in 1895 when the town of Vandergrift was born. But this story is more than one man's legacy. This is also the story of an industry and a community married through time to the same ideals. It is the history of a town moving through generations without losing its heart. It is a testimonial to those who seized the opportunity brought about by McMurtry's ideals and who, like McMurtry, believed that greater things could be obtained through investment into the lives of others.

McMurtry's Vandergrift became more than a town. It became a lifestyle. All towns are more than just a cluster of homes and streets. The people are the town, and every town reflects the very nature of its previous generations and current citizens. This historic tie between generations gives each town a spirit all its own. There is a spirit about this town called Vandergrift. You can hear it wisping through its beautiful trees every Spring. It wraps around you like a warm blanket in Summer. It floats heavy in the Autumn air and glimmers across the snow covered lawns in Winter. It seems a place of destiny. It carries that spirit of "something better than the best."

Reverend James E. Laero
Bethel Family Church of Vandergrift
Fourth Generation Resident of "Something Better Than The Best"

Chapter One

The Beginning

A wide sloping valley cradled at its base by a gentle river bend. Rolling hills blanketed in all directions with magnificent stands of oak. The river itself, swift and wild, flowing down from its sources below the foothills of the majestic Allegheny Mountain range to the east. Here, in this pristine setting of early American beauty, where only the soft swish of an occasional Indian paddle interrupted the scene, sat the backdrop for what was to become a 20th-century revolution of ideals between industry and social development. Here was a place where the seeds of one man's dream of excellence found good ground, grew, and flourished into a century of opportunity known as Vandergrift.

The exact date of that first Indian canoe slipping quietly down the Kiskiminetas River is not known. Presumably it was sometime in the early to mid-1600s. History records the Delaware Indians migrating to the area along an east-to-west track following a loosely tied string of streams and rivers between the Delaware Valley and Allegheny Mountains. Pushed west by a growing surge of European settlers, they found the solitude and natural habitat of the Kiski Valley perfect for settlement.

The Kiskiminetas River itself begins just upstream at Saltsburg where the Conemaugh River and Loyalhanna Creek join. It's a short river, only 25 miles from its source to its mouth. It was those early Indian settlers who gave birth to the name of the river, "Kee-akkshee-man-nit-toos" The exact interpretation of the name seems lost with the ages but "Cut Spirit," "Make daylight" (the impatient cry of a warrior eager to take the war path) and "plenty of walnuts" have been suggested. The Kiskiminetas by way of its tributaries was a main link to the Allegheny River and thus provided ready access to points west for the continuing migration of these native American Indians.

By the early 1700s, hundreds of native Americans lived along the banks of the Kiskiminetas and nearby Allegheny River. These early tribal settlements were soon accompanied by trading posts. Later in the 1700s the Indian settlers were driven on by white settlers and the conflicts of the French and Indian War. "Progress," a new word to this young land, was pushing the valley ever closer to its destiny.

Courtesy of Harold Doutt

Early 1900s Sketch of the Kiskiminetas River

Salt on the River

On March 9, 1771, the Pennsylvania State Assembly declared the Kiskiminetas River a "Public Highway." The assembly eventually set aside enough money to make improvements necessary for safe navigation along the river. Until then hazards such as "Kiski Falls" (a series of deadly rapids that had claimed many lives) made commerce and travel on the river extremely dangerous. Improvements came in the form of blasting and removing the large rocks from the threatening falls, thus creating boat channels in the Kiski River. (The site of the original falls is still evident from Roaring Run Trail along the old canal path just outside the community of Apollo.) These new river channels provided access to flat boats, which carried the valley's first significant economic imports. By the early 1800s, the area was sparsely populated by farm families; but with the river channels open, industry was not far behind.

The War of 1812 spurred the first significant industry of the Kiski Valley. Actually it was a side effect of the war that opened the valley to commercial productivity. The battle lines of the war cut off regular sources of certain supplies which had until then been imported to Western Pennsylvania from the east. One of the most critical items lost in this period was the preservative salt. Destiny was about to nudge this corner of the world a bit closer to its future sometime between 1795 and 1798 (or 1812 and 1813 depending on the historian), when salt was discovered among the rolling hills of the Kiski Valley. Soon the most productive salt springs in Pennsylvania were exporting the scarce preservative down river on flat boats to needy consumers. The war ended and the salt mines eventually closed, but the pattern cut by this early industry was the portent of this valley's future.

Mineral Builds Early Economy

The Kiski Valley's salt industry was big business in the late 1700s through the mid 1800s. In Saltsburg, Salina and down the Kiskiminetas River to Gravel Bar and Old Kiskiminetas Town were Gordon Salt Wells near the Hick mine, the Boggs & Anderson well, (just above Cow Bell Riffle). On the Westmoreland side of the river at Roaring Run were McCauley & Trux wells and a Mr. Gamble had yet another well just up river from Roaring Run.

Around 1826 another well was drilled at the site of Old Kiskiminetas Town. (This area is known today as Pine Run Bottom; and would be located near the site of the present day municipal water treatment plant just outside of Vandergrift Borough). They named the well "Hope Salt works" and worked the well for twenty years. Much of what they mined was shipped to Pittsburgh and points beyond by way of flat or keel boats with later canal shipments north to Warren, PA. In 1830 the Armstrong Company produced 65,500 bushels of salt at an average price of $2.50 per-bushel.

Boats and Trains to the Future

The Pennsylvania State Assembly provided the next opening to the valley's growth when it began construction of the Pennsylvania Canal in 1826. The canal would connect the Ohio River and Lake Erie to the Delaware River.

By 1829, canal boats were traveling up the Kiskiminetas River to points east. Soon afterwards, the main line canal to the valley became operational and prospered as more travelers, farmers, and industries used it.

Courtesy of Kittanning Leader Times and Doug Both

Walk into the past and hike along the "Roaring Run Trail" located a few miles upriver from Apollo. Imagine the dangers of river travel along the rapids of the Kiskiminetas River. Canal travel eliminated these and brought great improvement. Above, John Englert stands on Roaring Run Trail looking into the canal basin which was 40 feet wide and 4 feet deep. He stands along the bed of a former railway that had been built on the towpath for the canal.

Below, John Englert stands next to part of the past. It is a visible piece of one of 68 locks in the Western Pennsylvania division of the Pennsylvania Canal near Apollo. The material is concrete over brick.

Courtesy of Kittanning Leader Times and Doug Both

Courtesy of Leader Times, Kittanning, PA

Transportation By Canal Boat

The Canal and Canal Boats

The canal was constructed mostly by hand by Irish immigrant workers who earned 50 cents a day plus board.

Canal travel grew rapidly, and the number of boats on the canal increased. With the increase in passenger travel, accommodations were made available on the canal boats. It wasn't long before the owners started to incorporate dining rooms and separate sleeping rooms. In making these changes, the need for overnight stops at canal inns was eliminated. These canal inns had dotted the river banks in much the same fashion that the old stage coach inns dotted the turnpikes.

It took four days to travel some 394 miles from Pittsburgh to Philadelphia. The cost of this trip was $7.00 per person, plus meals.

The price of freight on the canals was considerably cheaper than freight by wagon. In the year 1853 the price of freight on the canal was about 3 cents per ton, while the cost of freight traveling on wagons was 15 cents per ton. Added to the wagon rate was the cost of staying at coach inns, which was anywhere from $3.00 to $7.00 a night, plus meals. Many businessmen made the canal system their choice for shipping freight.

Needless to say, the canal brought a boom to the small towns along its path, and particularly to the Kiski Valley.

Passengers traveled on fast "Packet" canal boats, which could make 80 to 100 miles per day. Charles Dickens, the English author came this way, as did the writer Harriet Beecher Stowe and the politician Henry Clay. The bodies of two presidents, William Henry Harrison and Zachary Taylor, passed by on the way to their final resting places.

In one of the few accounts of canal travel on record, a woman from Europe wrote,

> *The valley of the Kiskiminetas is like one noble fruitful park. Here and there were harvest fields of small grain, and of the tasseled Indian corn; and a few coal and salt works, some forsaken, some busy, showed themselves on reaches of the river; but we were usually enclosed by a circle of wooded hills, reposing in the brightest lights and deepest shadows. The canal commonly ran along the base of one of these hills; but it often let us slip into the broad livid stream of the river itself.*

Charles Dickens wrote,

> *There is much in this mode of travel which I heartily enjoyed at the time, and look back upon with great pleasure.*

Not long after the canal became fully operational, a new mode of transportation emerged–the railroad. The railroad was much faster and did not have to depend on a river for its direction of travel. The low

Courtesy of Harold Doutt

The "Cut", showing old Franklin Avenue bridge

cost of rail travel spelled the end for the canal and the beginning of greater opportunity for the Kiski Valley. The railroad was completed to Pittsburgh in 1857. The canal was sold to the railroad the same year, which began to salvage much of the canal for usable railroad supplies. The last canal boat delivered a load of salt to Blairsville in 1865. Soldiers leaving Apollo for the Civil War left by canal boat and returned by train. Powerful technology was now driving the valley to industrialization.

Making Tracks

In 1864, the Conemaugh Division of the railroad was built from the junction at the mainline in Blairsville to where the Kiskiminetas River empties into the Allegheny River near Schenley. At the future site of the town of Vandergrift, the railroad climbed up the side of the hill above East Vandergrift and passed through a 65 foot deep valley cut through the hill between what is now the Catholic Church and the number one fire department in Vandergrift. (During the 1920s the Cut was filled with slag and ashes from the foundry and is now a large playground and an attractive park extending from Franklin to Hancock Avenues. An old plank bridge that originally spanned the divide is thought to be buried several feet underneath Franklin Avenue.)

Remains of the Day

You can see evidence of the Pennsylvania Canal by hiking one and a half miles up the Roaring Run trail out of Apollo. Just before you reach Roaring Run, the trail passes the remains of Lock 15 and some stone work. Another dam created slack water upriver from this point. At Lock 15, the canal boats left the river and entered the canal and traveled three miles through Apollo along Warren Avenue and Astronaut Way to reenter the river in the Pegtown area. For information, contact the Roaring Run Watershed Association, P.O. Box 40, Spring Church, PA 15686.

Iron and Steel Roll In

As the new railroad dropped tracks through the valley the steel industry rolled in behind. In 1865 the first steel mill of the valley was built in Apollo. (The iron and steel making industry actually made an earlier appearance in the valley just upriver from Apollo in 1825, when James W. Biddle established an iron furnace there.)

Apollo was the first town established by settlers in the valley, being laid out in

Courtesy of Buttermilk Falls Publishing Company
Another view of the "Cut"

1816 along a new state road through the area. It was then called "Warren" (the town traces its origin to a stopping place on the Kiskiminetas Indian trail called Warren's Sleeping Ground).

The mill at Apollo was powered by a 20-foot diameter water wheel with a 20-foot face drawing excess water from the canal. The mill was updated to steam and went through a series of unsuccessful owners until changes significant to the yet non-existent town of Vandergrift occurred.

In 1886, the operation of the mill was taken over by the newly formed "Apollo Iron and Steel Company." Destiny waved its hand again as the Apollo Iron and Steel Company would lead two men to the valley who would soon birth "The Workingman's Paradise."

Men Of Vision Arrive

Among the original principals of the Apollo mill were Captain Jacob J. Vandergrift, the majority stockholder, and George G. McMurtry, stockholder and manager of the plant. Under McMurtry's direction, the Apollo plant prospered from negligible production levels to one of the leading producers of the world's galvanized iron supply. The success of the mill spurred McMurtry to search for a future expansion site within the valley.

As this early industrialist traveled the river bank through the valley, he came to admire a particularly inviting site just downriver from Apollo. The site, known then as the Townsend Farm, rested along a wide sloping valley cradled at its base by a gentle bend in the Kiskiminetas River where, nearly two centuries earlier, those first Indians had passed in their canoes.

In 1892, the Apollo Iron and Steel Company purchased the Townsend farm, the adjoining Hugh Jones farm and the Varner and Laufer farms further up the valley. At the time of the purchase, the Apollo plant was not ready to expand, but events just beyond the horizon pushed McMurtry to a decision that forever changed the steel industry and the social structure of the valley.

In 1893, workers in the Apollo mill went on strike for higher wages, refusing to abide by a wage scale written into a contract the company had with the national union. McMurtry swiftly broke the strike by hiring new workers. In a display of courage and determination, he led the new men through the picket lines himself. This led to irreparable bitterness between the former workers, the townspeople, and the company. It was apparent however, that McMurtry's dissatisfaction with union practices began well before the strike.

One practice in particular, that of filling vacancies in the plant with senior workers

George G. McMurtry: The Man Behind The Vision

George Gibson McMurtry was born near Belfast, Northern Ireland on May 28, 1838. He was orphaned at an early age and was raised by an uncle on a small farm. He became unhappy with the monotonous life of a farmer, and when old enough, he secretly left home to enlist in the British army as a bugler. His uncle persuaded him to leave the army after a short time and return to the farm on the promise that if George would work for one more year, his uncle would assist him to find a new position or send him to America. At the end of the promised year on the farm, he elected to come to the United States.

McMurtry arrived in America to find that opportunity was not so available as believed. He drifted from place to place finally arriving in Detroit with only seventy-five cents in his pocket. He began his work career in Detroit, but soon found a position in the Chicago office of the Jones and Laughlin Steel Company and was transferred by that company to Pittsburgh. Subsequently, he started a bolt and nut business under the name of Charles and McMurtry. His business career was interrupted at this point by the Civil War. George enlisted on the side of the North and served in the cavalry. He attained the rank of major.

After the war he was employed by the Volts Galvanizing Company of Pittsburgh which later purchased the works in Apollo which became the Iron and Steel Company. McMurtry was the manager and significant stock holder in this mill which in due course led to the founding a new plant and town in Vandergrift in 1895.

George G. McMurtry was truly an American success story. From humble beginnings, self educated and with hard work and vision for the future, he became an industrial giant. It was said that he was the first men in the tin industry whose vision was sufficiently keen to enable him to grasp the truth that in interested home owning, loyal workmen lay the secret of industrial success. Although shunning public appearances, he had a magnetic personality, was enthusiastic and optimistic even in the darkest business days.

His employees and associates found him to be absolutely trustworthy. He always treated them fairly and justly. Every man in his employ, regardless of position, knew that McMurtry viewed merit alone as the key to advancement and progress.

George McMurtry was a most generous man, giving great financial assistance in matter that would enhance the quality of Vandergrift and the welfare of its citizens. He gave the sites for the public schools, churches and fire departments;. provided financial help to build the churches, On his last visit to Vandergrift in 1902, he arranged for each church to have an organ. He assisted in the purchase of fire equipment, and musical instruments for the first band; provided the land and financial help to provide a cultural center for the town (the Casino; provided for the public library and lecture programs, and probably much more about which we are unaware.

George McMurtry died in Atlantic City on August 6, 1915 at the age of 77. He is buried in the Kensico Cemetery, Valhalla, New York.

"All hail the prince among men. All hail to the kindly, unselfish , genial friend who was a friend of man. Many men were the beneficiaries of his bounty. We shall not look on his like again. He has gone out of our lives forever, leaving them better for his having lived and planned and toiled. But he has left a heritage which we the living must guard and keep as he would have it kept.

from the Vandergrift News, *October 21, 1915*

Courtesy of "Vandergrift: First 75 Years"

The Parent Plant: Apollo Steel Mill

from other plants, cut hard against McMurtry's principles. McMurtry firmly believed that promising young workers should be advanced from within the plant itself as reward for hard work.

It was the combination of the strike and his dissatisfaction with the union apprenticeship program that prompted McMurtry to consider pulling out of the town ahead of schedule.

The final straw for McMurtry came in 1894 when the Apollo plant needed land adjacent to the mill for expansion. Hearing of the plant's needs, two speculators purchased the land expecting to gain big profits at the mill's expense. McMurtry, stubborn Irishman that he was, refused to deal with them and was able to persuade the company trustees that the time had come to build a new plant and with it a new town.

Considering the speed at which McMurtry's new plant and town would become reality, it is evident that this man of character had the dream in place well before these events transpired. This vision, which would become Vandergrift, was built upon years of laboring alongside other men in the trenches and reinforced through latter years as a successful executive in charge. McMurtry was now set to test his own ideals, with full power to instill his own spirit, free of the encumbrances that had led to this opportunity.

As McMurtry's plans unfolded, it became clear that this was not to be just another average steel mill concern with rows of buildings churning out steel. McMurtry now had the opportunity to incorporate all his social, labor, and industry beliefs in a revolutionary vision of life and work.

A glimpse of this dream is found in an April 1895 company letter to world-renowned architect Frederick Olmsted (the town's designer) stating,

> *"We desire to have a town that in many features will be unique, and in all respects more attractive than the average manufacturing town of the present day. In fact, we want something better than the best."*

With this vision in the hands of his architect, McMurtry seized the day and began his "Workingman's Paradise."

Courtesy of "Vandergrift: First 75 Years"

The Townsend Farm, circa 1890s viewed from Kepple Hill. This is the land where Vandergrift today sits.

The mill in the picture below, now owned by Allegheny Ludlum, sits on what is the slope in front of the house in the top picture. The farmhouse is believed to have been on a small bank just above and behind the mill. You can see a portion of the embankment at the far right above the mill in the picture below. For more information about the Townsend Farm, see "What Was It Like Before McMurtry Came To Town?" in *Reflections of the Times.*

Courtesy of Amy Myers

Over a Century Later: the Same Site from a Slightly Different Angle.

Reflections Of The Times

Stories of the Day

Early Native American Settlements

Early in the sixteenth century, the Delaware Indians were pushed westward by European settlers. The tribe migrated north following the Susquehanna River through the heart of the Pennsylvania and then west through the area known today as Williamsport, LockHaven, and Clearfield. At a point southwest of Clearfield, the Susquehanna's west branch diminished into a small unnegotiable stream at a little village known today as Cherry Tree. There the Indians would conceal their canoes in the woods and shoulder their goods for about a 10-mile trek to Two Lick Creek. (This is very likely the portage route described in historical documents as the Cherry Tree portage.) At Two Lick Creek, the Indians loaded their possessions into a second set of canoes and continued the journey. Following Two Lick Creek west past present day Clymer and Homer City, they entered Black Lick Creek, which ran into the Conemaugh River northwest of modern day Blairsville. Proceeding down the Conemaugh River, they arrived at the Kiskiminetas River near present day Saltsburg. There the Delaware had only a 25-mile voyage down the Kiskiminetas to the Allegheny River, which opened access to the south and west via the Ohio and Mississippi Rivers. This water route, which passed along what would one day be the town of Vandergrift in the Kiski Valley was a key link in east—west travel and trade for early Native Americans.

A Good Place to Live

The Delaware Indians found a bounty of plentiful fish, wildlife, and game as they traveled through the Kiskiminetas river valley. Old records report Delaware Indian settlements near present-day Apollo. By 1731 other native tribes such as the Shawnee had three towns (200 people in all) along the Kiskiminetas and Allegheny Rivers. The three towns mentioned are Black Legs and Kickenapauling (which were located at Saltsburg), and Kiskiminetas, (which was located near where the Kiski Valley water treatment plant sits today at the mouth of Pine Run).

In the beginning, these Indian towns were a loose collection of families living along the Kiskiminetas from present-day North Apollo to just above Leechburg in the Park's Bend region. Later, through contact with traders, a trading post was established and eventually a small settlement appeared, taking on the name "Kiskiminetas Old Town." (Years later, when salt was discovered in the valley, salt wells were drilled there. After that, a small shanty town grew up as coal was mined in the area. Little remains today of this settlement other than some old foundations and a small dam in a creek where people stored food to keep it cold.)

Evidence of Indian activity has also been found in East Vandergrift, where the grave of an Indian was uncovered during building excavation. Other local stories mention a Chief Warren having a sleeping ground in the Apollo area, and another says that Warren's burial place was in North Apollo (the old Griftlo Park area) near North Vandergrift.

The Indians abandoned the area when the French and Indian war broke out in the 1760s and more settlers moved into the area. But records indicate that these tribes were involved in several conflicts with settlers throughout the valley until about the 1790s.

What Was It Like Before McMurtry Came to Town?

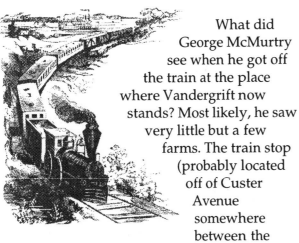

What did George McMurtry see when he got off the train at the place where Vandergrift now stands? Most likely, he saw very little but a few farms. The train stop (probably located off of Custer Avenue somewhere between the American Legion and Walnut Street) was called Townsend Station. It was apparently little more than a stop the train made so folks from the neighboring farms could board or possibly load their produce.

We do know a little bit about the old Townsend farm. In the library of the Western Pennsylvania Historical Society, a book published in 1908 by the *Vandergrift News* entitled, *Recollections of Yesterday at the Old Home* was written by N. E. Townsend, son of John Townsend, who grew up there in the late 1800s. He sketched out in poetic verse and prose his family history and his pre-Vandergrift memories of his childhood. Combined with bits and pieces from deeds, newspaper articles, and other sources, we can put together a pretty good picture of what this plot of land was like just before George McMurtry came to town.

N. E. Townsend's great-grandfather, Isaac, built a log cabin near Salina, PA., in 1778. His son, Isaac Jr., was born there and lived there until he married in 1818. Possibly in anticipation of a large extended family, Isaac (junior or senior, we don't know which) acquired some land in the area in 1821 from a James Baird who had received a land grant from the Commonwealth. This land grant, then known as "Poors Purchase," most likely was the Kiski Valley.

Again in 1827 according to more deeds, Isaac Jr. also bought land, but just where is unclear; we can only assume it was where he eventually moved. His son, John, was born sometime during these years.

N. E. Townsend noted that in 1833, after Isaac Sr. died, Isaac Jr. moved his family to the land where Vandergrift is today. At that time, a dense forest of huge oak trees blanketed this area, from the bottom land down by the river all the way up the hill. Here Isaac carved out a life for his family, developing a farm that would eventually produce grain, watermelons,

On the Trail

Indian travel through the region was not limited to the Kiskiminetas River. As the Indians hunted and traded, Western Pennsylvania became crisscrossed by trails in every direction. The Frankstown Path was overall "the most important and frequently traveled" trail across the Pennsylvania mountains. This trail began where Harrisburg is today and ran westward. Somewhere near Indiana, it split into two branches. One branch went to Kittanning; the other went to Tarentum and was called the Kiskiminetas Path. The earliest written mention of the Kiskiminetas River by name was in reference to this path. Conrad Weiser, a prominent negotiator with the Indians, wrote in his journal: "August, 25th, 1748. Crossed Kiskeminetoes creek and came to Ohio [Allegheny] that day, 26 miles." The Kiskiminetas Path branched off the Frankstown Path about six miles west of Indiana and ran due east to Tarentum (then called Chartier's Old Town). The path crossed the Kiskiminetas just downriver from present-day North Vandergrift. From Carnahan's Run (beside Lee's Woodland Lanes bowling alley), it crossed the river to the site of the present-day municipal water treatment plant, the former location of Kiskiminetas Old Town. It continued on to Chartier's Old Town, a large Indian settlement.

Another trail that ran through this valley was the Loyalhanna Path. It ran from a point near Latrobe along the Loyalhanna Creek to Saltsburg and ran northwest to meet the Kiskiminetas Path near Vandergrift.

and apples, among other produce; Isaac also worked a few saltwells in the area.

At this time the canals were in full swing. Local commerce using the canal boats to Pittsburgh made the Kiskiminetas River a heavily traveled "state highway." Also, the river was dammed up at Leechburg, creating the effect of a small lake all the way to Apollo.

Townsend noted in his book that "most of the grain raised in the bend [our area] was loaded on Canal boats and shipped to market" from a natural rock pier, near the Vandergrift—North Vandergrift bridge today.

Townsend wrote of a childhood spent fishing for "black bass and cat-fish" from that natural rock pier, of the swimming hole near where the old railroad station now sits, of the "old stone spring" that bubbled and chattered somewhere in the vicinity of where Welsh Printing is today, and of "Indian Rock," just downriver, that was his own private "resort." (The location of Townsend's Indian Rock is unclear, but there is a fantastic view from a rock overhang on Kepple Hill that juts out over River Road.)

Based on descriptions in his book and as best as we can tell, the Townsend farmhouse was located over the cliff on a what is now small brush-covered plateau behind Welsh's Print Shop and Keddie Chevrolet. Townsend's descriptions mention being near a spring and a brickshed of the mill. It was nothing fancy, but was comfortable for a family.

One Townsend descendant remembers whole families visiting, and children getting out of earshot of adults to play in the spring. As the town was being built, when Henry Nichols and his family lived in the Townsend farmhouse, the Kepples from across the river would come to the house for a religious meeting with several other families. And even a

few years earlier, *"Friends would come from far and near, would remain for a meal, a day or a week and were always welcome,"* wrote N. E. Townsend. *"If father corrected, we sure had a friend for mother in pity would always defend...."* At the end of a day of working on the farm, the dinner bell was anxiously awaited, as were his mother's bread, pies, and doughnuts that were kept in the cellar.

John Townsend was highly respected gentleman in the community. He was a school director for 12 years for Allegheny Township, which extended to the Kiski River at the time. He contributed greatly to the upgrading of the education of local youths and in the construction of school buildings. He also served as county commissioner for three years.

Townsend's wife, Eliza, was well known for her gracious hospitality and nurtured culture in her home in the midst of what only years earlier had been unbroken wilderness. Their family, it has been noted, "developed a taste for music" at an early age and reportedly did well at it. Their son Newton was a successful music teacher. With the Townsend family's variety of interests in the it's no small wonder that their home became "a center for political gatherings, business meetings, and social events."

When George McMurtry bought the Townsend farm from a consortium of land owners, the farm had already been parceled up and had passed out of John Townsend's hands. However, it is possible that Vandergrift founder George McMurtry once shook hands with "Honest John Townsend," one of the original settlers of pre-Vandergrift properties.

Villages Were Numerous Along Old Kiskiminetas

Henry Nichols was the construction supervisor for George McMurtry when he built Vandergrift. He and his family were among the very first families to move here, and they lived in the Townsend farmhouse. Years later, his son, H. W. Nichols, wrote in the Vandergrift News a series of columns about Vandergrift called "Fallen Leaves." In it he detailed life in early Vandergrift and on the Townsend farm. This and the next two stories are snapshots" of life here in the mid-1890s.

It hardly need be told that Kiskiminetas is an Indian name. In an endeavor to follow the Indian pronunciation it has been variously spelled by early historians and its meaning has had several interpretations. It is the name given to the beautiful Kiski Valley when it was known to the Indians as a happy hunting ground where fish and game were plentiful. This was before the coming of the white man with his towns and industries that pushed the natives west.

Indian camps and villages were rather numerous on the lowlands along the Kiski River and Indian artifacts have been found in various places including East Vandergrift and on the Kepple farm down the river from Vandergrift. Many years ago it was told that during excavations on or near what had been the Townsend farm a cache of Indian arrowheads had been unearthed containing enough flints to fill a wooden bucket. Who found them and what became of them I do not know. I do know, however, that with the Kepple boys I personally found Indian flints on the bottom land of the Kepple farm.

This brings me back to the old Townsend farm home that I helped to occupy in 1895—1896 while the new steel plant and town were being built. The history of "Vandergrift's First 75 Years" has a photograph of the Townsend farm setting in Section V. The house and surroundings were rather typical of the good farms of the day and something about them here should be of historical interest to Vandergrift enthusiasts.

The home was flanked by cool pine trees with a peaceful yard beneath them. Here in good weather the family and some friends spent many pleasant hours of an evening and on Sundays. Under the trees hung a long rope swing, that was capable of riding high and this was much in use by the young folks. Between two trees a hammock swung where at leisure time one of the adults could usually be found dozing. There was no garden furniture such as in use today but there were two homemade benches constructed from a log cut

Courtesy of Buttermilk Falls Publishing Company

This Field Is Part Of Vandergrift Today

in half and set up on peg legs. Other chairs were brought out from the house as needed and often quilts were spread upon the ground that was covered more with soft pine needles than grass.

Just off the low back porch was a rather deep watering trough about six feet long that had been cut from a solid piece of sandstone and at some earlier time had been laboriously scooped out with handtools. At one end of the trough was a cast iron pump, the handle worn bright by human hands. I have often wondered what became of this stone. Possibly it is an interesting antique now resting in some resident's yard, filled with flowers in summer.

Not far from the back of the house was a large wood-burning oven constructed of field stones. It evidenced much use and was still being used some for preserving, rending hot fat into lard and soap and for baking bread. Here my four-year-old sister Carolyn had her clothes catch fire that resulted in an heroic rescue which is another story.

South of the house was a large, white, frame barn with hayloft and stalls for numerous cows and horses. In our day it was used only occasionally to house visiting carriage horses and their rigs. Between the house and the barn there was a "Chick Sales" [outhouse]. It was a two "holer" with artistic moon and stars cut in the door. I do not recall the children ever using it.

A place with a sweet, agreeable aroma was the cool springhouse off in another direction. This was a small one-room building, some distance back of the house and built of heavy timbers and stone. Here milk, butter, eggs and other things were kept in brown crocks that stood on large flat stones in the floor that was constantly flooded with cold water from an underground stream or spring.

This pleasant, peaceful farm setting in 1895 was soon to be crowded out of existence by the clang and whistles of the encroaching steel plant. No room today to speak of the interesting interior of this old house. Perhaps in a later article I can do it.

"Fallen Leaves" by H. W. Nichols.
Courtesy of the Vandergrift News.

First House on Van Site Short on Conveniences

My last article was about the environs of the old Townsend farm house but there was not room to tell of its interior which should have some historical interest. Young people today, enjoying all our modern conveniences, might like to know more of how people, particularly farm people, lived here many years ago.

This was a rather commodious, comfortable home, as it is remembered, but it contained none of the modern conveniences that were to be plentiful in all the lovely, new homes soon to be erected in Vandergrift. There was no central heating, no electricity, no gas and no convenient plumbing.

The ground floor opened onto a small, open porch that looked out upon a pleasant landscape that sloped gently down to the lush banks of the River. Before the house itself was to give way to the march of progress, this pretty, pastoral view was to be cut off by the rising less pretty mill buildings.

Inside was a rather large, comfortable, family room, then called the parlor, with a large open wood and coal-burning fireplace at one end. This was built of fieldstone and the hearth was one large stone slab about six inches thick. The lights were coal oil burning lamps of which there were several.

Each day the lamps were replenished with oil, their wicks were neatly trimmed and hurricane chimneys polished. One of them I shall never forget. It was a large lamp with a round base receptacle that held the oil and a large ball-shaped shade that surrounded a clear glass chimney. Both the base and large shade were painted with red roses and as a boy I never tired of looking at it when lighted. I think it was the prettiest object in my life.

The fine Vandergrift Churches were yet to be constructed. In the parlor just described religious services were held on Sunday evenings. I think the leaders came from Apollo but what the denomination was I cannot say. I was allowed to sit in the little congregation of twenty or thirty, made up of neighbors and occasionally one or two mill officials who at times stayed with us. The neighbors came in horse drawn vehicles; some walked the country roads and across fields carrying lanterns after dark. Some of them including ladies wore knee-high, rubber boots. On one or more occasions the Kepples attended, coming across the river by rowboat. With the older folks came a vivacious, young girl who attracted my attention for I saw few children. I think it was at such a meeting that I saw Magdalene Kepple Wherry for the first time, and I have known her with pleasure for more than seventy-five years.

The kitchen had a huge wood-burning stove and in front of it we children got our Saturday night bath in a large wooden laundry tub. One thing that impressed me even as a boy was the floor of this kitchen. It had no covering such as tile or linoleum, but was of unpainted wide wood slabs. There were no detergents in those days and the floor must have been kept clean with lye or strong soap for it was immaculately clean and a very light tan color. Perhaps I remember it so well because Uncle Job our colored helper hit me rather hard with a large wooden spoon for tracking dirt from the yard onto this floor.

On the second floor were the bedrooms, one at least of which had an open fireplace. Each room had a double bed with a high oak or walnut headboard that extended nearly to the ceiling. Under each bed was a chamber, some of them with pretty flowers. Each bedroom had a washstand with a rear rack for towels. On each such stand there was a large porcelain washbowl used for face or feet. In each bowl stood a large matching pitcher that was filled with water each day. Beside these stands were what we called slop jars. Perhaps they had some more elegant name but I don't know it. They stood about eighteen inches high, were porcelain and had matching lids. They were supposed to receive the used bathing water but the children often found them more convenient than the chambers for other things.

More than once I knelt in front of these bedroom windows with my arms upon the sill and watched my father climb into the sky on the skeletons of the new mill buildings as he went about his work as a superintendent of construction; usually with a roll of blueprints under his arm or a ball peen hammer in his hand.

There was a bathroom of sorts on the second floor but all I remember of it was a rather ugly bathtub made of blue grey zinc sheets welded together. It was enclosed by wooden wainscoting the top of it burned nearly black by the long use of strong soap.

Narrow stairs led up to a spooky unfinished attic almost filled with thick dust and broken and discarded furniture. The children often crept up these stairs but never ventured farther than heads level with the floor. This was partly because one or two bats were always darting back and forth between windows festooned with ancient cobwebs.

I do not know if there was anything of value in this storage but I can well imagine the excited interest that would be shown by one of our modern itinerate antique dealers."

"Fallen Leaves" by H. W. Nichols.
Courtesy of the Vandergrift News.

Courtesy of Harold Doutt and Buttermilk Falls Publishing Company

The Townsend Farmhouse

Only Few Still Alive Who Can Recall Farm

There are not many people around today who can look back upon the Vandergrift townsite when it was farm land without streets or houses. There are but one or two who come to my mind. This is because of two reasons. First, they would have to be children in 1895—1896 and except for those in the old Townsend home, children were rarely seen on the land. Next, Old Father Time who swings his scythe over all fields has cut most of us down.

My first visit to the Town location was on a Sunday afternoon when with my Mother and Father I was taken across fields on what seemed like a very long, upgrade walk from the old Townsend farm home to what was to be the Town Center of Vandergrift. It was then only a field with an unobstructed view in all directions. There were no streets or sidewalks but many evidences of the work of surveyors with ground stakes, lines and flags. Along several future streets were excavations and piles of earth undoubtedly dug for sewers that had been or soon would be placed.

My Father carried with him a blueprint of the town layout and as we stood about where the cannon now stands my Father unfolded the map and pointed out on it, then on the ground, the place where he hoped to buy and build our home when the lots were put on sale. I remember well my mother's concern as she told Dad she thought the location was *"very far out."* She was then told that we would only be one block from the business section that would be built on Washington Avenue. As it developed later some of the nicest residences were built on Washington Avenue and most businesses came to Grant Avenue.

On a subsequent walk we went up to the top of Grant Avenue and from the east side of what was to be Franklin Avenue looked out over what was later Morning Sun. My mother liked it only as a view and said *"Oh! I wouldn't like to live away up here."* Later she thought the Franklin Avenue development very nice but she never tired of the lovely home that was built for her on Grant Avenue which, as later developed, was really near the business section.

Major Altman came early to Vandergrift to be connected with the Steel Company and later on became a Justice of the Peace and I believe the Town's first Municipal Judge. Out, what is now Sherman Avenue and at a point about where Hamilton Avenue joins it, there was a farm house somewhat smaller than ours. The Altman family consisting of the Major, a very sweet Mrs. Altman and two late teen-age Daughters Julia and Lula, moved into this house while the Town was building.

The Nichols and Altmans became good friends that lasted so long as they lived. They visited back and forth between farm houses and laughed over many a game of hearts for small stakes. Neither family owned horses at this time and the visits were always made by shanks' mare. It was quite a walk, and after dusk they carried lanterns and had to be careful not to fall into new excavations. And there was one other serious danger. In the neighborhood of the Altman farm house there was a marshy area with a quicksand bottom. Here one evening a man unfamiliar with the land and not carrying a light wandered into the marsh and was waist deep in quicksand before Major Altman, my Father and others got him out with the aid of planks and logs. This marsh was later successfully drained by the Town engineers.

Later when the red brick business building was erected on Washington Avenue facing Custer, the Altmans moved into an apartment there. Here Lula was taken seriously ill. There was no bridge across the river at Vandergrift but there was a wooden bridge at Apollo and doctors made hasty trips by horse and buggy from Apollo through the old railroad cut in a valiant effort to save her. They could not and she was one of the first people to die in Vandergrift and I am quite sure the first young person.

"Fallen Leaves" by H. W. Nichols.
Courtesy of the Vandergrift News.

Courtesy of Harold Doutt

McMurtry's Dream

Chapter Two

Building The Best

The beliefs and character of any man can be seen by what he produces. George G. McMurtry was a man of great dreams and ideals. Through his years of experience in business, labor, and life in general, he had developed a vision that truly reflected his own character. In this valley of beauty and fullness, McMurtry's vision found its destiny.

The dream was not intensely noble. It was centered around profit. But unlike other industrialists of his day, McMurtry believed profit began with productivity and that productivity began in the work force. His vision was simple; *productivity in the plant depended on a healthy, happy work force.* With this in mind, McMurtry set about the tasks of developing a town where his workers and their families would find not only employment, but contentment as well. Truly a revolutionary ideal for that day.

It is common knowledge that early steel towns had not been established out of concern for workers. The meager housing supplied to early steel workers was used by unscrupulous owners to control the labor supply by regulating living conditions. Companies were paternalistic, as they exercised control over town government, and private affairs of the residents. Some have equated mill towns with the feudal system of past centuries. No one could own property and residence there was at the whim of the company. The social atmosphere was oppressive and conditions demeaning. The drab sameness of the houses, the lack of parks or other recreational facilities only added to a deplorable lifestyle.

Author Ida M. Tarbell, writing in 1916, described one mill town like this.

> *There are no pavements, no fences, no space for gardens or flowers. Refuse and filth are allowed to collect in the alleys. Rains had cut gullies and piled up banks, all covered with the dirt and grime from the mill. Over it all roamed pigs, geese and children. There were no sewers, and no water piped into homes. The lack of proper water supply and sewage disposal was the cause of serious and deadly outbreaks of disease of all types.*

Before McMurtry planned his own town, he traveled the country and to Eu-

Courtesy of Buttermilk Falls Publishing Company

Vandergrift - the Town of Winding Streets

rope studying the best mill towns then in existence. Selecting the good and discarding the bad aspects of each town, he formulated his ideas for his company's model town.

His plan was announced in a pamphlet called The New Town. He planned to start with,

> *A site of natural health and wealth and beauty; drained; graded; flat but convenient; good roads and walks, not in squares, but according to the lay of the land; such water as flows from mountain springs brought into houses; sewers; expanse of grass; trees; outlook; modern above and below ground; electric lights, telegraph, telephone. Every man to choose his part with the means at hand of supporting that part; The people to own their houses and control their pursuits. The means of health and enjoyment of life within reach of all inhabitants. Liquor not to be sold there.*

He also proposed that each home should have a bathtub, a rare thing for the 1890s. *We intend to make a better town than there is in the world for physical, health, and comfort.*

When George McMurtry first envisioned a town that would be "something better than the best," he set out on a journey in search of people and modern ideas that would ensure his town's success. He drew concepts from visits to towns in Europe there enlisting the aid of men involved in landscaping. In his venture to build "something better than the best" he wisely sought out those who themselves possessed this very quality in their own professions.

Frederick L. Olmsted was a key choice in this process. Olmsted, of Brookline, Massachusetts, was considered the best landscape architect of his day. But it was his understanding of McMurtry's particular needs that made Frederick Olmsted perfect for the task ahead. Like McMurtry, Olm-

Frederick L. Olmsted

The Dean of McMurtry's Dream Team

Frederick Law Olmsted, a world-reknown landscape architect whose revolutionary designs impacted 19th century cities across the nation, is best known for his design of New York City's Central Park.

Before becoming interested in design, Olmsted served as a seaman aboard ships in the China trade, journeyed throughout the American South as a newspaper correspondent, and even operated a farm on Staten Island.

Through years of experience and study in the field of town planning, Olmsted developed revolutionary designs that provided tranquility in the midst of an industrial revolution.

Vandergrift was the first industrial town planned by the Olmsted firm and takes its place with previous noteworthy designs by this firm such as Central Park; the Boston and Buffalo Park Systems, Niagara Falls Park (U. S. side), the Chicago World's Fair, and the grounds of the Capitol in Washington, D.C.

sted was a man of vision whose own dreams would find full opportunity in this dream town.

During a tour of England in 1850, Olmsted became aware of the problems the industrial revolution had wrought upon cities, and previous attempts to remedy the situation through town planning. Upon his return, he published a book about what he had seen.

While planning Central Park in New York City in 1858, Olmsted and his partner, Calvert Vaux, incorporated the first principles of what would become a design signature for Olmsted. Key to their plan was the inclusion of numerous stretches of green grass. Big American cities in the mid-1800s had minimal access to any rural setting, but in Central Park, Olmsted instituted the importance of the idea of parklets and boulevard-type, tree-studded avenues within a metropolitan area. Suddenly citizens had an escape from their urban concrete world. Olmsted's concept, borne in the design of Central Park, would one day find full expression in the creation of the town of Vandergrift.

In 1869 Olmsted was able to further develop his ideas as he and Vaux designed a new town in Illinois called Riverside. It had a network of curvilinear streets, contoured to the lay of the land. He went on to develop bits and pieces of ideas in other various projects over the years, including the concept of worker-owned homes. But in Vandergrift, he and his firm would find opportunity to put all the pieces together as the designer of McMurtry's town. Vandergrift became the canvas for his design brush.

From the initial layout of the new town's streets, it was clear that Olmsted was preparing for one of his greatest design achievements. The streets did not cross

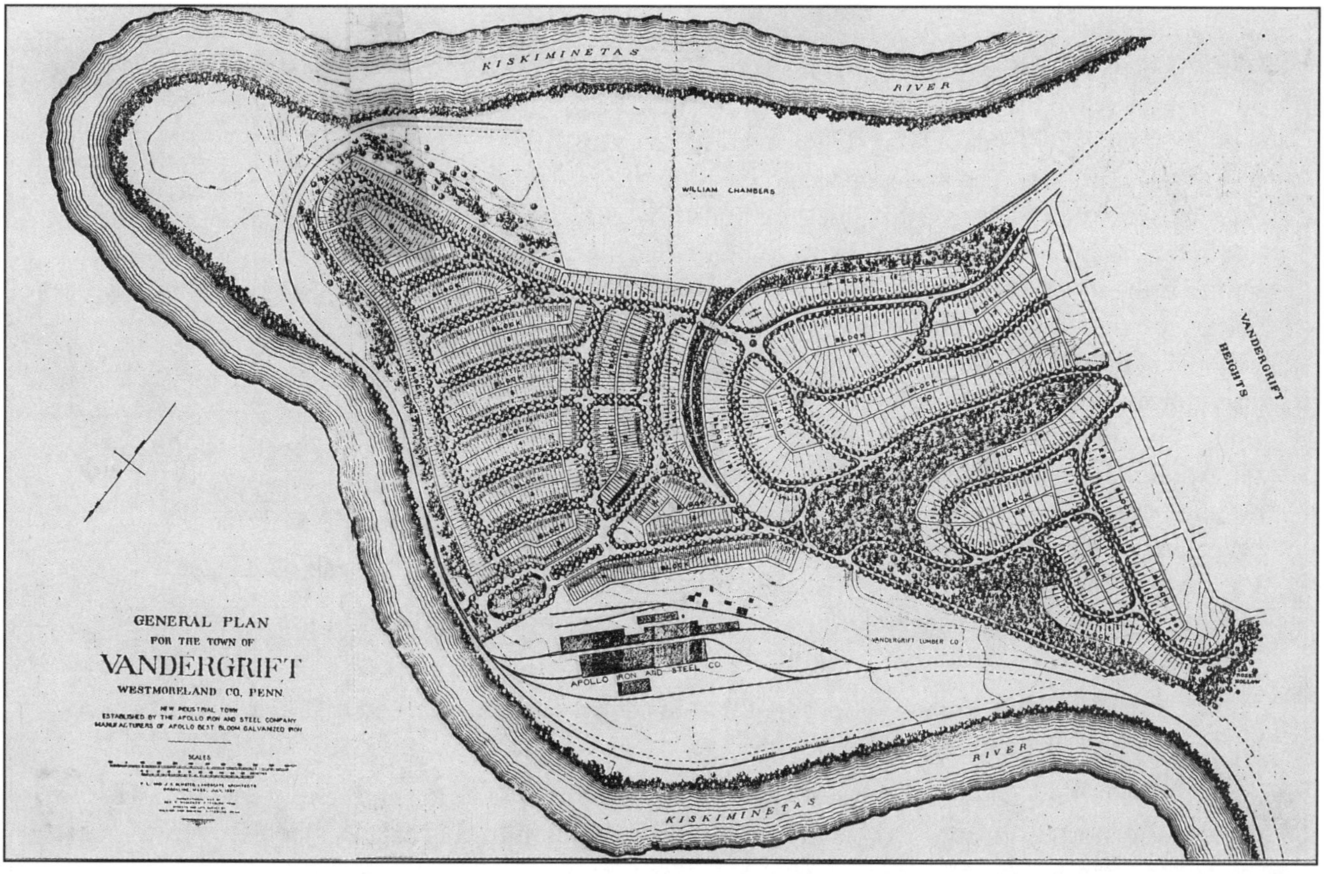

Courtesy of the Pittsburgh Press

Olmsted's General Plan for the Town of Vandergrift

each other at right angles, but formed arcs of a circle, gently curving with the contour of the land with a number of adjoining ornamental plots, now described as parklets. As design plans progressed, Olmsted's genius went into full swing. The dreams of two men, McMurtry and Olmsted, were about to produce a revolutionary marriage between industry and community.

With the dream in motion, the time had come to choose a name. After considerable discussion and several rejected suggestions, McMurtry, in typical form, finally declared, *Hell, boys, We'll call it Vandergrift for Captain Vandergrift.* Captain Jacob J. Vandergrift was McMurtry's friend and a strong supporter of his vision. McMurtry's choice was truly an honor but very much in line with his own ideals as his friend was himself a living representation of the character this new town was to display.

The land is purchased, the decisions made, the plans drawn up, the town is named, lets get the show on the road!

Follow the Yellow Brick Road

Standing at the corner of Washington and Grant Avenues on May 1, 1895 (the business district of present-day Vandergrift), you would have found yourself in a farmer's pasture contemplating a quiet rural scene. But soon these fields would be crisscrossed with gently curving streets paved with yellow brick. Hundreds of thousands of bricks were to be laid by hand

Captain Jacob J. Vandergrift

Captain Jacob J. Vandergrift was born in Pittsburgh on April 10, 1827. At age 15, he left home to be a cabin boy on a river steam boat. He proved to be industrious and hard working and rose to the position of captain of the boat. He eventually owned one boat and had interests in several others. He is credited with being first to utilize space on the front of the boat and to develop a new method of towing barges. He moved to Oil City, PA, and became the first profitable oil pipeline operator and founded the Imperial Oil and Refining Company. Eventually he became the principle investor in the Apollo Iron and Steel Company. As a business partner, personal friend, and supporter of George McMurtry's "Workingman's Paradise," he financed the building of the Vandergrift Block Building (an early town office and apartment complex) and several homes at the lower end of Farragut and Sumner Avenues in Vandergrift before the turn of the century.

It was said of Captain Vandergrift that his entire life was marked by strict integrity and honesty of both principle and practice.

He held the firm conviction that wealth was a gift of God for high and noble use. He was most generous throughout his life to church and philanthropic causes. Jacob J. Vandergrift died on December 26, 1899.

Courtesy of Harold Doutt

Vandergrift Homes, early 1900s

throughout the town. You can still find evidence of these original brick streets in many of the town's alleys and under the present topping of asphalt.

Stone from nearby quarries would be cut into curbs and installed to contain the bricks and rain runoff. (These stone curbs are evident all over town.) Miles and miles of pipe for water and sewers would be installed. The water line would run about three miles south of town where artesian wells would provide the town with the best water in the area.

There was no power company to provide electricity nor a county water system to provide water to each home; arrangements had to be made for that. A forest of trees would be planted and a forest of poles to carry electrical and telephone lines would be needed.

Untold tons of construction steel for girders and the corrugated walls and roof for the new mills would soon be arrive, along with heavy machinery, red and white brick for homes and businesses, and lumber, much lumber for most of the homes.

All the people and material to create a town would arrive by railroad or by horse and wagon.

Freedom and Opportunity Built In

McMurtry had planned that the building and operation of the town and the mill

This Is Expensive!

Residential lots sold for 25 cents a square foot; corner lots for 40 cents. Business lots sold for 75 cents a square foot, with corner business lots going for 85 cents. In 1907, new lots on East Adams were selling for $750.00. It is not known if this expensive situation was planned or an oversight. Lower paid people were certainly needed to operate the mill and the town. But they could not afford the lots at the prices for which they were sold, even though they seem drastically inexpensive to us. Therefore, they bought lots outside the original town of Vandergrift.

Courtesy of Harold Doutt

The Top of Hamilton Avenue Where It Winds off of Franklin Avenue

Courtesy of Harold Doutt

Fourth of July Parade Coming up Farragut Avenue

should be separate entities to avoid the problems mill run towns had encountered in other areas. Creative planning and organization would be needed to solve all the problems of developing this "Better Than The Best" of towns.

Courtesy of Harold Doutt

Home interiors, Vandergrift early 1900s

After thirteen months of preparation, the Land Company announced, *We are ready to sell lots. Have waited until the place is entirely ready. Now you can judge its value and buy intelligently.*

By June 8,1896, the company had 814 lots ready to sell. Two hundred of these lots were for businesses. During the first week of sales, 276 lots were sold to working men and businessmen. Speculators were turned away because only prospective employees were offered home sites.

With all of the improvements in place, these building sites were not cheap by 1896 standards. The average cost of a lot was $1,000. This high cost would restrict the buyers to the skilled, well-paid mill workers and businessmen. Laborers, store clerks, and other low-paid residents would find other arrangements in communities that would develop around the town. It is not known if this situation was planned or just an oversight, because lower paid workers were certainly needed to successfully operate the mill and the town.

There were no zoning laws when the town was founded. No stipulations were made as to the style, size, or cost of homes to be built. Every man was guided by his own taste. Early deeds did forbid the sale or manufacture of liquor.

Iron Age Magazine wrote this about the homes in 1901:

> *Instead of erecting plain or homely structures, they were inspired by their surroundings to study architectural graces and numerous beautiful houses were built in the infancy of the town. Today it is one of the prettiest towns to be found anywhere.*
>
> *Every house, of course, has its own bathroom and other sanitary conveniences. Every house uses natural gas for cooking and sometimes for heating and lighting, although, elec-*

Vandergrift Land and Improvement Company

Being the astute manager that he was, George McMurtry created a separate corporation called the Vandergrift Land and Improvement Company to handle the development of the town. This corporation would be responsible for the layout of the town, the construction of the streets, and other infrastructure necessary to operation of the town; it would also sell the building lots. Separate companies would be formed under the improvement company to provide water, electric, and telephone service. The most notable early president of the company was John F. Horne.

On May 2, 1895 with the plans and organization in place, without ceremony, ground was broken for Vandergrift. There were no bands, no flags or banners, no speeches, just—let's get busy and get the job done—that was so typical of McMurtry's operations.

James Sansom Whitworth
Attorney, Bank President

The man who negotiated the farmland purchase on which Vandergrift was built, James Sansom (J. S.) Whitworth, obviously liked the community he helped to found, he spent the rest of his life managing its institutions and living there.

Whitworth was an attorney for Apollo Iron and Steel Company whose manager was George G. McMurtry. McMurtry trusted Whitworth to secure the farms owned by John Townsend, Hugh Jones, William Lauffer, and James Verner, approximately 600 acres.

All Whitworth reported about himself in an article on the town's history for the *Vandergrift News* was that a bank was opened with him as president. That bank was the Vandergrift Federal Savings and Loan, and he held that job until his death July 28, 1934, at the age of 77.

Courtesy of H. Reynolds Clawson III

The Whitworth Mansion, circa 1900

Whitworth was born in Apollo, where he attended public schools, then went to Slate Lick Academy. In 1876 - 1877 he taught at New Texas. After more study at a school in Ohio, he returned to Apollo and was principal of their public schools for three years. While he was there former Vandergrift Burgess Jack F. McIntire was among his pupils. Whitworth studied law at night, and was admitted to the bar in Armstrong and Westmoreland counties in 1882. He opened a law office in Apollo and became attorney for the Apollo Iron and Steel Company in 1886.

On July 15, 1897, he came to the home he built at 107 Custer Ave., Vandergrift, to live. His descendants, granddaughter Caroline Clawson and great grandson Harry R. Clawson III, who is a banker, as is his father, at National Bank of the Commonwealth, still reside there.

His death was the big headline story in the *Vandergrift News* July 30, 1934. "Mr. Whitworth's history was the history of Vandergrift," it said. "He had been identified with every phase of the town's development. His death took away an inexhaustible source of history and anecdote concerning this model city.

He became, in the twilight of his life, a figure almost legendary. His physicians advised daily walks for his health. He followed their instructions. Every day, except when the weather was inclement, he strode for miles along the highways of the Kiski Valley, swinging his light cane, greeting acquaintances, and occasionally stopping to chat."

An Interesting Story...

Mr. Whitworth was a crafty philanthropist. It is reported that, while walking through the Heights, he noticed children playing baseball with a stick. He gave them money on that day to buy a bat, or ball, or glove, and off they would race to get the item.

As he passed by again the children hid what they'd purchased, so he would give them more money to buy another needed item. This continued until, by the account of one resident, the whole team was outfitted. Mr. Whitworth of course knew what was happening.

tric lighting is generally used. (All of this was quite unusual for its day)

Within one year, 150 houses and one church had been built, and the population had grown to an estimated 600 and would continue to grow. Vandergrift officially became a borough on May 15, 1897.

McMurtry established the First National Bank of Vandergrift in June 1897 to meet the town's banking needs and to provide financing for homes, businesses, and town improvements such as schools. It was located in the Vandergrift Block Building. Employees of the mill were expected to transact their financial business with this bank. It soon became apparent that the limitations on national banks in making loans hampered efforts to aid development of the town.

Park, showing P. R. R. Station,
Vandergrift, Pa.
Courtesy of Buttermilk Falls Publishing Company

Washington Avenue, the widest street in town

(In 1902 the National Bank was replaced by the Vandergrift Savings and Trust Company. In 1905 it moved into a new building at the corner of Washington and Grant Avenues, which is now the home of the Integra Bank.)

Almost every aspect of the town's development seemed to be in the hands of talented people. To satisfy the plan for parks, trees, and shrubbery, McMurtry hired Count Van Aubery, a German forester. In a short time, he had young trees lining the streets and had beautified the parks. His military presence, it is said, frightened those inclined to disturb his work. True aristocrat that he was, he added dignity to the town after the same fashion as he implied the saber cuts on his face added dignity to his person. Could he but wonder at his handiwork if he could see the town now when spring breaks forth along its streets, or see the glorious fall colors that brighten the town annually.

Not everything went as planned however. You might take note that the widest street in Vandergrift, Washington Avenue, was intended originally to be the main business street in the town. However, business men for the most part shunned the high-cost business lots on Washington Avenue for the lower cost lots along Grant and Columbia Avenues. Thus, the evolving business economy filled the much narrower streets which had not been designed for heavier traffic.

Another interesting challenge befell McMurtry when the high cost of the building lots in Vandergrift caused a boom in sales of home sites in Morning Sun (now East Vandergrift). McMurtry attempted to dissuade people from buying there by making it difficult to get to the mill and businesses in town. He did this by having a 14 - foot high wooden fence built from the cut to the foundry, causing quite a detour for men coming to work at the mill. The wall proved to be little inconvenience as holes were cut where passage was desired, and soon it was removed.

At one point when the sale of building lots lagged, McMurtry threatened that, *If you don't buy our home sites, you can't work in our mill.* It does not seem that this threat was ever carried out because many workers continued to commute from Apollo and other surrounding communities.

These challenges proved insignificant in light of the many successes yet to be realized by McMurtry.

More than a Good Home A Good Place to Live

Mr. McMurtry was convinced that a good worker required more than a good home to live in. He believed that church-going men were honest, hard working, and less likely to cause problems on the job. He also realized the importance of educational, cultural, and recreational opportunities to a productive work force. McMurtry filled these needs through generous support of schools, churches, parks, and a community theater.

Education

It is interesting to note that 1895 is also the anniversary of the Pennsylvania law that mandated compulsory school attendance. Children from the age of 8 to 13 were required to attend class at least 70% of the days school was in session. Children from the ages of 13 - 16 were not required to attend school if they had a job. As early as May 1897, the town had elected a school board, which immediately began plans for the Custer School on land donated by McMurtry. Until this school was built, classes were held in the basement of the Methodist Church and in Grimm's Hall in

Ouch That Smarts!

Early discipline in the Vandergrift Public Schools was a bit tougher than what exists today. In the early days of the Custer School, teachers would frequently slap students on the back of the hand with a ruler for such offenses as whispering or making slate pencils squeak.

Other frequently used forms of discipline included confinement, either to the cloak room or to the corner of the room. The child could not move or look at the class until the teacher permitted. One teacher would give offenders a good shaking. She would put both hands inside a boy's shirt collar and shake them violently.

But the really painful punishment came as you moved into the higher grades. There, resting on the window sill of each classroom, was a rattan whip. Being whipped this way would leave ugly red marks on the back, thighs, and calves of the unfortunate students who faced this punishment. After some years, the rattan whips were replaced with paddles.

These memories were collected from a column called *Fallen Leaves* written by H. W. Nichols. Nichols favored the discipline practices and his opinion of the early Vandergrift Public Schools was a very positive one. *"In all these years the schools were splendid and whatever success I have had in life I owe largely to the sound foundation for learning acquired in Vandergrift."*

Teachers On Wheels

Did you know that once Vandergrift Heights Public School teachers could not attend the roller skating rink? In 1907 a rule was passed to this effect: *Hereafter the attendance of any of the Heights teachers at a skating rink will be taken by the school board as a resignation.*

You may ask why such a drastic measure was passed. The school board stated that some of the teachers were devoting too much of their time in the evenings at the skating rinks. It was also alleged that some were neglecting their school duties and were not in the best fashion for their work the next day.

the Presbyterian Church. Vandergrift Public School opened November 15, 1897, and had its first graduating class of 15 girls in the spring of 1902. Few boys attended high school, preferring to work rather than attend school. Early graduation services were held in the Casino.

The growing population prompted the building of a second school, the Lincoln Building, in 1900. Like the Custer Building, it contained eight class rooms, plus a 350 seat auditorium and gymnasium.

In short order, the school board was required to add a third school, the Sherman Building (1911). The Lincoln School served as the high school until 1919 when a new school was built to accommodate the growing community.

Education was not neglected in Vandergrift Heights either. (see Chapter 3 for story on Vandergrift Heights) Students began classes in a wooden school building in 1898 that was followed by the Longfellow Building. The Wilson Building (named for Woodrow Wilson) was completed in 1911, the same year the wooden grade school was demolished. (The Wilson Building is still located on Longfellow Street; it is privately owned.) Vandergrift and Vandergrift Heights schools consolidated in 1915 when the towns consolidated.

The public school was not the only source of an education in Vandergrift's early days. There was the Vandergrift Commercial College, which was first located on the second floor of the Beamer Building on Grant Avenue (next to Elliott Electric Supply). Sixty-nine students were enrolled in a variety of business classes in 1903. In 1906, increased enrollment caused the college to move to the Pennington Building. The last information about the college appeared in the *Vandergrift News* in 1924.

Freedom of Worship

The Land Company donated some of the best corner lots in town and offered to pay half the cost of a church building if the church congregation would put up a building worth at least $15,000. The Methodist,

Courtesy of Buttermilk Falls Publishing Company

Two of Vandergrift's first schools: The Custer and Lincoln Buildings

Worshipping

The Vandergrift Churches: In the beginning...

George McMurtry's idea for "something better than the best" included a revolutionary provision for freedom of worship believing that "good people would want good churches." Through the Vandergrift Land and Improvement Company, he offered a clear deed for choice lots, plus a check for $7,500 to any denomination who would agree to build a church in the new town costing no less than $15,000. In addition, McMurtry personally provided each a new organ.

His agent in this matter, J. I. Bachman, explained McMurtry's motives in the offer to a prospective presbytery this way, "Gentlemen, do not misunderstand us; we are not a benevolent organization. This is not charity we are offering you. It is simply a business proposition. We want good citizens in our town and we know that good people will want good churches."

According to Henry W. Nichols, his father was already host to a group of those good people in 1895. He reported 20 or 30 people crowded into their sitting room to hear a clergyman from Apollo preach several times a month.

FIRST EVANGELICAL LUTHERAN CHURCH

The Lutherans were the first to accept McMurtry's offer. The Rev. John W. Poffinberger, pastor of Hebron Lutheran in Leechburg, took the proposition to Conemaugh Conference in May 1896. The cornerstone for the new church at the corner of Washington and Custer Avenues was laid in November 1896, even though the church was not yet organized. Organization took place on May 16, 1897, with 117 charter members. They dedicated their church building on June 22, 1897.

FIRST PRESBYTERIAN CHURCH

In June 1896, the Presbyterians in Apollo who expected to move to Vandergrift appointed a committee to ask their presbytery for permission to organize a church there. Permission was granted, and the first services of the new group of 40 were held in a rented hall until McMurtry's' offer could become brick and stone at the corner of Washington and Columbia Avenues. They laid the cornerstone in April 1897 and began to meet in their new building in September 1897.

METHODIST EPISCOPAL CHURCH

Methodists in Apollo were doing the same thing at almost the same time. Rev. Noble G. Miller helped organize the board of trustees for a new church in September 1896. Their cornerstone was laid July 1, 1897 at the corner of Custer and Lincoln Avenues. The first service in the sanctuary was February 14, 1898. When the dedication took place in April of that year, the Methodists had 263 members.

UNITED PRESBYTERIAN CHURCH

United Presbyterians of the Conemaugh Presbytery discussed the founding of a mission in Vandergrift as early as December 1895. At the time a group was worshiping in private homes in 1896 under the ministry of Rev. R.A. Jamison of Apollo. This group chose land from Mr. McMurtry at the intersection of Washington and Franklin Avenues. They worshipped in the First Presbyterian Church until their own building was completed in early 1898. The church was officially established December 10, 1898, with 43 charter members.

VANDERGRIFT FREE METHODIST CHURCH

Vandergrift Heights (then a separate town) was also in the process of establishing its own place of worship. A group of Apollo Free Methodists living on the Heights formed a group under the leadership of William McKim in November of 1897. By the next September, Miss Ada Pearce was appointed first pastor of the society. From home meetings, they moved into a local schoolhouse until their frame church on the 300 block of Emerson Street was dedicated in the summer of 1903. In 1988, the facility became the home of Bethel Family Church of Vandergrift.

ST.GERTRUDE'S ROMAN CATHOLIC CHURCH

Easter Sunday, April 10, 1898, marked the town's first Roman Catholic Mass. The mass was celebrated in a small church erected on a knoll at the east end of town. Eleven years later that first church was replaced by the existing Romanesque style St. Gertrude's Church, which was blessed on

In Vandergrift

March 11, 1911, by the Most Reverend Regis Canavin, Bishop of Pittsburgh.

FIRST REFORMED CHURCH

Not far from St. Gertrude's Church on Franklin Avenue, the First Reformed Church of Vandergrift was organized on August 24, 1899, at a meeting in the United Presbyterian Church. Services were held in a rented hall while a small chapel was built in 1901. The present church was erected in 1902 and is known today as the First Reformed Church of the United Church of Christ.

FIRST BAPTIST CHURCH

Another group of Christians had also been meeting in rented halls for several years. This was a mission outreach of the Apollo Baptist Church. As attendance grew, the group decided to set January 1, 1900, as the date for the beginning of the First Baptist Church of Vandergrift. Thirty-two charter members and their families purchased land on the corner of Adams and Franklin Avenues in 1901 and completed the church in 1905.

ST. PAUL'S LUTHERAN CHURCH

By 1901, Rev. Poffinberger of the First Lutheran Church had begun a branch church school on the Vandergrift Heights. This work grew quickly and in May 1902, St. Paul's Lutheran Church was organized on Emerson Street. There were 69 charter members under the care of the Rev. George Beiswanger.

ALL SAINTS EPISCOPAL CHURCH

September 1, 1903, marked the first worship service for Episcopalian folks. They met in the Reformed Church under the leadership of Rev. Thomas Loyd, the first rector. The group opened All Saints Episcopal Church March 25, 1906, on Sherman Avenue.

The town settled down to work and build their lives between the years 1903 and 1913. No new churches sprang up during those years but seeds were being planted in tent meetings, home gatherings and ethnic groups that would soon sprout and grow. From those seeds came five more churches after 1913, the Holy Trinity Slovak Catholic Church, the Greek Orthodox Church, the Gospel Tabernacle, the First Church of God, and the First Baptist Church of North Vandergrift.

A Slovak group obtained permission to leave St. Gertrude's Church in 1913, but it was not until 1916 that the ***Holy Trinity Slovak Catholic Church*** was blessed and the first Mass said in their new sanctuary in East Vandergrift. Rev. Father

Courtesy of Harold Doutt

The Lutheran, Methodist, and Presbyterian Churches, Circa 1900

Worshipping in Vandergrift

Sigismund Szydlowski, O.S.B., was their first priest.

The ***Greek Orthodox Church, Saints Constantine and Helen,*** began in a rented hall. The group bought land on Lincoln Avenue in April 1914. The church was officially incorporated March 25, 1916, and a building built shortly thereafter.

Mr. and Mrs. William Difibaugh moved to Vandergrift from Jeannette and began holding prayer meetings in their home in 1912. This group formed ***Gospel Tabernacle***, and called Rev. Lewis C. Hill as their pastor. He and the men of the congregation constructed their worship site in 1916 on Sherman Avenue.

In 1918, a group comprising local residents began worship services in a private home on Longfellow Street. From this group the ***First Baptist Church of North Vandergrift*** was formally organized in January of 1920, and soon after, moved into a new church building in North Vandergrift.

The group that became the ***First Church of God*** began as the result of tent meetings held years earlier. They called the first full-time pastor in 1916 and dedicated the church building at the corner of Walnut and Franklin Avenues in 1921.

Vandergrift's Jewish Congregation: B'nai Israel

People of Jewish faith were among the throngs who came to the new town for employment. By 1907 or 1908, Max Copstein and Isadore Rubin formed the required 10 men into a congregation that was later named B'nai Israel. They worshipped and taught in the Conservative tradition of Judaism.

Isadore Rubin wrote home to his father, Rabbi Reuben Rubinowitz, in Vasiliski, Lithuania, that the group needed a copy of the Torah, the Laws of Moses (the first 5 books of the Old Testament). Rabbi Rubinowitz brought a Torah to this country in 1910, and this Torah became the treasured centerpiece of worship and instruction for B'nai Israel.

Early meetings were held in rented halls on Washington Avenue and in a room Jack Rubin owned above his Ladies Department Store on Grant Avenue. Small weekly Sabbath services and the Sunday school and Hebrew school meetings were held at the Grant Avenue site. For larger meetings, such as the High Holidays of Yom Kippur and Rosh Hashana and for Bar Mitzvahs, B'nai Israel the congregation rented one of the larger town halls such as a the fire hall, the VFW hall, or the Sons of Italy hall.

As the years passed, the congregation grew until at its peak 47 families, comprising about 200 people in the Apollo, Leechburg, and Vandergrift areas were calling B'nai Israel theirs.

During these robust years, B'nai Brith (Sons of the Covenant) was in operation for the men, and a Hadassah chapter existed for the women.

B'nai Israel never had an official rabbi, but Isadore Rubin frequently lead the worship, as did other men of the congregation because requirements to lead were simply, "clean hands, a pure heart, and knowledge of the service." When Rabbi Rubinowitz came to live with Isadore, he led services only on holy days. In later years, Jack Rubin often led the services and taught in the Hebrew school.

Meetings were held at the Grant Avenue site until the early 1970s. By this time most of the Jews had moved from the valley eliminating the required ten men attending. B'nai Israel came to an end.

Jack Rubin said, "No matter where the Jews went, they held on and tried to continue with their religion. That's why they have survived as a people." In keeping with that tradition, in 1993, the B'nai Israel Torah scroll was given to a Kollel, a special group of Jews in the Squirrel Hill section of Pittsburgh, whose mission is to learn the laws of Moses and to teach them to others.

Courtesy of Harold Doutt

The Casino Theatre and Municipal Building, circa 1900

Lutheran, and Presbyterian churches took advantage of this offer. In addition, McMurtry financed a trip to Europe for three of the town's clergy to broaden their education. McMurtry's generosity to the churches continued when in 1902 he offered each church in town a free organ.

Ida Tarbell wrote of the churches in 1916:

> *The churches are most aggressive in attacks on evil doing with strong community backing. There are nine churches in Vandergrift and the suburbs with a population of 12,000. On one Sunday 5,500 attended church by official count.*

Did the churches have an impact on evildoing? They must have, because one story relates that *only two policemen are on duty, one during the day and one during the night. The town is so quiet that when police help is needed you can usually find one sleeping on the steps of the theatre.*

A Taste of Culture

Most people arrived in Vandergrift by train. As they approached their destination, they must have wondered just what their new town would be like. Would it be like the other dirty dreary mill towns they had seen or heard about?

We can but wonder what their thoughts were as they left the station and looked up Washington Avenue. The streets were bright with yellow bricks and handsome new buildings lined the street. Across the street a beautiful park with grass, flowers, and trees extended up a slight slope to a majestic white building fronted by tall Roman columns. There at the crown of this elegant concourse rested the center of culture for this worker's paradise, the Casino Theater.

It was unusual for a town the size of Vandergrift to have such a fine theater facility. The average turn-of-the-century working man had few opportunities to experience culture other than his own. But this was McMurtry's dream. Always *Better Than The Best.*

In 1906, the Casino Company offered to sell the Casino building to the town for $15,000. The offer was placed before a vote of the town's residents. The voters rejected the offer leaving the Casino in the hands of the stock holders until 1925 when the town purchased it.

"In a Day or Two, That Won't Do"

While on the subject of fine buildings, two others of interest should be mentioned, the Vandergrift Block Building and the Sherman Inn.

The Vandergrift Block Building was located at the corner of Washington and Sherman Avenues. This building, financed by Captain Vandergrift, was likely one of the first large commercial buildings built in the town. It contained the mill offices, the bank, Land Development Company Office, Post Office, the telephone office business, and apartments on the upper floors. It was a busy place and must have been the center of the town's early expansion activities. It

The Casino

Part of George McMurtry's plans for a contented work force in his Workingman's Paradise centered around the creation of cultural opportunities within the town. One of his greatest philanthropic investments in this area was his support of the majestic Casino Theater.

Before 1900, the town had no adequate place for large group meetings, or for a library, or offices for the administration of the town. George McMurtry supplied land and $14,000 toward the construction of a $32,000 building to meet these needs. The Vandergrift Casino Company was incorporated to finance the balance of the cost. The Casino was completed in June 1900 and served the town as lecture hall, Vaudeville and movie theater, and provided a stage for live theater. The theater was used for school programs and graduations; some churches had their beginnings there. The building also provided meeting rooms for the town council and space for a library. It also housed the mayor's office and town jail.

The Casino Theater opened the evening of June 23, 1900 to a packed house presenting Henrietta Crossman, a star of legitimate theater. Many plays, stage shows, and lectures were to follow. On November 24, 1906 Bob Fitzimmons, the World Middle Weight and World Heavy Weight Champion in the 1890s appeared at the Casino in a play titled,"A Fight For Love." It was headlined as a dramatic and scientific event. Seating prices ranged from 35 cents to $1.00

During World War I, many plays and speakers appeared to encourage the war effort. In 1918, a military musical spectacle titled, "My Soldier Girl" appeared with a smart swift and saucy cast with a brigade of wonderful girls. In March 1918, the Casino Theater hosted former President William Howard Taft. The *Vandergrift News* wrote in an article, "We are indeed honored to have a man of Mr. Taft's prominence, standing and ability come to a town of our size. Mr. Taft's topic was "The Great War."

Following dramatic restoration efforts the Casino now houses the Vandergrift Museum and recently reopened its doors to live theater presentations. It remains today a majestic legacy to the rich historic culture of the community.

Courtesy of: "Vandergrift: First 75 Years"
The Vandergrift Block Building. Note the Sherman Inn at far left.

days."

McMurtry laughed. *"In a day or two, that won't do, start the building in the morning,"* he commanded. Although it was 10:30

was torn down in 1965.

Another building across Sherman Avenue from the Vandergrift Block was not nearly so imposing, nor did it play such an important role in the development of the town. The plan to construct this building did however shed a great deal of light on the character of George McMurtry. When he wanted something done, he wanted it DONE! Mr. McMurtry was concerned that important visitors, who would undoubtedly be coming to see his model town, had no adequate lodgings or place to eat.

He told his contractor, H. W. Nichols, of his concern and Mr. Nichols replied, "I'll draw a sketch and have it ready in a few

then, when Mr. McMurtry returned two hours later, a sketch was ready. With only minor changes it was approved. The temperature Nichols reported, was below zero. The ground was frozen and had been for several days. Excavation was almost impossible.

"The ground," Nichols said, "is frozen two feet deep."

"I'll attend to that," McMurtry answered.

Calling workmen, he ordered enough steel sheets to cover the earth (at the building site). At four o'clock in the morning, the lot was ablaze with flames (gas was piped under the steel sheets to thaw the ground.)

Courtesy of: "Vandergrift: First 75 Years"
The Sherman Inn, Vandergrift's first hotel, may have been physically moved as many as 3 times.

Henry W. Nichols

Planner, Builder, Mayor, Postmaster, Retailer, Husband, Father

Henry W. Nichols, Vandergrift's first mayor, may have had a knack for being in the right place at the right time. Born in Utah in 1863 to a prosperous family, he was taken by his father to the historic ceremony near Promontory Point, Utah, when the golden spike was driven to join east and west by railroad for the first time. This occurred May 10, 1869, when Henry was six years old.

He grew up in Salt Lake City, then became a successful architect and builder. In 1893 recession ruined his business. Leaving home and family, Nichols reversed Horace Greely's admonition to "go West" and headed East instead to find work. Two years later while in New York City, he met George McMurtry. McMurtry hired Nichols to supervise construction of a new steel mill in Vandergrift, Pennsylvania.

When Nichols got to Vandergrift, his family joined him. They lived in the Townsend homestead on mill property until their home could be built at 157 Grant Avenue. He and his wife raised four children in Vandergrift.

Not only was Mr. Nichols the first mayor (or Burgess as it was known then), but in 1896 he was appointed the first postmaster. He held this post until 1904.

After the mill was completed, he designed and built the Vandergrift Inn, completed in just under four weeks in midwinter, at Mr. McMurtry's command. He helped build many of the houses in town and supervised construction of the Lutheran Church and parsonage. He and a brother also operated a variety store on Grant Avenue for a time.

At seven, teams were dragging a scoop. The original conversation took place on January 31, 1897. *"We want lunch served in the dining room,"* McMurtry added, pointing to the sketch, *"on February 28."*

It was hard work for Nichols and his men, but lunch was served on the day appointed. Mr. McMurtry was a guest that day and as he quit the room, he complimented both the hotel and the caterer (Leonard Elswick).

In only 28 days, the Sherman Inn had been built! With such a dominating personality, it is little wonder the town grew quickly and as planned.

The Sherman Inn is no longer at its original site. It was reportedly moved to a new location on Sherman Avenue to be used for a residence. Ropes and pulleys were attached to large metal stakes driven into the street and pulled by mules to move the inn up Sherman Avenue.

Reflections Of The Times

Stories of the Day

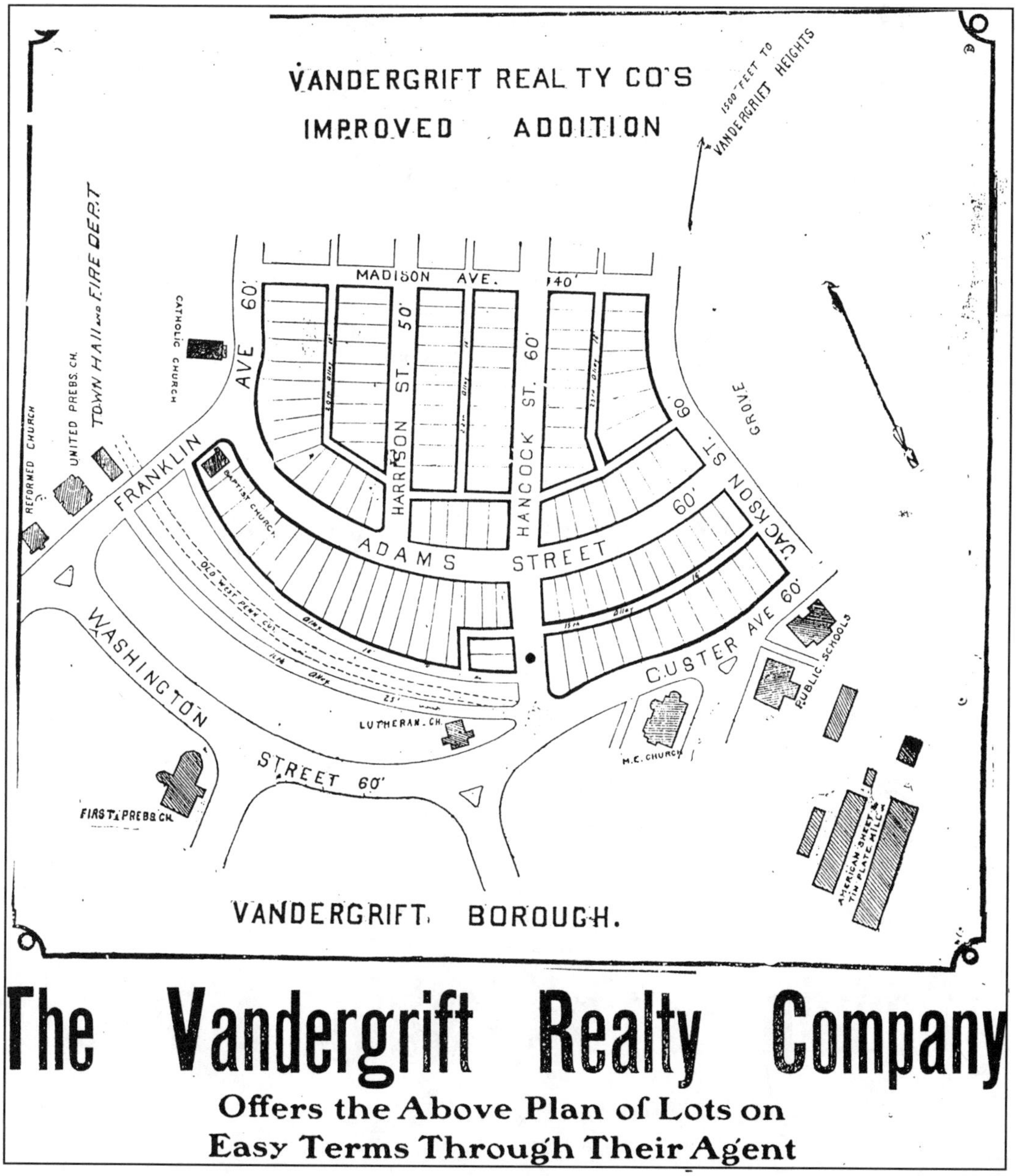

Courtesy of Buttermilk Falls Publishing Company

Lots were selling fast in 1907 and new sections of town were opening up. This section became known as "Pumpkin Center." Such ads (this one actual size) were often found on the front page of the local newspaper. *(From* The Vandergrift News, *April 11, 1907.)*

Satisfaction Guaranteed. **Low Prices Always.**

Penningtons

All Suits and Overcoats 25 Per Cent Off

Instead of offering a few odds and ends or a few undesirable leavings of the season, we offer our entire stock of Mens', Boys and Children's Suits, Overcoats and Raincoats at 25 per cent. less than our original price. Our stock comprises an up-to-date assortment and our prices are always the most reasonable.

Suits marked	$ 8.0	now	$ 6.00	Overcoats marked	$ 8.00	now	$ 6.00
" "	10.00	"	7.50	" "	10.00	"	7.50
" "	15.00	"	11.25	" "	15.00	"	11.25
" "	20.00	"	15.00	" "	20.00	"	15.00

All Trousers at 25 Per Cent. Off.

We are offering our entire stock of Dutchess trousers and other makes, nothing reserved.

$6.00	Trousers now	$4.50	$3.50	Trousers, now	$2.63
5.00	" "	3.75	3.00	" "	2.25
4.00	" "	3.00	2.00	" "	1.50

Don't wait until it is too late.
COME NOW.

Pennington's Clothing Stores,

Authority on Styles

Vandergrift and Indiana

Courtesy of Buttermilk Falls Publishing Company

Look at these prices! We have come a long way since 1907. *(From* The Vandergrift News, *January 24, 1907.)*

Composition Contest.

THE Vandergrift Business College will give a free scholarship for either a Book-keeping or Shorthand course to the person writing the best composition on the subject, "Why should a young man or woman take a business course," second, third and fourth prizes will be certificates for $35.00, $25.00 and $20.00 respectively, the next five will be certificates for $15.00 and the last five for $10.00. In sending the composition do not sign your name on it but write it on a separate sheet, so the judges will not know the name of the contestant before giving their decision. All compositions must be received at this office not later than October 30, 1911.

Vandergrift Business College

C. R. ANDERSON, Principal.

Vandergrift Block, Vandergrift, Pa.

Courtesy of Buttermilk Falls Publishing Company

Higher Education

Vandergrift had a college! There were as many as 5 different names found for Vandergrift training schools existing between 1897 and the mid-1920s. At least three were separate institutions. Such schools were needed to train the bevy of workers needed to support industries in a new mill town. (*From* The Vandergrift News, *October 12, 1911.)*

Counterfeit Gang Apprehended

On Saturday evening of December 5, 1912, a North Vandergrift merchant noticed that he had been paid with "queer." Queer was the term used for counterfeit money. Upon his discovery he telephoned the Vandergrift Justice of Peace telling him that he thought he knew who had passed the queer money. Together, the merchant and the Justice of Peace laid a trap that would uncover a Western Pennsylvania counterfeiting gang.

During that initial call, the Justice instructed the merchant to keep quiet about the incident and wait for the counterfeiters to return. He further instructed the merchant to call him when the suspects arrived. The Justice lived just down the block and could hop a trolley and be there within minutes. They didn't have long to wait.

Later that very evening, the counterfeiters returned again and passed more queer to the merchant. The Justice got the word and hopped the trolley as planned. Pulling up at the next stop, the counterfeiters boarded and paid the conductor with more queer—right in front of the Justice! They were of course immediately arrested and brought to the Vandergrift lockup. The counterfeit money was made of babbit steel and resembled the silver dollar of that era. Twenty-five or thirty known pieces were distributed before the gang was apprehended.

The suspects apprehended were a man from the Vandergrift Heights and a woman from Parks Township which is just across the river near Leechburg. During a search of the man's residence, officers found the beginnings of a counterfeit money plant. Upon further investigation it was discovered that he was in the process of ordering further materials for counterfeit production. However, after a third arrest and interrogation of a gang member from neighboring Leechburg, it was discovered that the existing counterfeit coin was coming to the area through a former Vandergrift Heights man who was running his operation out of Indiana, PA 40 miles to the northeast.

At this point, the U.S. Secret Service was called into the investigation. After a local investigation, the Secret Service investigated the Indiana leads and moved the prisoners to the Allegheny County Jail in Pittsburgh.

The leads in Indiana did not pan out when the Secret Service found that the suspect location had been cleaned out before they arrived. In January 1913, the three local suspects were tried in Federal Court in Erie. All pleaded guilty of passing funny money. The Vandergrift Heights man was sentenced to two years in prison at Levenworth, Kansas; the two women were sentenced to one day in the Allegheny County Jail.

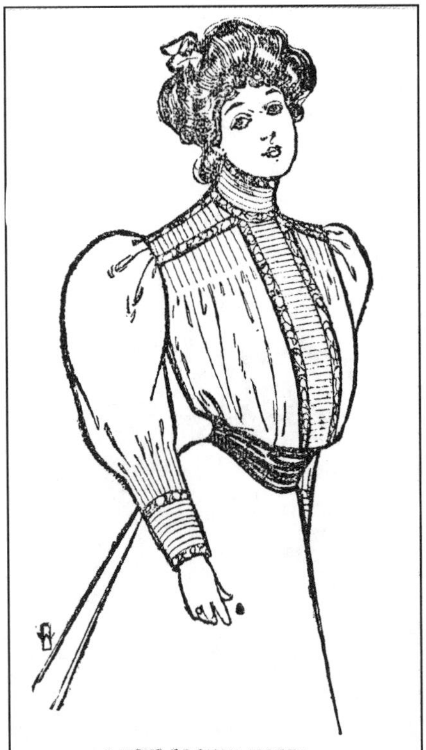

A NEW BLOUSE MODEL.

The Newest Fashions in 1906

from "Our Fashion" section of The Vandergrift News, *November 29, 1906.*

Things to Buy

The Phillip's Harness Company was located on Bancroft Street, which is now Hancock Avenue.

From The Vandergrift News, *November 26, 1908.*

Hi-Tech

Vandergrift goes first class into the 20th Century with the newest thing in 1907.

From The Vandergrift News, *August 1907.*

Ads on this page courtesy of Buttermilk Falls Publishing Company

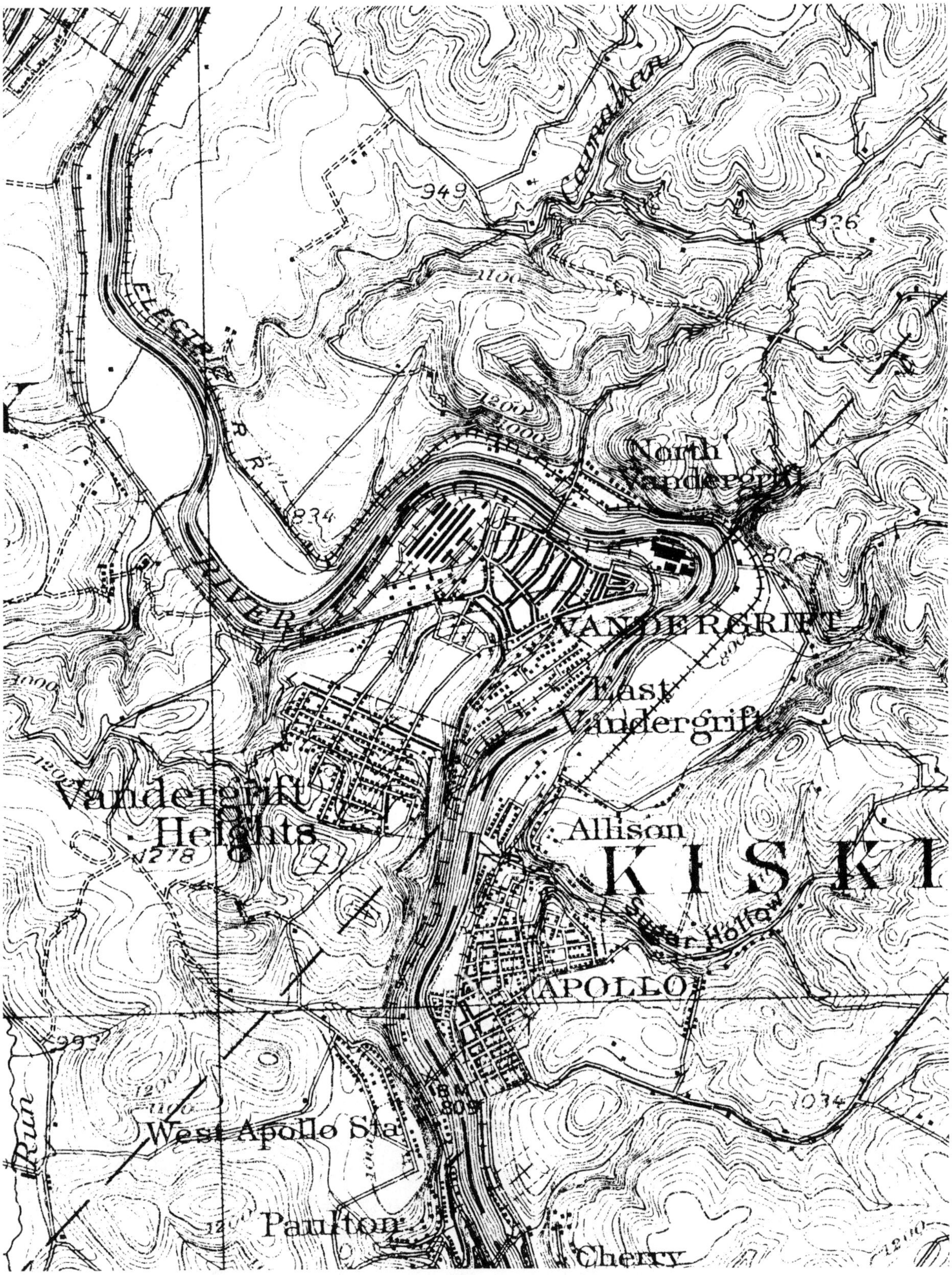

Courtesy of Greg Bothell and U. S. Geological Survey

Vandergrift, 1907

Vandergrift and Vandergrift Heights are shown here as 2 separate towns before their consolidation in 1916. Note the space between the 2 towns. The close contour lines show the Grove, a deep ravine where Davis Field is today. The Cut, the old railroad gorge on Vandergrift's outskirts, can be seen nearby. Across the river, the tracks for the trolley line can be seen.

Chapter Three

Growth through Consolidation and New Communities

As this model town, this Workingman's Paradise, rose swiftly from the valley floor, another community began just south of the border on the valley's upper slopes. Named the Vandergrift Heights, it was anything but a model town or a paradise.

Vandergrift Heights was started about the same time as its neighboring Workingman's Paradise and had parallel growth with it under the control of the Vandergrift Land and Improvement Company. The Heights officially became a borough on December 8, 1897, just seven months after Vandergrift achieved the same distinction. The Heights, however, lacked almost all of those features that the planners of the model town used as selling points

Comparing the two towns makes it apparent that Mr. McMurtry did not believe that the unskilled, low-paid workers in the mill needed the same high-quality living standards as the skilled workers, because no provisions for them are mentioned in the early plans for the town. It could be that circumstances caused by the opening of low-cost building lots in East Vandergrift forced the land company to arrive at a hasty solution to this competition. To be competitive, lots on the Heights were sold for about $150; 5 dollars down and 5 dollars a month. By 1916, there were 500 houses in the town, all but 8 of which were owned by laboring men. Most of the homes were owned by immigrants.

Instead of the gently curving streets of Olmsted's design, the more common checkerboard pattern was laid out for the Heights, and it would seem, laid out by someone not too aware of town planning, for some of the streets fell on almost impossible grades and very steep slopes. Streets were unpaved and sidewalks, those that existed, were made of boards. When the original water tanks for the town's water supply were replaced with metal ones, the wood from the tanks was used to make the boardwalks. One can only imagine what the street conditions were like when it rained.

The town council meetings were filled with complaints about the impassable intersections and the deep ditches created

Courtesy of Harold Doutt

Vandergrift Heights' Lowell Street in the early 1900s

by water run off on the steep streets. The task was beyond the efforts of the street department, which consisted of one man, a wheelbarrow, and a shovel. In 1907, the council took action to buy a railcar load of bricks to install paved ditches. The bricks cost $4 a thousand delivered at Vandergrift Rail Station!

At one point Longfellow Street was almost impassable because of deep mud stirred up by the constant horse and wagon traffic. To aid their customers, the businessmen built a boardwalk across the street at Longfellow and Wallace Streets. Unfortunately, they had it built so high that it impeded the regular street traffic and it had to be removed. It was not until 1911 that Longfellow and Emerson Streets were paved. As late as the 1950s, 60 some years after the town was founded, many streets and alleys on the Heights remained unpaved (Bryant and Poe Streets, just to mention two.)

Whereas every home in Vandergrift had a bathroom, every home of the Heights had an outhouse (many of which were still available to be tipped over on Halloween night into the 1940s.) Another sanitation difference was garbage disposal. In 1906 the council decided to fine people who threw their garbage into the alleys. This brought an angry crowd to the next council meeting to object to the fines. What objection? The town had no provisions for garbage pick-up. The council then granted a license to a man with a horse and wagon to pick up garbage on a subscription basis.

History notes only one small park in the Heights, McGregor Park, on the west end of Lowell Street. It was reportedly named after John McGregor, a Free Methodist minister who was a councilman. He was a kind and gentle man, who was so well thought of that the park was named for him.

The Heights had its own business district located primarily on Longfellow Street centered around Wallace Street. Many small stores were built and operated in scattered areas of the town. If you look carefully as you drive around, you will note the buildings that had

Courtesy of "Vandergrift: First 75 Years"

First Italian Grocery Store and Foreign Exchange

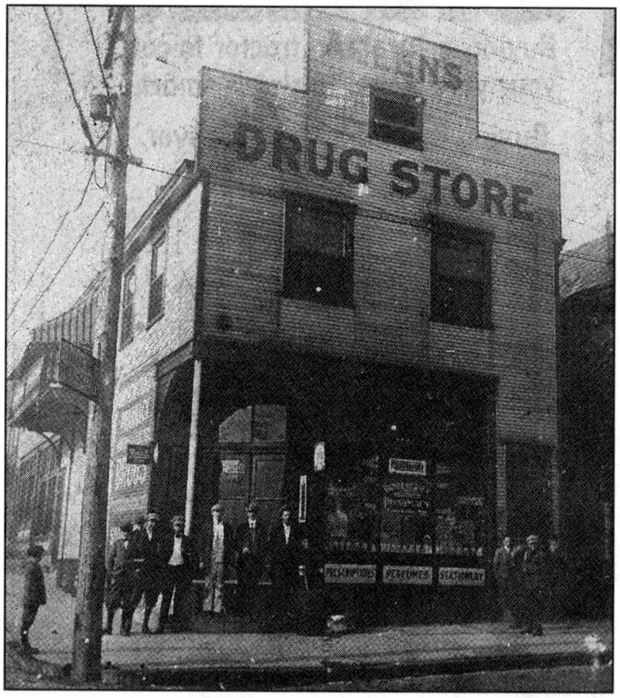

Courtesy of Harold Doutt

Allen's Drugstore, corner of Longfellow and Wallace

store fronts, but are now residences. No grand community theater served the cultural needs of the Heights populace—only a simple Nickelodeon on Lowell Street (operated by Ben Conti.)

The Turning and Singing Society is often mentioned in records of the town. This organization was apparently dedicated to gymnastics and singing. The group operated a gymnastics school and held gymnastic exhibitions and dances. The Society was said to have had one of the finest halls in Western Pennsylvania with a grand dance floor made of white maple. Turners Hall was at Longfellow and Holland Streets, where the Ambulance Service is now located. At some point, the Turners Hall became the Owls Club, a fraternal organization. The building burned in the 1950s.

Old Cemetery Moved

Mr. H. W. Nichols, a pioneer resident of our town, related this story in his "Fallen Leaves" series which appeared in the *Vandergrift News*.

Early Vandergrift ended at the railroad cut south of Washington Avenue. Across the cut, extending from where the Baptist Church now stands about two blocks toward Custer Avenue, there was a cemetery. In this cemetery, the farm people of the territory had buried their dead for several generations. Nichols estimated that 100 graves, marked with various styles of markers, were contained in the cemetery. It was said to include some graves of Revolutionary War soldiers.

It was about 150-feet wide, with the north side on the cut and the south side facing bright, rolling open green fields that extended from the cemetery to the Heights. It was surrounded by a split rail fence, which was broken in places.

The fields above the cemetery made a wonderful playground for the boys of early Vandergrift. They spent much time there on ballfields and playing in homemade tents and shanties. The cemetery had a several tall pine trees that provided a cool, quiet respite from the sun of the open fields. The boys would eat wild blackberries and red raspberries that grew along the fence. Sometimes they played spooks among the tombstones and bushes. Covering themselves with pieces of tent canvas or burlap, they would make ghostly calls from their hiding places.

Nichols believed the cemetery was abandoned about 1902. He watched as the trees were cut down, the graves dug up, and the tombstones and remains (such as they were) hauled away. He did not say where these relics were taken.

A taste of the Wild West could be found at the Corral owned by Ed Lane, a former Rough Rider in the Spanish American War. Horses were broken to saddle and harness in the large corral located between Holmes and Bryant Streets, where Poe Street is now located. There was great excitement when a new shipment of ponies would arrive to be broken. Crowds would gather to watch the riders, who dressed like cowboys, do their work. Many residents kept a cow or two with a few keeping as many as six. Boys drove the cows to and from pasture beyond the cemetery to fields on the Owens Farm and to a field adjacent to the water company's reservoir. This practice ended at about the time of World War I.

If the Wild West did not interest you, how about running away with the circus? A real honest-to-goodness traveling show had its home in Vandergrift Heights. Labanna Steele promoted the show, which was stored at his livery stable at the west end of the block above Longfellow Street

The Labanna Steele Traveling Road Show

In 1902, LaBanna Steele established a traveling road show, called Al Steele's Uncle Tom's Cabin Show. Al (Alfred) was LaBanna's son. This show had a large tent and 36 gilded wagons. The show originally portrayed the popular story from the book, "Uncle Tom's Cabin." The high drama came as little Eva ran across painted canvas ice cakes pursued by fierce blood hounds, which were in reality, Great Danes that were so gentle they had to be led across the stage. Many a tear was shed as Little Eva lay dying. This show was fairly popular and was on the road for two years.

In the third year of the show, the format was changed to that of a circus and included a contortionist, a trapeze artist, a man who swallowed his face, and a man who went up in a smoke-filled balloon. The circus did not fare as well as the Uncle Tom's Cabin Show and eventually was closed with some assets being sold and other pieces such as the brightly painted wagons allowed to rot away at the back of their livery stable.

The show and the circus both wintered in Vandergrift.

between Wallace and Hawthorn Streets. Besides providing a home for the show, of course, the stable provided horse and vehicle rental for passengers as well as freight and horse boarding facilities. The stable was destroyed by fire.

The Two Become One

Vandergrift Heights was its own town, being incorporated and having its own town government, schools, fire department, and shopping district. A 1912 *News* advertisement for the Vandergrift Land Company states *We have opened and paved a new street between Vandergrift and Vandergrift Heights, called Hancock Avenue, and laid along this street and adjacent there to a plan of lots called South Hill Plan.* The completion of the South Hill plan would fill the space dividing the two towns, and Hancock Avenue would become the main connecting road.

In 1915, the progressive-minded people of the two towns began serious consideration of consolidation, which had been discussed as early as 1913. It was believed that the consolidation would achieve economic benefits by having only one administration. Most important would be the increased attention a larger town could elicit from county and state governments. Each town council appointed a committee to prepare the matter for presentation to the voters (during these negotiations it was proposed that the combined town should be named "McMurtry", but the idea apparently had little support.) All indications were that both towns had everything to gain from consolidation.

The vote was taken on June 5, 1915, with a small voter turnout. The vote to consolidate was passed in Vandergrift by only two votes, while the voters in the Heights were more favorably inclined. Vandergrift now boasted a population in excess of 10,000. In this way, the Vandergrift Heights government ended 18 years of service to its citizens.

The Vandergrift Heights was not the only suburb of the paradise. There were also East, West, and North Vandergrift, and the Park Plan, which all play a part in the town's history. Like Vandergrift Heights, these areas were "bedroom" communities providing housing for the workers in the industries located in Vandergrift.

The Morning Sun

Of all the suburbs, East Vandergrift is the only one that became, and still remains, a separate incorporated town. Its history stretches back to 1773 when John Montgomery of Carlisle acquired title to the land from Thomas and John Penn, William Penn's sons. It was known then as Three Bottoms. A small village grew up on this land and was administered as part of Allegheny Township. The village was called Morning Sun.

The land passed through many hands till purchased by W. S. Beamer of Apollo in the 1890s with the object of subdividing it into low cost building lots (low cost as compared with Vandergrift.) The sale of these lots to Vandergrift mill workers precipitated the building of the wall from the

Courtesy of "Vandergrift: First 75 Years"

Jozef Gallovich and children in Morning Sun

railroad cut to the foundry by George McMurtry to discourage buying lots there. It also probably brought about the early establishment of the Vandergrift Heights.

Morning Sun was incorporated as the borough of East Vandergrift on December 18,1901. Many old-timers still refer to it as Morning Sun. The town grew steadily. By 1920, the population was 1,969. The population growth displayed a phenomenon typical of many mill towns during the years of heavy immigration. The early residents of the town were primarily Scots-Irish and English. With the influx of immigrants from Eastern Europe, the original residents moved away, leaving a town comprising mostly Polish, Slovak, and Lithuanian immigrants.

There were a few stores and most significantly, a modern ice plant built in 1911, that produced 37 tons of ice per day for delivery throughout the area. The only other significant industry was the Cohn Lumber Company, which burned in a spectacular fire in 1912.

As in the Heights, the streets were unpaved and virtually impassable in wet weather. Boardwalks were installed on both sides of McKinley Avenue, only to be washed away in the 1907 flood. Sewers and street lights were installed in 1912. McKinley Avenue was paved in 1916. A ferry connected East Vandergrift with Apollo after the Apollo Bridge was washed away in the 1907 flood. Flooding by the Kiski River was a recurring problem for the town until flood control dams were built on the Loyalhanna Creek and the Conemaugh River in the 1930s.

Most of the immigrants were Roman Catholic and were served by Saint Gertrude's Roman Catholic church in Vandergrift. The people, however, yearned for churches and priests who could speak their native languages. With much effort and financial sacrifice, their dreams were fulfilled. St. Casmir's Lithuanian Roman Catholic Church was built in 1922; it was destroyed by fire and rebuilt in 1936. The

The Great Flood of 1907

The *Vandergrift News*, March 14, 1907: "The Kiski valley this week experienced the biggest flood seen here since the memorable Johnstown deluge [1889]. . All the towns along the river in this section are afloat, houses have been swept away and industrial operations throughout the valley are interrupted by the high water. East Vandergrift was covered. A forcigner whose name was could not be learned, was drowned. North Vandergrift was also under water as the river crossed the trolley track and reached back to the foot of the hill. Water covered the middle pier of the North Vandergrift bridge and the structure was said to be in danger. The mill and foundry were forced to shut down. The trolley line was put out of commission and all telephone communication between Leechburg, Apollo, and Vandergrift had been cut off.

In East Vandergrift water reached the second story on houses between the tracks and the river. By noon today, the water had covered the railroad tracks making the town one unbroken sheet of water.

Vandergrift saw the advantage of its location when the other places were flooded out. On the Heights the heavy rains damaged the streets considerably, Wallace Street being particularly cut up."

From the March 21, 1907, paper: "A Vandergrift resident who has kept records on the floods says this flood was the greatest known. The stage of the water reached last week was two feet above the record Johnstown Flood."

Slovaks built Holy Trinity Church in 1916; it was torn down in 1993. The Polish residents built the All Saints' Roman Catholic Church in 1924, which was destroyed by fire in the 1980s. St. Casmir's is the only remaining "immigrant" church in the community, and its name has been changed to Our Lady Queen of Peace.

The first school was a two-room, two-story building, which was later expanded to eight rooms. The school burned in 1933 and was replaced with the help of the Works Progress Administration (WPA) in 1939. This school on McKinley Avenue is now used as a church. East Vandergrift students attended Vandergrift High School. No schools are now operating in the town because their system has been incorporated into the Kiski Area School System.

The fortunes of East Vandergrift are tied closely to the events in Vandergrift, where the rise and fall of the steel industry had major influence on the economies of the two towns. The town and homes are well maintained and show the great pride of the people who live there.

Courtesy of Jean Panza

Elm Street in the Park Plan

The Secret of the Park Plan

The Park Plan came into being in 1907, when the Vandergrift Land Development Company offered lots for sale on the west side of the Grove (see the article on the Grove elsewhere in this book), over to what was known as Frozen Hollow. The area had

Foreigners Riot

A group of culprits, referred to as "foreigners loaded with booze" in the newspaper account of that day, apparently got out of hand on the streets of North Vandergrift one Sunday evening in June 1910.

When Constable Anderson attempted to quiet the revelers, a riot broke out. The crowd turned on the officer beating him with sticks and stones and driving him from the community. When he returned with back up, he found the rioters barricaded in a boarding house.

With pistols drawn, the officers and deputies fought their way through the dark boarding house arresting the suspects with much struggle. During the melée, one of the rioters escaped through a window. As one of the deputies took up the pursuit, the fleeing suspect took five shots at the officer who also got off several shots during the chase.

No one was seriously injured during the riot. Nine "foreigners" were jailed and fined. According to many newspaper accounts from the early days of Vandergrift, this was not an uncommon occurrence. In fact the article that related this event in 1910 was not even headline news. It was contained in a small two-inch by six-inch side column in the local paper. If this occurred today it would probably not only make the headlines in local papers but probably would be covered by CNN.

Courtesy of Mrs. Hallie Griffen and Buttermilk Falls Publishing Company

Vandergrift and Vandergrift Heights were two separate towns. Above is a picture that was taken from Longfellow Street looking toward the Northeast. The picture shows nothing but fields between the two towns. To the right of center is St. Gertrude's Catholic Church, while to the left of center, partially hidden by tree branches, is the grandstand of the old athletic field, now the site of Vandergrift Elementary School.

Below is an ad taken from the *Vandergrift News*, May 23, 1907. It explains how the Park Plan got its name.

VANDERGRIFT - PARK - PLAN

The Baseball Ground

has been laid out into a

PLAN OF LOTS

by the

VANDERGRIFT LAND AND IMPROVEMENT COMPANY

which will be placed on sale
commencing

JUNE 14 AND 15, 1907

Full particulars can be had at the Land Office

Courtesy of Buttermilk Falls Publishing Company

contained a ball park, thus the name "Park Plan." The Park Plan was laid out on a grid system, with the streets being named for trees. This area was settled primarily by Italian immigrants. A few of small grocery stores and other services were scattered along Linden Street, which was the main street. If you want to see and feel what the old streets of Vandergrift were like, take a ride on Linden Street, which is still paved with bricks. The conditions in the town were more like those of the Heights than those of Vandergrift. There were initially no paved streets or town amenities as in the "Paradise".

Park Plan contained one of the few company-owned housing areas in what is now Vandergrift. In 1896 the Land Improvement Company sold a parcel of land in the lower part of Park Plan overlooking the mill to Lewis B. Hicks, a coal operator. In 1907 Hicks had 10 double houses of the mining town variety built for his employees. The atmosphere of the company town prevailed here to include the violence perpetrated by the coal and iron police during the labor troubles of the 1920s. The land remained in company ownership till 1953. The houses were subsequently sold to the tenants. All but two were torn down to provide for the Route 56 Bypass during the late 1960s and early 1970s.

The Park Plan was part of Allegheny Township until 1918 when the residents of the plan petitioned that the town be annexed by Vandergrift. On August 3, 1918, Vandergrift's population increased by 1,500 and its boundaries extended to the small deep valley of Frozen Hollow on the west. Still in question at the time of the vote was

Community Threatens Vigilante Action: Murderers Taken Out The Back Way

Imagine this; You are a police officer. You have two accused murderers in your custody who need to be transported three miles to a neighboring community for arraignment. No problem, right? But not so easy in the year 1909 in Vandergrift, as this story reveals.

On the morning of July 17, 1909, two brothers got into an argument on a sidewalk in North Vandergrift in front of the home of Mr. Gurney Coles. The two were barbers who lived and worked in Vandergrift just across the bridge. As the argument ensued, Mr. Coles came from his house to send the brothers on their way. A scuffle broke out as Mr. Coles took matters into his own hands and began beating one of the brothers. At that point, one of the brothers pulled a revolver and shot Mr. Coles point blank in the neck. As Mr. Coles fled bleeding, he was shot again and dropped to the sidewalk. Witnesses carried Mr. Coles back to his home where in spite of medical attention, he died a few hours later.

In the meantime, the two brothers returned to their apartment in Vandergrift unaware that Mr. Coles had died. They were arrested later that day and put into the Vandergrift lockup.

The outrage over Mr. Coles' murder drew large crowds from North Vandergrift and Apollo during his two-day funeral. As news of the murder spread, the Vandergrift police were notified that the North Vandergrift community would "do bodily harm" to the two brothers when they were transported through that community en route to Apollo for arraignment. As a result of the threats, a group of officers from Apollo were called on to join with the Vandergrift officers to form a protective caravan, which hauled the prisoners out of town the back way over the Vandergrift Heights and into Apollo from the south side. From the arraignment in Apollo the prisoners were whisked off to the Armstrong County Jail in Kittanning, PA on a train.

whether the taxes collected would cover the installation of sewers, fire hydrants, paved streets, and other town amenities. The Plan had no schools or fire department when annexed.

North Vandergrift And The Levi Plan

As the creation of a new mill caused the creation of Vandergrift, so it also caused the development of the village of North Vandergrift in Parks Township, Armstrong County. The land occupied by the village was owned by Levi Stitt, an early settler in Parks Township. Mr. Stitt and his brother John Franz Stitt built and operated a famous flour mill on Carnahan's Run (Stitt's Run), called Stitt's Mill. When a person wanted to compare the quality of something, a common expression for 75 years was, "As good as wheat in Stitt's Mill." The expression has been used across the country wherever Armstrong County people located.

Courtesy of Buttermilk Falls Publishing Company

The First Vandergrift Bridge and the Village of North Vandergrift

Levi Stitt had the village laid out in lots in a plan recorded on December 22, 1898. An additional plan called the "Levi Plan" was filed on September 11, 1911. When Mr. Stitt died in 1902, he gave his children lots in the town and "nine acres, more or less" of hillside land. He also gave a 50-foot front of land on the river for the first bridge between the two towns. The Stitt family also gave the land for the first school, which was located where Stitt's Machine Shop is today.

North Vandergrift became the home for many immigrants who came to find work in the mill. Slovaks, Greeks, and African Americans settled there, along with a few other nationalities. The Slovaks especially wanted a home site where they could keep a cow. The social life of the community centered around the ethnic clubs, like the Slovak Club, and the churches.

The men crossed the river to work in the mill by boat at first, then, by one of the three successive bridges, the first being built in 1900. When the bridge was replaced in 1932, people crossed the river on a pontoon foot bridge made of 55-gallon drums. This bridge was built by Rankin Euwer. Children especially enjoyed crossing the pontoon bridge, with its creaking and sighing sounds, to go to town for movies and other activities.

In 1906, the Western Pennsylvania Traction Company completed a streetcar line from Leechburg through North Vandergrift to Apollo. This was a real benefit to the town because all the workers coming to the mill from these towns had to disembark and embark in the village. The bridge would be filled with men coming and going during the shift changes at the mill. As a result, many businesses were established in the town.

Levi Gilmer Stitt
Master Mechanic

Levi Stitt was a local man who emerged as a notable figure in the development of the Vandergrift Mill during the early years of the mill's development.

At the age of 10, young Levi was found by his father tinkering with a milk can. When the father asked what he was about, the 10-year old announced that he intended to build a steam power plant for the grist mill that the family owned on Stitt's Run.

Still going strong at the age of 88, Mr. Stitt related the following events, which introduced him to the steel business:

Levi Stitt was a young journeyman carpenter, a member of a crew of carpenters under the supervision of James Owens involved in the construction of a new building at the Apollo steel mill. During the project, Supervisor Owens was called to jury duty. At his departure he designated Levi Stitt as temporary supervisor until his return. Levi recalled, "There I was, a young man in charge of all those older carpenters."

When the project was finished, James Owens took a rolling job in the mill, and young Levi Stitt was retained as supervising carpenter. This first event in the rise of the young carpenter probably occurred about 1882 when Stitt was 22 years old.

The second documented event in 1895 indicates that the young Levi rose from journeyman carpenter to master mechanic in 13-15 years. When the first steel was rolled at the new plant of the Apollo Iron and Steel Company plant in Vandergrift on October 29, 1895, listed among the officials and operators was Levi G. Stitt, Master Mechanic.

In December 1896, Levi Stitt was engaged in the design and installation of the sheet mill along with W. D. Hall, mechanical engineer of the Apollo Iron and Steel Company. The Vandergrift plant was at that time the Vandergrift Works of the Apollo Iron and Steel Company.

A device generally credited to the ingenuity of Levi Stitt was the cooling rack in the bar mill. This device served to hold for a short time the product of the bar mill. This product was in the form of bar stock about 30 feet long by perhaps 1 inch in thickness and 10 inches wide. A rotating shaft about 30 feet long held projections in the form of the spokes of a wheel, but without the rim. Mill product was lifted from conveyors and retained on the spokelike members, while the shaft rotated 180 degrees and deposited the bar stock on conveyors on the opposite side of the shaft. This ingenious design by Levi Stitt offered a delay reaching the bar shears, allowing the material to cool to a workable temperature before it was sheared to ordered length.

Mr. Stitt's creativity and energy touched every area of his life. He kept daily weather data in a notebook where he made notations about weather, temperature, etc. Well before electric service was available outside the town's limits, Levi Stitt's Parks Township home had electric lights and power supplied by his hand-built electric power plant which was run an internal combustion engine.

Water systems outside of the towns were also very few, but Mr. Stitt devised his own windmill system to pump water to his house and barn from a nearby spring and well. His house contained a curio room in which he had a collection of artifacts from the area. The collection was carefully catalogued. Mr. Stitt's interest in progress and new technology lead him to be among the first owners of an automobile in the Vandergrift area.

The only evidence of education beyond grade school is found in historical family documents noting Levi and Benton Stitt, a brother, attending night school to study mechanics.

The home that he designed and built (and rebuilt after a destructive fire destroyed the partially completed structure) is now the principal building of Pine View Personal Care Facility, in Parks Township. In his 90s, Levi Stitt was still walking the distance from his Parks Township home to Vandergrift.

There were three hotels, the Wares Hotel next to the bridge on the upriver side which burned, Taylor's Hotel located on Lincoln Avenue which catered to African Americans, and another at an unknown location. Rowley's and Papas's stores were adjacent to the bridge and were particularly busy places. Papas's store burned; Rowley's is still in operation.

Numerous bars and drinking establishments sprang up and drew especially good business because Vandergrift was a dry town and the sale of alcoholic beverages was prohibited. On Saturday nights, the town was really jumping, full of people from across the bridge who came to indulge in the forbidden fruits.

Emote Rhodes operated a slaughter house in town, and he also owned a row of houses next to his business. Cattle would be brought by train, unloaded in Vandergrift, driven across the bridge, and herded through town to slaughter. On occasion, hot dogs were handed out to children. The smells from this business were very bad, especially in hot weather. The business was washed away in the 1936 flood.

The Supreme Ice Cream Company was part of the ice house in town. At the icehouse, they would freeze fruit or vegetables into a block of ice and put it on display to show how clear and pure their ice was.

A blacksmith shop was next to the old ESSO station (both now replaced by the Veteran's Memorial.) Mr. Thomas Stitt, great grandson of Levi Stitt, was born above the blacksmith shop. It seemed that every time his mother wanted to put him to sleep, someone would bring in a horse to be shod. What an interesting place to live, above a blacksmith shop!

The first school building was a two-room wooden structure. In 1927 two rooms of a new brick building were completed, and both buildings were used as schools. About 1930, the brick building was expanded, and the students in the wooden school marched to the new building to begin classes. The wooden school was torn down. The new school is now occupied by McGinley Real Estate. Students attended high school in Vandergrift.

In 1918, early African American settlers in Vandergrift gathered in a private home on Longfellow Street to have church services. By 1920 this nucleus formed the First Baptist Church of North Vandergrift and soon had their church built there. The Brethren Church held its first services in the Vandergrift Heights Municipal Building, then located to a building next to the North Vandergrift Baptist Church. They outgrew this building and moved to a new church on Kepple Hill. A Methodist congregation moved into the building previously occupied by the Brethren Church and held services there for a time.

The town never had a fire department, relying on Vandergrift's departments for fire fighting until the Parks Township Fire Department was established.

Levi Stitt's nephew, Levi Gilmer Stitt, was a noted master mechanic in the steel mill, known for developing new procedures and techniques. Quoting from the *History of Armstrong County (1914)*:

> *He [Levi G. Stitt] built the present fine plant at Vandergrift, which is the most modern in the country. Levi G. purchased the first automobile in Vandergrift on March 17, 1903. It will have a special sprocket made according to Mr. Stitt's suggestion which will give it a decided advantage in the way of hill climbing over the regularly built machines of the same make."*

Another resident of North Vandergrift, who made his mark on local history, was the Rev. John Carter, an African American minister and steel worker at the Vandergrift Plant. Mr. Carter helped organize the C.I.O. (Council of Industrial Organizations—now the United Steel Workers of America) in Vandergrift. He was the local C.I.O.'s first president and succeeded himself for several terms.

In the 1920s the Vandergrift Grays baseball team (an African American team) was the runner up in the state championships and placed three players on the state all-star team (C. Johnson, C. Chestine, and J. Moore.) They were judged the best sportsmen in the tournament and were awarded a trophy.

Like Vandergrift's other satellite towns, North Vandergrift and its people made a significant contribution to the early history and growth of the town. The fortitude of the settlers there is exemplified by the fact that after disastrous floods, the town would rebuild and retain its special character. The town was never incorporated as a borough and retains the status of "village" in Armstrong County. No mention of Vandergrift's annexing the town was found in research. Nonetheless, most have always considered North Vandergrift to be part of Vandergrift in spirit, if not legally.

With consolidation and new neighboring communities, McMurtry's dream continued to grow in spirit as well as size. With the growth came a unique mixing of diverse cultures from around the world. Vandergrift became a melting pot within the melting pot that was America.

Courtesy of Doyle Rowley

Rowley's Store, T. J. Rowley on Left and Joe Wright on Right

Reflections Of The Times

Stories of the Day

A Washing Machine That Drains Itself

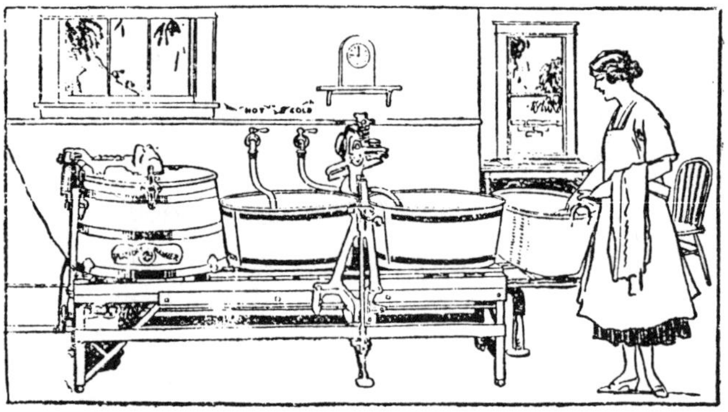

It IS A VOSS PLATFORM WASHER— the most highly developed wash machine in the world. You are even relieved of lifting water or tilting tubs. It not only washes your clothes and wrings them for you, but ALL THREE TUBS DRAIN THEMSELVES.

You must see this washer to appreciate its many advantages. We will be more than glad to give you a personal demonstration. Get the Voss Book "PRACTICAL INFORMATION FOR THE WASHING MACHINE BUYER".

H. J. KUHNS

101 Grant Avenue **Vandergrift, Pa.**

New Break-through! Thinking about buying a washing machine? In 1919, you could buy one that actually drained itself! *From the* Vandergrift News, *1919.*

.....BUICK CARS.....

1912 MODEL

Model 34, Roadester	$ 900.00
Model 35, Touring	1060.00
Model 28, Roadester	1075.00
Model 29, Touring	1250.00
Model 43, Touring	1800.00

Cars at above prices include the following equipment: Mohair Top and Dust Hood, Wind Shield and Prestolite Tank. For further information phone or write

W. H. GEORGE

GARAGE PHONE 56 P. O. BOX 166 RESIDENCE PHONE 1341

VANDERGRIFT HEIGHTS, - - PENNA.

PUBLIC NOTICE

The Vandergrift Ice Company announces that the price of pure distilled water ice delivered is 1-2c a pound retail or on credit with a discount of 20 per cent for cash. Cash coupon books can be obtained from the drivers or at the office. No coupon books can be obtained on credit. Wholesale trade in Vandergrift 75c per block.

VANDERGRIFT ICE COMPANY

Chilling News

1913 Vandergrift featured an ice company. Before refrigerators, ice was a hot commodity for local citizens. *From the May 8, 1913,* Vandergrift News.

This Is Not Your Father's Oldsmobile... But it could have been your dad's Buick. And believe it or not, windshields were part of the equipment included in the price. *From the Oct. 11, 1911,* Vandergrift News.

J. I. ALLEN

THE DIAMOND STORE

149-151 Columbia Avenue **Vandergrift, Pa.**

See our line of thin Dress Materials for Summer Dresses at low prices. Very pretty patterns.

White Voile Waists, just a few left, regular **$2.00 numbers. Special $1.50 each.**

UNDERMUSLINS

Ladies' and Children's Gowns at **75c to $1.75 each. Camesoles,** silk and muslin at **50c to $1.60 each.**

Light and dark Percales at **35c** per yard

Lancaster Gingham at **25c** per yard.

Nice quality bleached Muslin at **30c and 35c per yard.**

Just a few Pabonia 81x90 Sheets at **$1.50 each. Mohawk Sheets 81x90 at $1.75 each.**

SPECIAL—¼ OFF in Henderson and Nemo Corsets. Just a few numbers left.

Good quality Window Shades at **70c each.**

SPECIALS IN RUGS

9x12 Axminister Rugs at..............................$32.50
9x12 Tapestry Rugs at ....$20.00 and $22.50
9x12 Body Rugs at $50.00
Small Rugs, 36x72 and 27x54 at ....$6.50 and $4.25

SPECIAL FOR SATURDAY

Best grade of Mixed Nuts, while they last, per pound........**15c**

Unmentionable Prices

From a 1918 edition of the Vandergrift News.

All ads featured in this section courtesy of Buttermilk Falls Publishing Company

The Ladies Bazaar
THE STORE ACCOMMODATING
New Spring Suits AND Coats
New Spring Dresses
Special for Friday and Saturday at $14.98
Splendidly made of Satin Taffeta and Georgette in all new colors.
New Spring Millinery
Special for Fri. and Sat., $5.00 value at $3.98
In all the new Mushroom, Poke and Sailor Shapes in Black and Colors.
Waists
$4.00 and $5.00 Values Georgette and Crepe de Chine Waists, slightly soiled, at
$2.98
Sweaters
New Spring Sweaters: Special for Friday and Saturday, all the new colors, at
$5.98

The Latest Fashions

From a 1918 edition of the Vandergrift News.

You Ought to be in Debt

EVER since you could understand you have heard just the opposite advice from that given above. Even since you began earning a dollar for yourself you have been warned against getting in debt.

The advice was well meant, of course, but it was not sound, because the surest way to save money is to have an obligation to meet, a debt which must be paid off at regular intervals. But it must be a *good* debt. There are bad debts, you know, and many of them, and they are a millstone around the neck. A *good* debt, however, is a blessing and has taught many a family to economize without discomfort, to save without worry and to accumulate without becoming miserly.

Of all good debts, none is better than an investment in a Home, because while you are paying off the debt you are enjoying a return greater than the debt's interest, by reason of being rent free. And also, the home owner has wide credit, high standing in the community, and much confidence in the future, with which encouragements a man can accomplish great things.

Don't wait for a Home until you think you can afford it; go into debt for one *now* and learn how really to save with profit.

You have your choice of 84 beautiful 40-foot lots extending along both sides of Franklin Avenue on the Eastern Hills of Vandergrift, overlooking the river and the hills beyond, and making ideal home sites. The new location is to be called

EAST VIEW ADDITION

and belongs properly to the well-known South Hills Plan. Every lot is well situated and well drained. Some of them are very deep, allowing ample room on the slopes at the rear for poultry, gardens and fruit. The Eastern exposure of some of the lots makes them especially attractive.

Come into our office any time and let us show you the plans and tell you about the very easy terms we are willing to allow you. Ask any of the people up in the South Hills district what they think of these lots and especially what their future value will be when all improvements are made.

Vandergrift Land & Improvement Company

Home Investment

This ad and the one on the next page were typical ads by the Vandergrift Land & Improvement Company. They were usually on the front page and appealed to or stirred up town pride. *From a 1916 edition of the* Vandergrift News.

Vandergrift Payroll Goes Up

DO you recall that along back in 1913 we ran some advertisements in this newspaper showing the great sum of money being paid out monthly in Vandergrift? In those advertisements we pointed to the largest pay which had ever been distributed by the American Sheet & Tin Plate Company mills here, and to the bulging payrolls of other Vandergrift industries as indicating how good a town this is in which to live and work and bring up your family. Since 1913 these payrolls have steadily increased until they are today nearly $350,000 a year greater than they were then. Take one example:

Payroll American Sheet and Tin Plate Company May, 1916, . . .	$326,938.00
Payroll American Sheet & Tin Plate Company May, 1913, . . .	$302,500.00
Increase,	$24,438.00

This is at the rate of $273,256 a year, and adding our other big industries, our trade and commerce, the total today is around $350,000 more yearly than it was three years ago.

Do you know of any other community which does as well by its inhabitants as this? Do you know of any better way of showing your faith in Vandergrift than by investing a part of your savings in a home?

Come into our office and look over our plans, get our terms and select your lot. We will assist you in every way we can.

Vandergrift Land & Improvement Company

Well-Paid...

by 1916 standards. *From a 1916 edition of the* Vandergrift News.

Christmas Talking Machine Club

A Carload of Talking Machines to Choose From

Get your Talking Machine while our stock is complete. We have Talking Machines in all styles—Mahogany, Oak and Walnut. Look over this list of the many attractive outfits we offer you, then come in today to see and hear them. It is practically impossible to get standard goods at this time as many of the large factories have been tied up with labor trouble, consequently there will be a shortage of machines, greater than it has ever been before. Come in today and avoid disappointment,

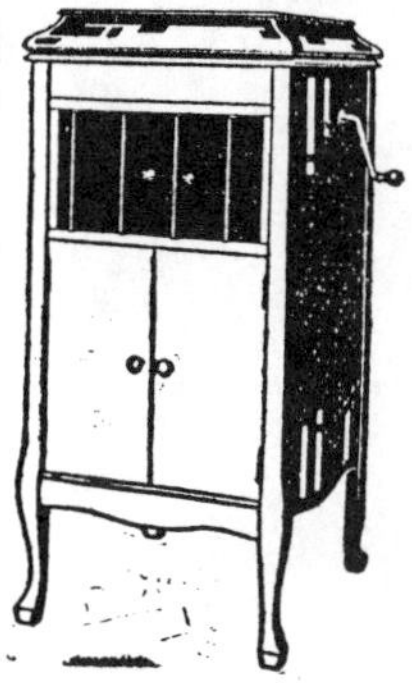

$110.20

This beautiful Columbia Grafonola in any finish, with 24 selections, your own choice, and 300 needles.

$10.00 Down, and the balance in 12 Easy Monthly Payments.

$125.20

This beautiful Columbia Grafonola in any finish, with plush lined individual record rack; just push the button and record comes out; including 24 selections, 300 needles and record index.

$12.00 Down, Balance $10 Monthly.

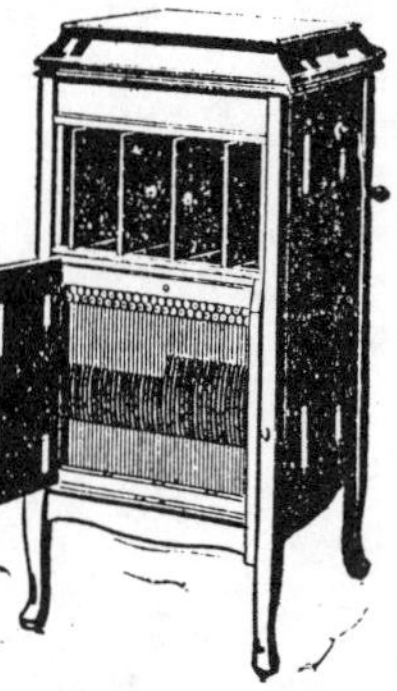

$142.95

This beautiful Columbia Grafonola in any finish, latest model with new automatic non-set stop; including 24 selections, 7 record albums and 300 needles.

$15.00 Down, and the balance in 12 Easy Monthly Payments.

$212.75

This beautiful Columbia Grafonola in any finish, 30 selections, 7 beautifully bound record albums, record index and 300 needles.

25.00 Down, Balance $15 Monthly.

We carry a large stock of Records, Player Rolls and Sheet Music. Come to our store and hear the latest music—in booths arranged for your convenience.

VANDERGRIFT MUSIC CO.

ood Pianos
hone 36
Open Evenings

"The New Music Store"

VANDERGRIFT, PA.

Expert Tuning and Repairing

121 Grant Avenue

A Machine That Talks?

So new, so revolutionary, it really didn't have a name. The Vandergrift Music Company sold the wonderful talking machine, and they were not cheap - by 1919 standards. *From the November 6, 1919* Vandergrift News.

Courtesy of Harold Doutt

Vandergrift Mill Workers, September, 1913

Chapter Four

The People of the Melting Pot

The more one knows about the people who settled in Vandergrift, the more one admires their strength and fortitude. Unlike today, there were no bilingual educational programs, no welfare, Social Security, or health care programs. It was just a man and his family striving to succeed on their own without outside help; they were independent and had to be responsible for their own actions. Religion had a great influence on them as evidenced by the numbers who attended the many churches they built. In the face of what seemed impossible odds, they did succeed and their children were successful.

The immigrants were called foreigners in those days, and they were treated as such by the American-born citizens.

The settlers in Vandergrift (the paradise part of town) were primarily the offspring of earlier American immigrants who settled in the United States from the British Isles and Western Europe; they were of Irish, Scotish, and German descent. Their families had been the first settlers in the surrounding towns, villages, and farms. Before settling in Vandergrift, they had worked in other local mills, or nearby farms or had traveled from neighboring states. They were mostly Protestant and had a deep suspicion of certain other religious groups (as those groups likewise had to them). They spoke a common language and had common customs and ideals. These were the Americans who had the better jobs in the mill and could afford to build homes in the "paradise" part of Vandergrift.

A New Wave

As the town and mill were being established, a new wave of immigration was underway. These immigrants were coming from southern and eastern Europe. Many of them were peasants who came from very poor rural backgrounds and had limited education. They did not speak English—in fact they did not even speak a common language among themselves. The mill had to post safety signs in six languages! They had strange customs, ate strange food, and had names you could hardly pronounce. To top it off, they were mostly Catholic. Many were downtrodden and bewildered after coming from countries where they had been oppressed by conquerors and dictators who tried to strip them of their culture.

In 1936, Pennsylvania historian Wayland F. Dunaway wrote this about the immigrants who arrived after 1890:

> *In the opinion of some, this new population has added practically nothing to the moral and cultural progress of the state, has lowered the standards of living, and has perpetuated racial animosities and prejudices.*

Rises in the rate of illiteracy, unemployment, pauperism, disease, vice, and crime were blamed on the immigrants, but, these claims were largely unfounded.

In addition to the foreign immigrants, a group of native-born Americans was treated with the same prejudice and disdain as the foreigners. These were the African Americans who moved here to find jobs from other parts of the United States. The anti-union policies of the mill aggravated the prejudice problems for African Americans and immigrants because many of them were brought to town as strike breakers.

The Ku Klux Klan, violently anti-Catholic and anti-immigrant, increased its influence in Pennsylvania during these early years of the new town. They burned crosses to intimidate the new arrivals. Reportedly a cross burning took place on a hillside (Kepple Hill) overlooking the valley in full sight of the town of Vandergrift.

Cora Mae Campbell

Today's supermoms have nothing on Cora Mae Campbell. Born Cora Krotzer in Clarion County in 1871, Cora married William Campbell and moved to Vandergrift as it was being settled. William worked in the mill, and Cora worked everywhere. She bore 11 children, and raised 9 of them, plus 3 grandchildren and, in addition, she took in an assortment of waifs, strays, and orphans.

An expert in organization, her children learned to help her and each other as soon as they could walk. One daughter recalled standing on a box to reach the sink, so she could help an older sister do the dishes. Cora baked bread, cooked, sewed, and washed clothes, cleaned, made soap, butter, and cheese, quilted, knitted, and crocheted, all without modern conveniences. After all that, she still had time to be actively involved in founding the Free Methodist Church on Emerson Street.

Perhaps she was best known for her skill as a practical nurse and midwife. She had no formal training, but she was respected and recommended by every doctor in town.

Someone who remembered her told this story:

> *In the days of segregation, a black woman in North Vandergrift was having a difficult time birthing her child. The black midwife sent two men with a wagon and a team of horses to see if Mrs. Campbell would come help. The men got as far as Holland Street in Vandergrift Heights where white men stopped them with drawn guns. 'What do you want up here?' they demanded.*
>
> *'We've come to see if Mrs. Campbell would go with us to help deliver one of our women. Our midwife sent us to fetch her if she'll come.' When Cora was notified of the request she promptly took off her apron, washed her hands, pinned on her hat, took her coat, and left with the men. When the baby was safely delivered and the mother resting, the men brought her back to the Heights.*

The fact that she did not hesitate to cross the color barrier to help someone was told all over town, but to those who knew her it was no surprise. Cora Campbell was like that.

Courtesy of Grace Kakais

Greek Coffee House, Columbia Avenue

With these types of prejudice in place, the immigrants faced a difficult time in their new town. This problem was offset partially by the fact that they were able to settle in ethnic groupings where they did have much in common with one another.

The largest immigrant group was the Italians. They settled primarily in the Heights, especially on Lowell Street, and in the Park Plan. East Vandergrift became home to immigrants who came mostly from Slovenia, Poland and Lithuania. When the immigrants moved into East Vandergrift, the American-born families moved out.

North Vandergrift became home to Slovaks, Greeks, and African Americans. The Greeks also became well established on Columbia Avenue, in the main part of town, and built a church on Lincoln Avenue, which is said to be the first Greek Orthodox Church built in Pennsylvania by its own congregation.

The social life of the immigrants revolved around their churches, social clubs, and fraternal organizations. There were Italian and Slovak marching-concert bands in town, complete with uniforms.

The Greeks put their own special twist on socializing by having as many as three coffee houses on Columbia Avenue. Mrs. Grace Regas Kakias, whose family operated one of the houses, recalls that the Greek men would gather in the coffee houses to drink Turkish coffee, eat Greek pastries, and drink Ouzo, the strong licorice-flavored Greek liquor.

Many hours were spent reminiscing about their native land and playing cards and backgammon. On weekends, belly dancers were brought in to entertain the customers. Many of the local residents did not approve of such merrymaking and the newspapers reported complaints about the noise and suspected gambling originating from the coffee houses.

The move from their mother countries was a harrowing experience for these newcomers. The routine went something like this for most immigrants: the young men would arrive in town alone, without their families. They would live in crowded, low-cost boarding houses, and save every penny they could until they had enough money to send for their families. Many returned home to bring their families back to this country. Once one family was settled, they would help other relatives make the trip.

The crowded conditions in the boarding houses and the separation from family were often the cause of tense situations resulting in fights and shootings. The tenants of the boarding houses often hired someone to teach them English. We can only imagine the terrible conditions and loneliness these newcomers tolerated. Imagine the joy when the men could afford to buy a house and send or go home for their families.

Customs and Character

Those early immigrants helped shape Vandergrift with their sweat and toil. Their labor in this "Better Than The Best" community remains a legacy to their investments.

These industrious early citizens sacrificed beyond imagination to establish their own places of worship and these churches became the focal point of not only their religious activity but other social activity as well. The people sustained their churches, and the churches sustained the people in times of adversity. In 1916 Ida Tarbell wrote that by official count, 5,500 persons attended church on one Sunday. Summer Bible school became so well attended at one point that it was conducted in the new high school on Franklin Avenue. In the decades to follow, every Sunday morning, the streets were full of people dressed in their Sunday best on their way to church.

For many people, church dinners, bazaars, and festivals were the highlights of

Greek Boarding House Party Gets Rough

On Sunday evening, July 20, 1912, the local constable was called to break up a party at a Greek boarding house that was located in the alley between Farragut and Columbia Avenues in Vandergrift. The celebration apparently had gotten out of hand. The constable arrived to find beer bottles flying from the windows and furniture being smashed throughout the boarding house.

When the constable knocked at the door, the celebration abruptly ceased. What occurred next could be likened to a version of the Keystone Kops.

As the constable entered the house, the revelers began to scramble for any avenue of escape. Some tried leaping from windows, others hid under beds, while some others even tried to climb out the chimney. But in the words of the newspaper account, "the constable got 'em all."

The line of 16 prisoners was marched across town to the lockup. But there was a problem. The jail was too small. The mayor had to be awakened to hold a special session of night court. The revelers were fined a total of $73.44 for disorderly conduct and desecration of the Sabbath day and sent on their way. It is reported that the fine was enough to pay the constable's salary for the month.

an otherwise dreary existence. The immigrants held ethnic festivals on holidays that had been celebrated in their home lands. These provided additional means of preserving their customs and traditions as well as a diversion from hard work. The Scots, for example held an annual banquet complete with bagpipes, Scottish songs, and food to commemorate the famous poet Robert Burns.

Hard Work and Self-Sufficiency

Hard work was truly the order of the day. The mill, mines, and foundry made this virtue readily attainable. The normal work week was 6 days, 12 hours per day. The work in the sheet mills was so strenuous and demanding that a 3-shift, 8-hour day prevailed. McMurtry tried his best to see that most men were off on Sundays. Into this type of schedule, time was found to maintain homes and gardens. (Visitors always made note of the well-maintained homes.)

Being self-sufficient was important. Those people who were not were frowned upon. Many homes were surrounded by vegetable gardens (especially in the immigrant areas). Women were adept at canning and preserving home-grown produce. Many people in all parts of town raised their own chickens to provide meat and eggs. In fact, a big event in Vandergrift in those early days was the annual chicken show. At one show, 600 chickens were displayed for the judges' opinions. Of course, having a chicken coop in your backyard was a real temptation for those folks of a less honest nature; there were frequent stories in the newspaper about chickens being stolen. Some people raised rabbits and pigeons, and some on the Heights even had cows.

An early story in the *Vandergrift News* found the editor being quite sarcastic about the immigrants' attempts to be self-sufficient. It went something like this.

> *Have you seen the beautiful Romanesque (an obvious reference to Italians) wall built of old fruit crates that has risen on the spare lot on Grant Avenue? It really is beautiful. It would even be more beautiful if it were put up ten miles out of town. If you peek through the holes in the fence, you will see that a garden has been started. We plan to make a daily inspection to watch the spaghetti grow.*

The Italians were incensed over the story, for in fact, the wall and the garden were the work of the Greeks. This is just one example of prejudice by the editor and an example of the determination of the people to make it happen on their own.

Many people had horses for transportation. As you ride through the alleys of the town, keep your eye open for the older garages that have a small door above the main doors. This door most likely was used as the access to the hayloft.

With all the animals being kept in town, you might wonder what became of all the animal droppings. Mr. Walter Steel recalls that the H. J. Heinz Company would buy the manure for use on their vegetable farm at Allison Park (later, Griftlo Park, which was in the area behind the Dairy Queen on the river road between Vandergrift and Apollo.)

Courtesy of Vandergrift: First 75 Years

The People of the Melting Pot!

Above is the Greek population of Vandergrift in 1916, having a religious ceremony at the excavation for their church on Lincoln Avenue. Below is the Vandergrift Heights Fire Department of 1909. The fire hall was on Emerson Street.

Courtesy of Harold Doutt

Jack the Hugger Stalks Vandergrift Women!

Headline story - *Vandergrift News* - March 13, 1913

The police are searching for a beast of a man who for sometime past has been insulting women, who happen to be on the streets at night without escorts, by exposing his person and otherwise offering insults. He is a slippery customer and has a habit of disappearing as if the earth had opened up and swallowed him .

In lonesome parts of town he has chased women clear home as if he took keen pleasure in frightening them. Husbands of the women he has frightened are getting their heads together and a strenuous effort will be made to catch the creature whom they say will be punished in a way that will suit the crime.

Jack the Hugger, as he came to be named, carried on a four-month reign of terror on the streets of Vandergrift from February through May 1913. Apparently "Jack" found strange satisfaction in exposing himself to ladies after dark and chasing them naked through the streets shouting lewd comments. Jack's stalking became so prevalent over the months that the women of town became prisoners of fear in their own homes, going out only under escort.

Jack truly was slippery. In fact, several months after the newspaper story quoted above, Jack the Hugger was captured by an angry mob. As the group of men and women grabbed him, he somehow broke loose and outran his pursuers into the darkness of the night. But Jack's time was running out.

Only days after his near capture Jack tried to rent a room in a local boarding house. Apparently when the female owner of the room arrived at the door to collect his rent, Jack showed up in the hallway stark naked. The woman called in the authorities not realizing who the man really was. After an investigation of his room and from the testimony of more than a dozen female victims, the man was identified as the infamous Jack the Hugger.

Four months after his reign of terror began, Jack, now identified as a man from Ford City 20 miles north of Vandergrift, was hauled off to the county lockup. His only comment was that he thought "Vandergrift has a nice lot of women."

People with a Common Bond

Although self-sufficient, the people of Vandergrift were not necessarily self centered. Many civic, fraternal, and veteran's organizations flourished during this time. In the civic organizations, people worked to improve themselves and their town. They supported worthy charitable causes and provided opportunities for those of like mind to socialize and become informed.

The fraternal organizations were formed to provide mutual aid and benefit to their members in times of distress. The purpose of one group was to visit the sick, relieve the distressed, bury the dead, and care for the orphans. And that pretty much sums up the purpose of all the fraternal groups. They assisted any of their brothers (fellow members) who were in need. They also supported orphanages, hospitals, and retirement homes. These organizations provided recreational diversion for their members by holding picnics, railroad excursions, dances, and sponsoring sports teams. Besides supporting themselves, they also provided support for worthy causes in the town.

The veterans groups worked to protect their rights and privileges earned through military service, which were often threatened by an unappreciative government and populace. They promoted democratic and

Courtesy of Harold Doutt

William Harry Davidson, First Vandergrift casualty in WWI

patriotic principles and strove to preserve and honor the memories of their fallen comrades. These groups served the town in many ways by sponsoring sports teams and other civic activities. For example, the American Legion at one time provided the salaries for the summer playground supervisors. The American Legion Post is named in memory of Harry William Davidson, who had lived on Hancock Avenue; he was the first citizen of Vandergrift to be killed in action in World War I.

In May 1913 in the *Vandergrift News*, we find the first mention of a company of Boy Scouts being organized in town. Their aim was to promote the ability of the boys to do things for themselves and others.

In the Line of Fire

Of all the fraternal and volunteer groups that existed, one deserves special mention. It was, and still is a group that seeks only to serve the members of its community. They voluntarily accept the responsibility of safeguarding our community and its resources from nature's most destructive force—fire. These volunteers can trace their lineage to the first volunteer fire company founded by Benjamin Franklin in Philadelphia in 1736. Historian John Morrison wrote, *The volunteer fire company is a symbol of Americanism, it is a continuing spirit of the minuteman.* Vandergrift is and has been blessed with dedicated men who routinely risk their lives for their fellow citizens in the service of their town.

The risk of fire in the early days of the town was much higher than it is today. Oil lamps, gas lights, and fireplaces created great fire hazards. A July 20, 1911, *Vandergrift News* story tells of one of the most spectacular fires that ever occurred in Vandergrift. A fire broke out in a pool room on Columbia Avenue and eventually destroyed eight buildings. Only a brick building impeded the further spread of the fire to Grant Avenue. Visualize the firemen attempting to contain such a fire with hand-drawn hose carts.

Courtesy of Harold Doutt

The George G. McMurtry Fire Department, circa early 1900s

The Number One (downtown) Fire Department was organized in the fall 1897. At that time George McMurtry presented the new company with two hand-drawn hose carts. He also provided the first steam fire alarm whistle and had it installed on the power house of the Vandergrift Electric Light and Power Company. Because of his generosity, the fire company was named the George G. McMurtry Fire Department.

The hose carts were kept at various privately owned locations and the Casino Theater until the firemen moved into their new fire hall on Franklin Avenue in 1903. The original equipment consisted of hand-drawn hose carts with 300 feet of hose. In 1902, a hook and ladder wagon was added. A hose and chemical cart were purchased in 1906. This equipment was all drawn by hand until 1910 when horses were used to pull the equipment. In 1912 and 1919, the company was upgraded with new motorized fire trucks. In 1912, the company was granted a charter by the courts of Westmoreland County.

Courtesy of Harold Doutt

Vandergrift Heights Fire Hose and Ladder Company

The Vandergrift Heights Fire Hose and Ladder Company, as it was first known, was organized in June 1899, when the townspeople recognized that the impassable road conditions between the towns caused long delays in the arrival of the downtown company. McMurtry donated one hand-drawn hose cart to the company; it was kept in a livery stable on Longfellow Street. The school bell was used to sound alarms.

By October 1899, the Heights borough building was completed at Wallace and Emerson Streets where space was provided for the fire company. Because of the steep streets on the Heights, a new cart was purchased in 1903 and placed at Samuel Shaffer's residence at the corner of Whittier and Wallace Streets. The downhill grade from this point improved the reaction time of the company considerably. A chemical cart was purchased in 1911. The company went modern in 1915 when it obtained its first motorized fire truck.

When the two towns were incorporated, the fire department obtained the whole borough building for its use. This original building was replaced in the 1930s. The townspeople donated money to install a fire bell on the municipal building; it was replaced by an electric siren in 1919.

In Their Spare Time

The residents of Vandergrift had few labor-saving devices in the early 1900s. The men worked long, hard hours. The women did too, having to tend to coal furnaces and stoves, tend gardens, and a myriad of things that modern women do not have to contend with. Yet, these resourceful people found time for recreation and entertainment. Radio was relatively new, and television nonexistent. Phonographs, complete with 300 extra needles, were just coming on the market and were very expensive. But these were not the main source of entertainment in their idle hours.

The number and variety of activities available to Vandergrift's early residents were quite impressive. These activities were in addition to those provided by church, social, and fraternal organizations. This is probably far from a complete list. Among the opportunities were the roller rink, dances, movies available in at least six theaters (even an occasional talky), live theater, lectures, vaudeville, gun clubs, tennis club, auto club (with driving excursions), baseball and basketball games, horse racing, street fairs, traveling shows, carnivals, the circus, Wild West shows, picnics, the Hippodrome, band concerts (there were at least three bands in the area), parks and playgrounds, great holiday celebrations like the 4th of July, and the most ambitious of all, the Chautauquas—all happening right here in Vandergrift.

Courtesy of Phyllis Murphy Gumbert

Bicycle Race Held after a 1902 Fourth of July Parade. Location is believed to be on the site of the current Vandergrift Elementary School.

Like so many aspects of Vandergrift's history, a separate book could be written on the subject of entertainment alone. Here are some of the more memorable activities.

The skating rink (on Custer Avenue across from the Lincoln school building) was a very popular place. Besides skating, dances were held there on occasion. A big treat for the school children would be a skating party. The rink was so popular with the young school teachers from the Height's schools that the school board felt they were spending too much time there and staying out too late, which was detracting from their teaching. The board sent a letter advising the teachers that being present at the rink would be the same as a letter of resignation! Can you imagine such a thing today? The skating rink continued in operation into the 1940s.

A modern bowling alley was installed on Lincoln Avenue in 1911 (there were previous ones). There were no pin-setting machines in those days; young boys reset the pins by hand and were paid a small amount for each line of bowling. Occasionally a satisfied customer would throw a small tip down the alley to the pin boy. Another small bowling alley was located in the basement of the building on the northwest corner of Longfellow and Wallace Streets.

Movies were a very popular diversion; the proof of this would be in the number of movie theaters and nickelodeons found in town. Live theater and movies were shown at the Casino, which later became the Iris Theater. There were the Star, the Idle Hour, the Mullen, and the Marmac Theaters; and early *Vandergrift News* advertisements were for nickelodeons on Grant and Columbia Avenues and on Lowell Street. Movies were popular enough that stories of coming attractions were often found on the front page of the paper.

The better movie houses contained fine organs to accompany the silent movies. The Idle Hour theater had the latest device in musical instruments—a piano orchestra that was a whole orchestra in itself. A story in the June 6, 1910, paper tells of the Mullen Theater obtaining Madam Blanc and her "talking" pictures from New York for three days only. This is the first mention of "talkies" in the news.

The MarMac Theater

This theater will be the most up to date in its equipment of any moving picture house in Western Pennsylvania. The front is by Charles E. McKenry and decorated by a celebrated Italian artist. The decorations and lighting are beautiful and make the lobby one of the prettiest in the United states.

The inside decoration will be in pink and red, paneled in white stucco work panel mould and the lighting will be in suspended bowl form of indirect light. The screen is of the new plastered type and will give a soft light so as to not hurt the eyes even from the front seats.

Seats are of a comfortable type furnished by the American Seating Company. The orchestra piano is of the latest improved type and furnished by W. J. Benjamin, and costing $1,000.

from an article appearing in the Vandergrift News, early 1900s

The famous Mack Sennett productions were not only noted for outrageous comedy but also the beautiful girls who appeared in them. The Sennett girls — *will come from California—yes sir, themselves, in person to Vandergrift* before the feature movie.

The movie "Tillie's Punctured Romance" was said to be so funny that the management of the Casino hired two tailors to sew on buttons that were likely to come off whenever this picture was shown.

Movies were so popular that Mark A. Mullen of the Mullen Theater arranged to have a movie made of Vandergrift in 1913. The citizens were urged to put their lawns and surroundings in good shape for the filming. There would be a parade and baseball game. The stars of this movie would be the citizens of Vandergrift. It was planned that the film would be shown all over the United States and the world and be a great advertisement for the town. The movie was made and shown to sellout audiences at the Mullen and Marmac Theaters in June 1913.

The Vandergrift Gun Club had a skeet range (location unknown) and the automobile club held excursions during which the members would travel to other towns as a group. On one trip, the group was to leave Vandergrift at nine in the morning with plans to arrive in Ligonier at noon for lunch, then return to town (driving distance was approximately 50 miles, and the driving time about six hours!).

The Case of the Mysterious Missing Movie

In 1913, Mr. Mark A. Mullen, owner of the Mullen Theater arranged with the International Education and Industrial Film Company of New York to make a movie of the entire town which would include street scenes, homes, our people and anything else that gets in camera range. It was planned to make the film on the opening day of the baseball season as one of the "—most auspicious and spectacular opening days of the national sport."

G. M. Stehle, the photographer and his assistants arrived in town, and all was in readiness. At one o'clock on May 10, 1913, a "circus day" crowd lined the streets along the parade route. First to pass by the camera were 800 school children carrying small flags, then the city fathers of Vandergrift and the Heights, followed by the fire departments with their fire-fighting equipment. The next parade division included 80 automobiles loaded to capacity and three auto trucks carrying brass bands. After traversing the streets of both towns, the procession arrived at the ballpark.

The mayor of Vandergrift threw out the first pitch to the mayor of Vandergrift Heights, and the big game was underway, all being recorded on film. The Vandergrift team soundly trounced the Pittsburgh Independents, 9 to 4. The 3,000 people in attendance were well pleased with the results.

The movie was shown in Vandergrift the following week to sellout crowds at the Mullen and the Marmac Theaters. According to the *Vandergrift News*, it would be distributed across the nation, and shown "in the finest theaters in Europe." That was the last information found on this film until 1994 when Joseph Retter of Arkansas, received a newspaper article on this film from Jim and Francis McGee. Mr. Retter was the grandson of Mark Mullen (the gentleman who brought the film company to town) and had the two original reels until 1942, when he loaned the films to a friend in Arnold to have copies made. Mr. Retter lost contact with him shortly thereafter and never saw the film again. His friend died in the 1950s and relatives still living today have been very helpful but have no knowledge of the movie.

Members of the Tennis Club (location also unknown) played here and in other towns. George McMurtry provided a loving cup for the champion player for several years.

Baseball was a very popular sport for players and spectators. A number of teams were formed from nearby towns with men from the mill, foundry, and civic organizations. Stock was sold to organize a baseball team (semipro team?). A baseball field was built between Hancock and Franklin Avenues where the present elementary school is located.

The Circus, the Chautauquas, and the Hippodrome

Several circus and carnival companies made summer stops in Vandergrift. They arrived by train and began their show with a parade through town. One Wild West show arrived with 250 horses. The Sparks World Famous Show arrived in 1919 in two trains of "monster railcars," with "tents that are positively waterproof" and claimed to have seats that would comfortably seat 5,000 people. One story tells of a highly

Courtesy of Buttermilk Falls Publishing Company

The Circus Comes to Town. Note the smoke stacks of the Vandergrift mill in the background.

trained ape that escaped from the circus and ran into the mill where it ran between two furnaces and was killed instantly by the heat.

One activity that speaks volumes about the character of the people of the town was the Chautauquas that were held in the summer for several years. Chautauquas were programs that combined religion, education, and entertainment. This activity was started by a Methodist minister and a Ohio businessman at Chautauqua Lake, New York. Extremely popular programs of political oratory, inspirational lectures of the hearth, home, and heaven variety and first-class entertainment were scheduled to appear in different towns for a seven-day program, starting and ending on Saturday. A 1916 news article states their purpose was to give entertainment while constantly directing the thought of the community upward with the idea of making every town a better town in which to live and do business. The programs were held in tents

The Chautauqua Remembered

The Chautauqua programs brought well-known entertainers and lecturers to communities across the nation, in an effort to "stiffen the national morale through good entertainment and stirring lectures." It was a program of cultural enlightenment, moral reinforcement and patriotism. The Chautauqua programs spanned seven days, running from morning to night. The mornings were for children, with songs, craft contests, prizes and stories. Afternoons presented lesser-known performers while evenings presented the daily big shows. There were generally two plays per week, Shakespeare and a comedy. Musical groups performed in the evenings with the big name lecturers. William Jennings Bryan, of the famous Scopes "Monkey Trial" delivered a lecture at one of these evening sessions.

As a young girl, Betty Heckman of Franklin Avenue attended the Junior Chautauqua part of the weekly program. She recalls every program beginning with the theme song of the Coit Albert Chautauqua. Here are the words to that song:

I am proud of my town. Is my town proud of me?
What we need are citizens trained in loyalty.
When we work, when we play with our fellow men,
Good citizens we will be, and I'll be proud,
Be proud of my home town, and I'll make her proud of me.

Courtesy of Buttermilk Falls Publishing Company

that could seat 1,000 to 1,500 people. Children's programs were provided along with the main program.

To have a Chautauqua come to Vandergrift, a minimum of 1,000 week-long subscriptions had to be sold in advance. The price for the seven-day program was $2.00 for adults, and $1.00 for children. That may seem cheap enough, but it was the equivalent of two days' pay for many people. The Chautauqua set up its tents where the elementary school on Franklin Avenue is today. The first one was held here in 1913. It was billed as

> SEVEN PATRIOTIC DAYS WITH THE SINGLE PURPOSE OF STIFFENING THE NATIONAL MORALE THROUGH GOOD ENTERTAINMENT AND STIRRING LECTURES.

A popular diversion in 1911 was the Hippodrome. It was set up in the Vandergrift Works baseball park where *—sensational acts of every description and nature* were booked including a lion tamer who made the kings of the forest do everything but talk, jugglers, a two-year old acrobat who performed on the rings, and revolver sharpshooters. The sharpshooter performers gave lessons in revolver shooting to the local police.

Parks and Race Tracks

The list of recreational and entertaining opportunities available to the public of the early towns seems endless, but what about those who just wanted a cool place to relax away from their homes for a few hours, or those who could not afford such opportunities? This need was especially pressing on torrid days (well before air conditioning or electric fans) and especially for those who lived in apartments with no yard. The answer was public parks.

At first, the Grove met this need. The Grove was a wooded ravine with rather steep sides that extended from Longfellow Street on the Heights to just below Davis Field. It was in the area now occupied by the Heights playground, Little League baseball fields, tennis courts, and football field. It contained large trees surrounding a band stand. People went there for recreation, to picnic and to enjoy the cool shade provided by the trees.

The Grove was a very popular place and its passing as a result of a radical proposal in 1919 was lamented by many in this town. The property comprising the Grove was owned by the mill company. In 1919, the company agreed to donate this area to the town—after it had been filled with ash and slag from mill operations. The company offered to level and put this area in good shape for a park when the ravine was filled. In the same year, the town council proposed to accept the offer and to enlarge the park area by purchasing some property along Jackson Avenue. A bond issue was necessary to accomplish this.

In August 1919, the borough proposed a $50,000 bond issue to purchase the Jackson Avenue property for "—making and enlarging public parks, parkways, and playgrounds, including swimming pools, bathing places, and gymnasiums in what had been the Grove. The bond issue passed a vote of the citizens by a 4-to-1 ratio. It was estimated that the park would be completed in two years. A news article supporting the park suggested that the open air and exercise provided by such a park would increase the health of the community 25 to 50 percent!

What of the beautiful park extending from the railroad station to the Casino? Wasn't it available? It seemed not! A news item in November 1911 reported that the council was preparing to open the park on Washington Avenue to the public. The trees were now large enough that the public could enjoy the shade and could be made comfortable by construction of walks and benches in the park. Nothing further of this park improvement was noted in subsequent papers.

In 1912, Dr. A. T. Ambrose lead a move to eliminate the dangerous and unsightly railroad cut that ran behind Washington Avenue and to replace it with a children's playground and park. In due course, the cut was filled with ash from the foundry, and Vandergrift had a much-needed "—cool and comfortable resting place for citizens to enjoy the outdoor and fresh air."

And what about the Sport of Kings? No paradise should be without a good race track where a beautiful, well-bred horse could thrill the crowd. Two-wheeled sulkies drawn by trotters and pacers vied for top prizes. From news reports, often on the front page, a track at the fair grounds in North Apollo seemed to be the most popular. Special attractions were added to the racing bill to draw the crowds. On one occasion in 1911, the famous airman Curtis Wright flew his famous "aeroplane" at the fair grounds. No betting was mentioned, but without a doubt, enterprising entrepreneurs laid wagers in the viewing stands. It is also reported that there were race tracks in the area of the Vandergrift Golf Course and on Kepple Hill; these may have been used for training local horses.

The many recreational opportunities that emerged in and around McMurtry's town provided valuable relaxation and temporary respites from what was truly a life of hard work in the mill and foundry. Just as McMurtry had speculated in his original dream, the cultural, educational, and recreational opportunities were key to a productive work force.

Courtesy of Harold Doutt

Above is the Vandergrift Athletic field located where the Vandergrift Elementary School is today. Horse racing and baseball were two favorite pasttimes of the era.

Below, Vandergrift citizens are celebrating July 4th with a community picnic in the Vandergrift Grove, now Kennedy Park.

Courtesy of Harold Doutt

Reflections Of The Times

Stories of the Day

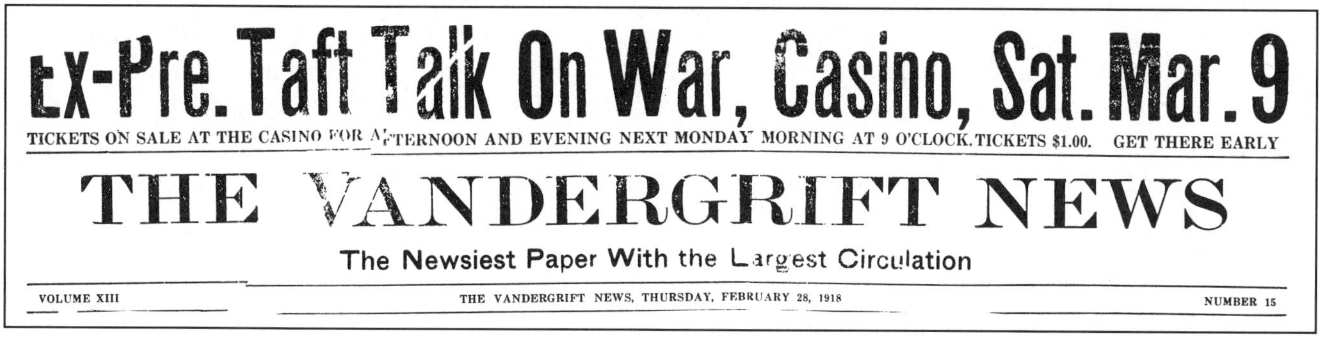
Ex-Pre. Taft Talk On War, Casino, Sat. Mar. 9

TICKETS ON SALE AT THE CASINO FOR AFTERNOON AND EVENING NEXT MONDAY MORNING AT 9 O'CLOCK. TICKETS $1.00. GET THERE EARLY

THE VANDERGRIFT NEWS

The Newsiest Paper With the Largest Circulation

VOLUME XIII — THE VANDERGRIFT NEWS, THURSDAY, FEBRUARY 28, 1918 — NUMBER 15

Courtesy of Buttermilk Falls Publishing Company

1918 Headlines

Nellie Bly

I always have a comfortable feeling that nothing is impossible if one applies a certain amount of energy in the right direction.

These are words that could have been spoken by any of the early settlers of the Kiski Valley region. It certainly could have been said by those who believed in Vandergrift and made it a thriving reality. It was Nellie Bly, an early Kiski Valley woman, whose words exemplified this pioneering spirit and determination.

Born Elizabeth Cochran at nearby Cochran's Mills on May 5, 1864, she earned her famous pen name and her first distinction as a reporter for the *Pittsburgh Dispatch*. In a business that admitted few women, she next took on Joseph Pulitzer's New York World and became known for her fearlessness. Her first story, written after becoming an inmate for 10 days at the asylum on Blackwell's Island, secured her fame and brought about changes in the treatment of the insane. It also set a pattern for her life and career.

Whether as a chorus girl or a war correspondent, Nellie Bly wrote about what she experienced first hand and investigated thoroughly. Her most famous exploit came in 1890 when she electrified the world she'd aimed at by circling it in 72 days, beating Jules Verne's fictional record and receiving his applause. Nellie Bly achieved in reality what others could only imagine. She became internationally famous, writing articles and books based on her adventures. She married a millionaire and ran her own major manufacturing company. She met and interviewed the famous and infamous and was actively involved in such causes as women's suffrage and child welfare.

By the time Elizabeth Cochran died on January 27, 1922, the investigative style of writing she had pioneered had become commonplace, as had women in reporting. Nellie Bly was no longer the world's daring darling, but it was never to be forgotten that a green-eyed girl from an obscure part of Pennsylvania took her home-grown determination and her dreams and presented them as a gift to the world.

Beautiful Grove

The grove was a gentle, peaceful valley that extended from Custer Avenue to Vandergrift Heights. It was called the Grove because of its beautiful large trees. Through the center of this grove was a spring-fed stream of clear, good water. On either side of the stream were fine, open, grass-covered spaces where families, Sunday schools and other groups could and did hold picnics in the cool shade that was not afforded any place else in town. There were comfortable paths where couples strolled. The boys had a grand time playing along the pretty stream. Here with small seines made from wooden bucket hoops and mosquito netting we could catch minnows that were never over two inches long. In quiet pools we sometimes seined tadpoles that we carried home in mason jars to watch them turn into frogs; which they never did. By turning over stones in the stream we could disturb small crayfish which caused us much fun as we chased them while they darted swiftly about.

People respected its beauty and opportunities for pleasure. There were picnic tables and benches, and long rope swings hung from a number of trees that were enjoyed by young and old alike. Regular weekly band concerts were held at the bandstand in the park. The young children sometimes were a nuisance dashing around the bandstand and in and out of the crowd when the older folks were patiently listening to the music, but the children were happy in a lovely place.

Courtesy of H. Reynolds Clawson, III

Fourth of July, 1896, at the Grove.

Arthur J. Pulos

When you talk about the American Dream or about America being the land of opportunity, you need look no further than former Vandergrift native Arthur J. Pulos. Born in North Vandergrift on February 3, 1917, he was the first-generation son of Greek immigrants. From his humble beginnings in Vandergrift as the son of a steelworker, he rose to world prominence in the field of silversmithing and industrial design.

Arthur's father, John, arrived in America from the Greek village of Kalamai. In America, he used the name Palukakos. His mother, Argyro, also Greek, arrived from the village near Izmir, Turkey. They were part of the wave of immigrants from Southern Europe who in the early 1900s had the great courage to leave friends and family to seek a new life in a strange land. They met in Vandergrift and established themselves in the Greek community in North Vandergrift, finally moving to Columbia Avenue. They had three children, Arthur, Mary and Tina.

Arthur Pulos attended Vandergrift public schools and graduated from Vandergrift High School in 1935. He attributes much of his success to Viola Sullivan, an art teacher, who encouraged his interest in art. His early art efforts can be seen in the 1933 and 1934 Vandergrift High School year books.

Recognition of his budding talent brought him a scholarship at Carnegie Institute of Technology (now Carnegie-Mellon University) where he earned a degree in art education. He traveled back and forth to college by train and bus and worked at an all-night restaurant to earn expense money. He earned a Master of Fine Arts Degree in silversmithing at the University of Oregon in 1943 and he soon received wide acclaim for his modern silver designs. His talent in art education and silversmithing led him to teaching positions at the University of Oregon and University of Illinois. He was a consultant to Colonial Williamsburg on restoration of their 18th century silversmith shop.

Pulos's works were widely displayed at exhibits and shows including the American Pavillion at the Brussels World Fair in 1958 and State Department traveling exhibits in Europe and Asia. He has received many awards and prizes; six museums now have his creations as part of their permanent collections. Records and working drawings of his work are on file in the Archives of American Art of the Smithsonian Institution in Washington, D.C. A 1957 *Vandergrift News* article stated that Arthur J. Pulos "was one of the most renowned silversmiths alive in the world today."

Pulos is the founder and president of Pulos Design Associates, an industrial design company. He and his company are responsible for the design of many products. The following are a few items representative of their many achievements:

- Fiber optic opthalmoscope/ otoscope for the Welch Allyn Company that is carried on the manned space flights. Its design earned it a place in the permanent collection of the Museum of Modern Art in New York City.
- Desk top dictation equipment for the Dictaphone Corporation which raised the company to a high position in a competitive market.
- The Green Line series of power tools for the Rockwell International Tool Company. Pulos was the first to design colored power tools and with these products, introduced the use of double insulation into United States consumer products.
- The exterior color schemes and interior furnishings for aircraft of the Piper Aviation Company.

This would have been success enough for most people, but Arthur Pulos felt a calling to a broader application of his art talents. Although art was an expression of an individual to satisfy the individual, he believed that these same art concepts could be applied to industrial design as a service to humanity.

With this philosophy, he became a pioneer in modern industrial design. He was a professor and chairman of the Department of Industrial Design at Syracuse University. Largely through the work of his graduate students and Pulos's notoriety, Syracuse, New York has become a principal center of industrial design in the United States.

Pulos is held in high regard by the design community, and has served as president of the Industrial Designers Society of America and the International Council of Societies of Industrial Design.

Through the auspices of the United Nations and the United States State Department, he has presented seminars, lectures, and other programs in 25 countries. He has written six books and many professional articles on industrial design; his most noted books are *A History of Industrial Design to 1940* and *The American Design Adventure 1940-1975.*

The spring 1983 issue of the *Journal of the Industrial Designers Society of America,* "Innovation," had this to say about Arthur Pulos:

Service to society is how Arthur J. Pulos perceives industrial design's primary commitment...This was the motivation for his professional record as a designer...He is a leading industrial design educator, writer, and consultant...Honored many times over by the design community, Pulos has also contributed significantly to the body of knowledge from which industrial designer and educator can draw...He was a member of the generation, trained as both craftsman and designer, who pioneered in industrial design as a profession...He is the first American to put into perspective the alliance between crafts and industrial designs in U.S. history.

With all of his accolades, awards, and achievements, Arthur Pulos displays a rare humility by readily sharing credit for his success with his family, his teacher who encouraged him and his associates.

Arthur Pulos is now (1995) retired and lives with his wife, Elizabeth Jane, in Fayetteville, New York.

A Prodigius Boby

Whatever it was, it was the highlight of this 1910 Minstrel Show at the Casino. The Casino often played host to a variety of acts, as seen on these pages.

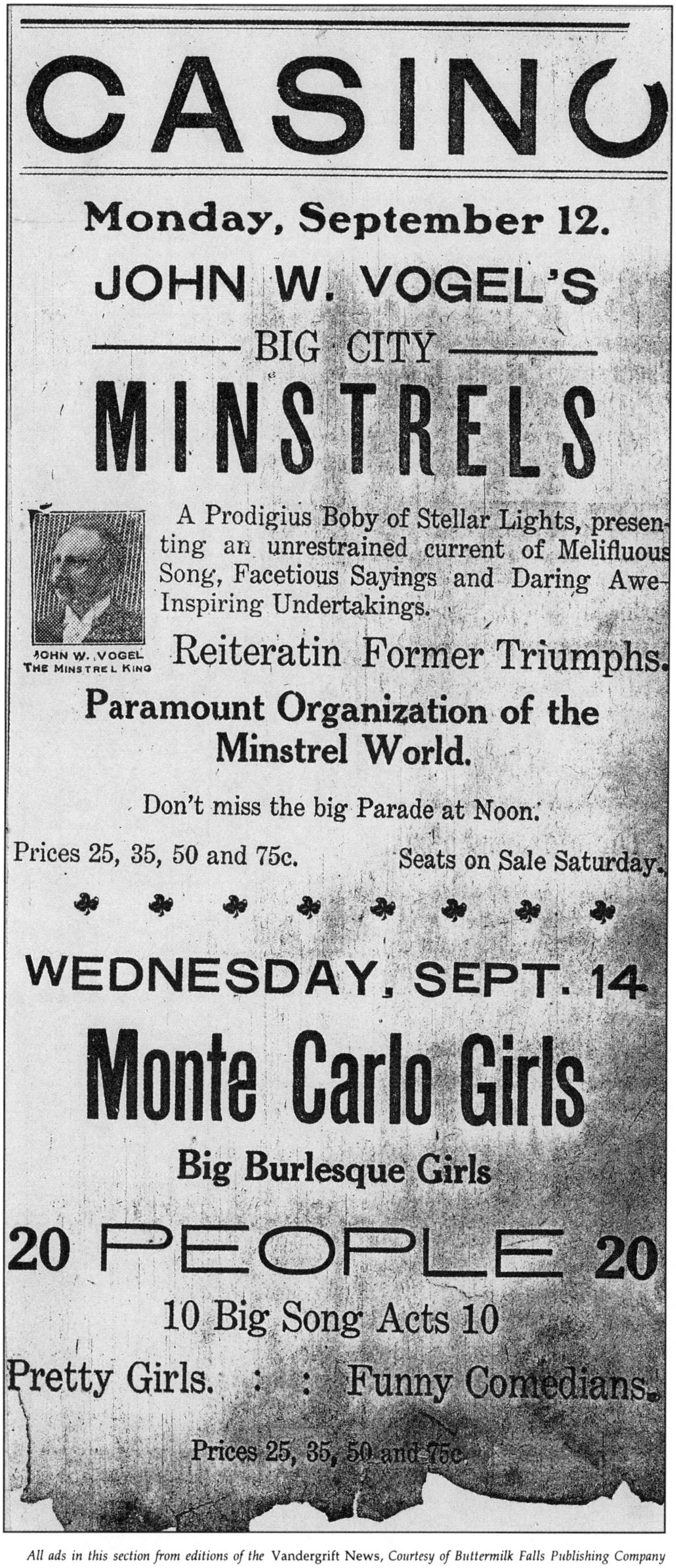
CASINO
Monday, September 12.
JOHN W. VOGEL'S
BIG CITY
MINSTRELS
A Prodigius Boby of Stellar Lights, presenting an unrestrained current of Melifluous Song, Facetious Sayings and Daring Awe-Inspiring Undertakings.
JOHN W. VOGEL
THE MINSTREL KING
Reiteratin Former Triumphs.
Paramount Organization of the Minstrel World.
Don't miss the big Parade at Noon.
Prices 25, 35, 50 and 75c.
Seats on Sale Saturday.
WEDNESDAY, SEPT. 14
Monte Carlo Girls
Big Burlesque Girls
20 PEOPLE 20
10 Big Song Acts 10
Pretty Girls. : : Funny Comedians.
Prices 25, 35, 50 and 75c.

All ads in this section from editions of the Vandergrift News, *Courtesy of Buttermilk Falls Publishing Company*

Courtesy of Vandergrift: First 75 Years

Vandergrift Mill, before 1898

Chapter Five

Industry and Prosperity

For younger residents of modern-day Vandergrift, it is difficult to imagine the sight of McMurtry's turn-of-the-century steel mill. The modern freshly painted facilities of the Allegheny Ludlum Steel Company now rest on what was once a foreboding stretch of black buildings lined with tall black smoke stacks that spewed the filthy black soot and smoke common to mills of that day.

When weather conditions were right, clouds of acrid smoke would lie thick and low to the ground, so thick that people occasionally had to drive with their lights on at noon. Night baseball games were often delayed when an errant wind blew the smoke across Davis Field.

The soot was an ever-present menace. Before clothes dryers, Mondays found almost every yard filled with laundry hung outside to dry. You can imagine the disgust of the housewives when they found their laundry flecked with black soot from the mill because of a wind change. It seeped through the most minute cracks to become part of every home's dust. To blow your nose was proof that you were breathing it as well.

In addition to the airborne pollutants, acidic wastes from the mill were dumped untreated into the Kiskiminetas River, effectively killing all life in the river. No green vegetation could be seen near the water. The once great fishing stream was no more. The once beautiful river became an ugly brown, smelly sewer for the valley's industries and communities.

What did all the smoke, soot and filth mean to the people who settled Vandergrift at the turn of the century? It meant jobs. By 1906, 2,200 men were employed in the mill. It meant being able to provide food and shelter for their families. It meant having the pride of work and achievement. It meant being able to attain the impossible dream of home ownership. It meant that a town would rise here amid the smoke and soot.

Work in most parts of the mill was hot, dirty, and dangerous. Many men worked in conditions that were as close to hell as you could get without actually being there. Working near molten metal, red hot bars and sheets was a day-to-day, hour-to-hour part of the job. Ash, soot, minute metal flakes made the job a dirty one. Men came off some jobs totally black except for their eyes and teeth. A friend told me of being so dirty that his own father did not recognize him when they passed.

The work was so dangerous, that the mill had its own hospital. They called it a hospital, but it was little more than an emergency room staffed by a nurse. A local doctor would be called to the hospital if needed. In the early days of the mill, a person with a serious injury who needed a regular hospital would be placed on the next train to Pittsburgh. The men who worked in the foundry had to contend with an additional hazard—silicosis, a disease of the lungs caused by inhaling silica dust from the sand used in the molding process.

There was no government Workman's Compensation Program for men who were injured on the job. Workers organized their own program to help their fellow workers. Members paid a small fee into the program each month based on their pay. When a worker was injured and could not work, he was paid an amount commensurate with his pay from the cooperative program.

In the midst of all the dirt, heat, and smoke, the mill had a greenhouse! A place where the workers could get plants to place in any area they might find where a plant might grow. Ida M. Tarbell, in her 1916 book, *New Ideals In Business* wrote about the Vandergrift mill.

Courtesy of Harold Doutt

Vandergrift Mill, circa 1900

They work in shifts of twenty and thirty minutes, intense work which requires an equal rest period. A group of men had used these rest periods in beautifying a corner for themselves. It was a spot perhaps eighteen feet square entirely surrounded by high walls. They had made here a grass plot with a merry little fountain in the center. Around it were benches painted a bright green. So unexpected was it, so evident an expression of their need of greenness and gaiety, that one could scarcely see it without a gulp.

What of labor-management relations? There was no union at the Vandergrift plant initially, a matter deeply resented by union members at other steel plants. McMurtry had no love for union practices; remember that it was a strike that helped prompt him to leave Apollo and build a new plant. The information we have indicates that McMurtry was a fair and honest man. The mill workers had a committee that took grievances to management, who must have settled them amicably because no evidence of demands for unionization among the local workers has been found. Efforts to

Who Was Ida Tarbell?

When one thinks of the name Ida Tarbell, more than likely the thought of muckraking journalism comes to mind. Although she was very famous for such works as *History of the Standard Oil Company*, and *The Tariff in Our Times*, Tarbell should also be remembered for her hopes as a Progressive looking for the social betterment of American society.

Ida Tarbell was born in Erie County, PA on November 5, 1857. She grew up in the oil regions of Western Pennsylvania, where her father had been in business as an independent oil operator. From a young age, Tarbell was exposed to what would be an ongoing struggle between small local businesses and large outside corporations. In 1870 her family moved to Titusville, PA. There she received regular schooling and finished high school.

Tarbell entered Allegheny College in Meadville, PA in 1876. 4 years later she graduated with a degree in biology. In 1883 she received a Master of Arts degree again from Allegheny College. During this same time she joined the editorial staff of *The Chautauquan* where she learned the magazine business thoroughly and became managing editor.

After spending time in Paris studying historiography, Tarbell returned to the United States to work for *McClure's Magazine.* While at McClure's she wrote several biographies of famous historical figures such as Abraham Lincoln and Napoleon Bonaparte. *History of the Standard Oil Company* was also published in McClure's during this time.

In 1906 policy differences caused the staff of McClure's to split. Tarbell and several other writers left McClure's and purchased *The American Magazine* to compete against McClure's. Tarbell wrote many works during this time. Around the year 1915, Tarbell shifted from a negative attitude toward business goals to a more positive attitude. This was also when she wrote *The Golden Rule in Business* which depicted big business in a much friendlier light. This article centered around Vandergrift. Tarbell first visited Vandergrift in 1914 and stated that the town impressed her as being fundamentally sound. Her second visit to the town was in September 1932.

On this second visit, Tarbell wished to research a book she was writing on the era of gigantic industrial development in America. She felt that Vandergrift was a good example of "the right sort of industrial town." Some might say that all small towns are the same. But of all the small towns in all the United States, Tarbell chose Vandergrift for what it had to offer.

Men of Steel

Workers at the #11 mill in 1913, from left to right: *front row* Orr Miller, Verne Shaffer, H. Collins, M. Robinson, Charles Knepshield; *back row* Roy Anderson, Homer Joyner, Lawrence Townsend, Oscar Shoemaker.

Below, workers at the #34 mill, from left to right: *front row* Vernon Elwood, Harry Raymond, Bill Ramsey, George Horne, Bill Campbell, W. Ed Doutt; *back row* Bill Sulkaikas, Ward Stitt, unknown, unknown, Elmer Kissinger, Abe Keirn

Both Photos Courtesy of Harold Doutt

Open Hearth Men Working with Stirring Rod

unionize the plant failed on a regular basis. Some years later, for reasons unknown, management signed a contract with the steelworkers union without pressure from their own employees.

The Mill Story

Ground was broken for the steel mill in June 1895, the same time the town was being laid out. Considering the magnitude and complexity of such a construction project in an area removed somewhat from large-city manufacturing, one would think that it would take time to bring production onto line. More than likely this was a point of great concern for the stockholders who were risking their money on McMurtry's venture. Probably in response to such concerns, McMurtry avowed that "they would roll steel before snow flies."

Being a man of his word, the first iron was rolled on October 29, 1895, just four months after construction was started. S. A. Davis, vice president of the American Sheet and Tin Plate Company had the honor of putting the first sheet through a mill operated by Harry T. Henry and his crew. George McMurtry kept his pledge with only one hitch—the iron for the roll had been brought to the Vandergrift Plant from Apollo. The first steel was produced in the mill on January 11, 1897, when the first open hearth furnace was tapped. With four rolling mills in place, the first work-turn in the sheet mill started on December 1, 1896. The mill was up and running quickly, which was good for the stockholders and the employees.

In 1907, the Vandergrift plant claimed the distinction of having the largest sheet

The First Sheet of Steel Rolled - October 29th, 1895

mill in the world. An April 18, 1907, *Vandergrift News* article claimed,

> *The sheet department of the Vandergrift mill has long been known as the largest in the world, and the new addition makes quite an increase (eight new mills). To enter at one end and pass through the entire length takes a walk of something over one-fourth of a mile.*

By 1913, 12 open hearths produced 276,329 net tons of steel.

The mill produced a variety of products including auto body sheets, terne plate, tack plate, and electrical sheets of various grades. In addition to its own production, steel sheets were shipped to the Vandergrift Plant to be galvanized from steelworks in Apollo, Leechburg, Saltsburg, and Hyde Park. In 1916, the mill output was 405,000 tons of finished products.

The Vandergrift plant was one of the first to produce silicon steel in quantity. This special process produced steel designed to conduct electricity and was especially useful in electrical generators and other electrical products. The process had been developed in England in the late 1800s.

In 1907, the mill also became the producer of an industrial chemical, sulfuric acid. The chemical plant was not the largest in the world, but in some respects was the most modern. Sulfuric acid is used in

The Character of the Workingman

The aim of the builders of Vandergrift was to attract a high class of workingman. This they have succeeded in doing. It is however a remarkable settlement of young people. Hardly a dozen persons can be found over 50 years of age. The skilled men employed in the mills, from superintendents down, will not average over 32. The workingmen are largely natives of the locality, sons of farmers or of workingmen in nearby towns. It is believed that not over 10 percent are foreigners, and these are principally employed in the galvanizing department where the work is distasteful.

Among such a high class of workingmen, a general spirit of good fellowship is shown. They freely and willingly assist one another, their relations being remarkably free from discord. It is a cardinal principle in the Vandergrift works that every man shall be treated as a man whatever his station may be. Any man having a grievance is invited to make it known to the management, and if on investigation the complaint proves to be well founded, the trouble is corrected. All superintendents to the highest, know the men personally so as to be able to call them by name and take pains to speak to them. Thus a bond of friendship and mutual interest is created and sustained.

All this has been largely due to the personal influence of George G. McMurtry, president of the company. It was his desire to make his employees as comfortable and as happy as possible and therefore he gave his personal supervision to the details. They realize this deep interest in their welfare and show their appreciation at every opportunity.

From an article in the Iron Age Magazine, *November 21, 1901.*

production of fine sheet steel. Production capacity was sufficiently high that acid could be sold to other companies. The processing was so well controlled that nothing escaped into the air to denote the presence of the new facility—something the townspeople were happy to make note of.

August 1919 saw the mill pay out a new record payroll, $541,945. The *Vandergrift News* had this comment:

> *This amount of money paid out in a community this size should make it the most prosperous in the United States. But these are every day matters here and that is the reason it is not noticed more. Vandergrift always has been unusually prosperous and if it ever comes to pass that this prosperity should cease for even a short period this prosperity would be more appreciated.*

Recessions and depressions seemed to have had little effect on the Vandergrift mill. During business downturns, the plant managers made every effort to offer work to the employees. Unfortunately, the mill and the town would soon taste the bitter pill that other towns frequently swallowed during bad economic times.

Early in its history, the mill established a profit-sharing plan and gave the employees an opportunity to take stock in the company. When profits were paid out to the employee stockholders, it was called *cutting the melon.* In 1909, the payoff was $19.10 a share plus a $5 bonus for each share of stock held. This was a sizable return for those with the foresight to invest in their own company.

Helping One Another: The Steel Worker's Relief Association

The dangerous work in the mill resulted in numerous injuries. The company had a policy of paying all medical expenses for anyone injured on the job and some compensation for time lost. In addition, the men themselves organized the Steel Worker's Relief Association. In 1912, it had 2,000 members divided into four classes predicated on earnings. For example, men earning under $60 a month paid 60 cents; men earning more than $100 paid $1.50 per month. After a person had been off work due to injury or sickness for 6 days, he would receive weekly payments from $5 to $12, depending on his pay class, for up to 16 weeks. The Association had a funeral division whose members agreed to pay 50 cents at each death. All proceeds were turned over to the family of the deceased. At the end of the year, any unused income was returned to the members by the way of a dividend. In 1911, $25,000 was paid in dues with $10,500 paid in benefits; after expenses, the dividend was 42 percent.

A Testimony of Contentment

A serious steel strike by the Federation of Labor steel workers union spread across the country in August 1919. Being non-union, the Vandergrift mill continued to work. The workers were being seriously pressured to join the strike by agitators from outside the mill. Vandergrift and Leechburg workers of the American Sheet and Tin Plate Company held a meeting at the Casino Theater. 40 speakers appealed to a capacity crowd to continue the open shop at the mills in view of the good working conditions and highest pay scales in the industry at their plants. The workers passed the following resolution by unanimous vote:

> *That we, the steel workers of Vandergrift and Leechburg works, here assembled do voice our sentiments and say that we will continue at work under present conditions for the benefit of ourselves, our families and the future peace and prosperity of*

Vandergrift and Leechburg. Also that we resent any interference by any union, outsiders or paid agitators to change the happy conditions which have existed in this community for twenty-three years.

This says a great deal about the loyalty of the workers to their employers and vice versa.

The newspaper took note of this action and pointed out that the first efforts toward improving conditions for the steelworkers were made at Vandergrift. George G. McMurtry, former president of the company was responsible for these improvements. He had given his common laborers the first opportunity they had to feel themselves decent, respectable citizens.

Not everyone was happy over the open shop policy; another news article tells of several men walking along Hancock on their way to work when shots were fired at them by two men from town in what was felt to be a strike-related incident. The perpetrators were captured by "soldier-deputies" who returned the fire, wounding one of the assailants.

Threats of violence "by the foreign element on strike" caused the state police to swear in many veterans of World War I as deputies. A large number of veterans were also sworn in as reserves to be called if needed.

Burgess McGeary issued a proclamation prohibiting groups from gathering, loafing, or loitering on the town streets. People were to keep moving and requested to refrain from the use of any language that might in anyway incite others to violence. The penalty—a fine of not more than $10 or 5 days in the borough lockup, or 30 days in the county jail. This all sounds like grim and tense times in the Paradise.

Keep in mind the phenomenal success of the mill up to this point, due in large part to the worker-management relationship that existed and how all that contributed to the growth of a unique town and people. Even bigger things were to come as the automobile and canning industries came into their own with increasing demands for rolled steel products such as those supplied by the Vandergrift Plant.

The Foundry Story

The foundry was started and grew along with the mill. It was originally the Chilled Roll Foundry Department of the

Courtesy of Vandergrift: First 75 Years

United Engineering and Foundry Company, Vandergrift Plant, 1901

Apollo Iron and Steel Company and moved to Vandergrift along with the mill. The foundry was in the business of casting brass, iron, and steel components of rolling mills. Being located near the largest rolling mill in the world would ensure its success.

Until 1897, low-cost, duty-free rolling mill components were imported from England and Wales making it unprofitable for U. S. companies to manufacture these products. The imposition of import duties by the McKinley Tariff of 1897 created a tremendous potential for foundries. This lead to the formation of the United Engineer and Foundry Company, which was headquartered in Youngstown, Ohio. The new company acquired the Vandergrift foundry in 1901. The company built complete machinery and equipment for iron, steel, and tube works, steel castings, machine-molded gears, forging presses, and steel, sand, chilled and adamite rolls. By 1916, the new company boasted to be the "Largest Roll Maker in the World—Makers of the Largest Rolls." The Vandergrift plant was a major contributor to this boast.

Courtesy of Buttermilk Falls Publishing Company

Inside the Foundry, in the Early 1920s

The hinges for the lock gates of the Panama Canal were cast at the Vandergrift plant. The foundry also produced the cylinders for hydraulically operated mechanisms that stretched heavy chains across the canal to prevent ships from crashing into the gates. An interesting story comes from production of the cylinders.

The cylinders were only 18 inches in diameter, too small for a man to do the chipping operation. The problem was solved by hiring a 14-year-old boy to crawl into the steel tunnels with chisel and hammer to do the job. The boy was paid a man's wages at the prevailing minimum scale—7 cents an hour.

By 1906, an increasing workload required that the size of the molding department be increased and was expected to be operational in the spring of 1907. In April 1907 the foundry announced a pay increase for all departments of the plant. The advances, entirely voluntary on the company's part, ranged from 1 and 1-quarter cents to 1 and 1 half cents per hour. The local newspaper reported that this advance would add quite a sum to the semimonthly wage fund distributed in Vandergrift. This raise sounds ridiculous by today's standards, but it was a 17.9 percent raise for the young chipper in the cylinders, based on the minimum wage of $0.07 per hour!

Courtesy of Vandergrift: First 75 Years

Hauling a Roll Cast at the Vandergrift Foundry, in the Early 1900s

Also, by 1907, important work marking the most advanced methods in steel casting was going on at the Vandergrift foundry. One item produced was a pinion 24 feet long, with a face 16 feet wide and 38 inches in diameter. This casting weighed 25 tons. It had not been many years since a casting of this size would have been considered impossible. The record weight of this casting would soon be surpassed as products of increasing size and complexity were produced at Vandergrift's foundry.

The progress of the foundry pretty much mirrored that of the mill during these years. It was noted however, that news reports of the strike in 1919 indicated that the foundry was more adversely affected by strikers staying off the job. No explanation was offered.

The foundry, like the mill, made a great contribution to the growth of Vandergrift. Its products were known throughout the steel industry and like the mill, its success is attributable to hard-working men who toiled under very adverse conditions.

Boom Town Industries

While the mill and foundry were the main employers in town, other industries and many businesses also were established to support the mills and the townspeople.

In 1909, the *Vandergrift News* announced the building of a box factory below the mill that would employ about 30 people. The new company had a contract with the mill and other firms to make crates for shipping steel and other products. The box factory was part of a larger company that had operations at New Castle, Youngstown, New Kensington, and other places

With all the hot and hazardous work in the mill and foundry, there was a need for protective clothing, especially for gloves. That need was initially met by the Vandergrift Glove Company. In 1915, the Hyde Park Glove Company bought out the Vandergrift company and moved its equipment to Hyde Park, PA. The company moved back to Vandergrift in December 1920 and located on Lincoln Avenue where the Welsh Printing Company is now in operation. The Hyde Park Glove Company was incorporated by J. R. and M. E. Milliron.

The glove company pioneered the manufacture of work gloves and was noted especially for the development and production of the hot mill glove, which was widely used in steel mills. They produced 30 types of work gloves and other safety items. At first, the glove components were cut at the plant and sewn at home by female employees. Eventually, the complete operation was done at the plant. A 1920 photo shows 13 employees.

Another large enterprise was coal mining. Little mention is made of this in early newspapers. In 1907 the paper announced the near completion of the facilities of the Pine Run Coal Company, which would be "the finest coal plant in the Kiskiminetas Valley." There was also the Hicks Coal Company, which built a row of "coaltown" type houses on the Park Plan. The mill had its own mine with many mine tunnels under the town which later caused homes to sink and streets to crack mostly on the Heights because of mine subsidence.

Small businesses of all types abounded in the town. Listed in the 75-year history of the town are businesses that advertised in the Vandergrift High School newspaper during the period 1919 to 1923. These numbers are hard to imagine, there were 21 food stores, 15 drygoods and clothing stores, 9 shoe stores, 8 restaurants, 8 candy and ice cream stores, 5 pharmacies; all told, 133 different businesses advertised during that period (there were probably more.) Not included on the list were the livery stables, the harness maker, and two Chinese laundries just to mention a few.

One other business worthy of special note was *La Stella D'Italia*, the only Italian newspaper between Pittsburgh and Philadelphia. It was issued by James Kyle and Company right here in Vandergrift. It was a 4-page, 6-column publication filled with matters of interest to the Italian residents of the Kiski Valley. The paper, doubtlessly, was welcomed by the many Italian immigrants in the Valley.

Few, if any, towns in the United States were built with the sound and comfortable construction that consistently marked the homes that sprang up in Vandergrift. Most of the homes were constructed of wood with a few of brick. During the first year after lots were sold in 1896, 160 homes were built. Tremendous amounts of building materials were needed for these homes and those yet to come.

The Vandergrift Lumber Company was a significant factor in the early development of the town. It was established and operated by Frank Jones in 1897 and was often referred to as the Jones' Planing Mill. It was located adjacent to the west end of the mill property where the box factory was located in later years. It was a very large operation with many huge stacks of lumber of all sizes, along with the planing mill. Outside the main building was a pile of sawdust as big as a house.

Then came the supply company of George A. Hunger who imported hundreds of rail carloads of building materials, much of which was delivered directly from the freight yard to the building sites. He also had a lumber and building supply store in the Hunger Building on lower Washington Avenue.

By 1906, H. L. Yerty had established a lumber mill on Washington Avenue where the high-rise is now located. It was destroyed by fire.

In 1928, the Donghia brothers lumber company was established in the Heights and is the only such company still in operation in Vandergrift.

Courtesy of Merle Yerty, Jr.

H. L. Yerty, Contractor and Builder, about 1914

Reflections Of The Times

Stories of the Day

James Sutherland, Roller

James Sutherland was born in Indiana, PA on April 19, 1874, the son of Charles and Mary (Miller) Sutherland. Jim started his career as a steelworker at the age of 19 in the Apollo Steel Mill. Hired as a roller, he was transferred to the new mill at Vandergrift. The rollers at this time held the highest pay rate in the mill. Jim started a pension plan for himself and his crew, setting aside $100 a pay. His insights and fortitude proved beneficial to all. In 1932, he retired at the age of 58. This would have been a typical story except that James Sutherland was an African American. In spite of the racial prejudice of the times, James advanced to foreman and was held in high regard and admiration by his crew. With Louis Landau, he went on to prosper through wise investments in the stock exchange.

Jim's life reflected the values of the times: God, Work, and Family. He married Lottie M. Lampkin. Born near Mayesville, PA on February 13, 1875, to Abraham and Elizabeth (Jones) Lampkin, she was the sister of J. L. Lampkin (Chief Yellow Lark), Indian Missionary. Lottie was an evangelist to Africa.

The couple had 4 children: Beryl, Blair, Arbutas, and Hulda. In 1905, they completed their home at 131 Hamilton Avenue in Vandergrift, one of the first homes built on that street (the original Sutherland house is occupied today by the Hutcherson family). Their son, Blair, would be one of the first to leave Vandergrift to fight in World War One. Blair returned to work in the steel mill. The family attended the Free Gospel Tabernacle on Sherman Avenue in Vandergrift where Hulda played piano in attendance until her death in 1957.

In 1945, after being confined to home and in poor health for many years, James Sutherland passed away at the age of 71

Courtesy of Harold Doutt

From left to right, #5 Mill Workers in 1913: *front row* J. Welsh, James Sutherland, J. Newhouse, W. Rakustraw, --Davis; *back row* Unknown, Unknown, --Stanley, Unknown, Unknown, S. Kunkle, H. McCollough.

Courtesy of Harold Doutt

Mill Blacksmith Department Workers, September 1913

Courtesy of Harold Doutt

Mill Pipe Department Workers, September 1913

Courtesy of Harold Doutt

Mill Office Workers, September 1913

Courtesy of Betty Heckman

Dough Boys Home on Leave - The Graduating Class of 1917, in front of the Casino.

Chapter Six

The Great War Years

Vandergrift was just 19 years old when events in Europe would reveal more of the town's character. In 1914, a conflict of undreamed of magnitude began in Europe with the assassination of Austria-Hungary's Archduke Francis Ferdinand and his wife by a Serb in Sarajevo, Bosnia. This incident led to war between Austria and Serbia which eventually spread to involve every continent. Because of this widespread involvement, the "Great War" or the "War to make the world safe for democracy," became known as the World War.

It became a war between alliances of nations. The major combatants were Britain, France, Italy, Russia, and in 1917, the United States together arrayed against Germany, Austria-Hungary, and Turkey with many other smaller states involved. It was the war where machines usurped the power of the individual soldier. Tanks, modern artillery, machine guns, poison gas, and airplanes created killing fields of unimaginable carnage. It was common for casualties to reach a half-million men in a single battle. In the battle of Verdun, France, the casualties exceeded one million. By the end of the war in 1918, casualties amounted to 37.5 million, which included 13 million dead.

The huge armies drew most men in the warring countries away from farming and manufacturing. The priority for all goods was to the military. The result was great shortage of food to the verge of famine, and a lack of consumer goods among the civilian populations.

The development of the submarine and its unlimited use by Germany against neutral and civilian shipping was the spark that finally brought the United States into the war on April 6, 1917. The United States began a major mobilization of military forces and a major effort to supply our allies with food and material. In 1918, the United States had sent enough troops to Europe to sway the advantage of numbers away from Germany and to the allies. United States Forces suffered 364,800 casualties including 126,000 deaths.

In the entrance of the existing Vandergrift Municipal Building, adjacent to the library, is a memorial honoring those from this area who served in World War I. It

War News from the Battle Trenches

The following excerpts of a letter from Corporal Arlie Stitt appeared in the Vandergrift News, *one of many such letters from soldiers that were in the paper from time to time:*

May 6, 1918

Dear Sis and All:

Just a few lines to let you know that I am well and happy... I am still living and everybody else in our battery is still living—nobody got hit yet and nobody will get hit if the boche (Germans) don't shoot a little straighter than he has been doing. They blew up a couple of shacks back of us but not close enough to get us...We blew up a lot of machine gun emplacements the other day and were called out three times last night for something. We fired a few shots and then went back to bed.

No fireman ever had anything on us for I haven't had my clothes off at night for two months. We are just like rats here—sleep in dugouts about ten feet under the ground; and believe me, we have some rats here, too. When they walk on you at night they are just like horses and make as much noise as 6 horses...The trees are all green here now and we have to change the camouflage so that it will look just like the woods...We have the French 75 mm, and she is sure a dandy; and we sure are making some marks with her.

Yesterday it was clear and about fifty airplanes flew around and the aircraft guns fired on them but didn't bring any down. Every clear day we have them fly around but they haven't located us yet. I have my hair all clipped off for you know fine combs are scarce here. Well sis, I guess I'll close. Write often and I will every time I can—writing paper is as scarce as girls here.

Arlie

somewhere in France

contains 995 names, including 57 who died while serving the call to arms. Many of the names are those original immigrants called to the service of their adopted country in the Great War.

And what of Vandergrift's contribution to the conflict? As you can well imagine, the mill was producing at full capacity to meet wartime needs. Major campaigns to sell war bonds (called Liberty Bonds) and food conservation programs were the major programs in town.

Psychological warfare and propaganda on both sides became highly developed during this conflict. To keep up the morale of the people, many speakers, plays and movies came to Vandergrift to extol the virtues of our position in the war. The Casino had numerous programs, including a lecture on "The Great War" by former President William Howard Taft. The *Vandergrift News* stated that it was indeed a great honor and privilege

> *...to have such a man of Mr. Taft's prominence, standing and ability come to a town of our size...We had not had a man of such national recognition among us before.*

The war had created a great worldwide financial crisis. Many of our allies were nearly bankrupt from the costs of the war, and our own nation needed to pay for the mobilization of our forces. In addition to taxes, a program of War Saving Stamps and Liberty Bonds was established; the bonds were loans to the government with tax-free interest. Liberty Bond parades were one method of drumming up support for the program. For one parade in April 1918, the schools were dismissed at noon on Friday so that all teachers and students could participate in the Liberty Bond Parade on Saturday; the small pupils were excused from marching but requested to line up on Hancock Avenue.

The real test was yet to come. In November 1918, a national program to raise $170.5 million was started. The amounts to be raised were apportioned out to each town. The amount apportioned to Vandergrift was $40,000; this in turn was divided and established as goals for various civic war work organizations. To achieve this goal, "everyone will be expected to give not less than one day's wages." Vandergrift's citizens did indeed go over the top on this drive, and raised $58,141—a proud and patriotic achievement for that day.

The real homefront contribution to the war became food. A newspaper headline of the period read, "Wheat Will Win the War. Eat It and You Help the Hun; Save It and

Courtesy of Buttermilk Falls Publishing Company

Front Page Editorial in the Vandergrift News, *May 29th, 1918*

You Fight for Freedom." This was no propaganda ploy, for our allies in Europe had only a 10- to 12-week supply of food on hand. Only the United States could meet this need, and failure to do so would mean famine and defeat. The American people were called upon to make sacrifices and send food to their allies In the final year of the war, the food shortage in Germany became a major factor in ending the war.

Europe needed 75 million bushels of wheat. To meet this need, Vandergrift's citizens were asked to cut down on their wheat use. A National Food Administration Office was established with branches down to the county level. Under penalty of law, residents were required to complete a form that appeared in the *Vandergrift News* indicating how much flour they had on hand and their estimated monthly consumption. The penalty for hoarding flour was $5,000 and 2 years imprisonment. People were called upon to eat at least 7 wheatless meals a week and to substitute corn meal, rye, and other cereals wherever possible. Even oyster crackers were counted as bread. The Food Administration ruled that oyster houses, restaurants, and other eateries should serve no more than 2 ounces of oyster crackers with an order of soup or oysters. This may have been a blessing in disguise for the restaurants, *"...for it is no secret in the trade that a great many customers consume at least one-third the value of their soup order in crackers that are served as a side dish."*

There were also severe shortages of meat, fats, milk products, and sugar in Europe. As we began to tackle the problem, the newspaper urged Vandergrift's citizens to eat meat only once a day, but as the magnitude of the problem became more evident, these headlines appeared, "Eat No Beef—If You Must Have It Confine Yourself to 1 and 1/4 Pounds Per Week."

Rules For Patriotic Pennsylvanians

These are the rules for patriotic Pennsylvanians, as announced by Howard Heinz, U. S. Food Administrator for Pennsylvania in 1918.

Beef Saving Rules In The Home

Eat no beef whatever, if possible.

Allow yourself, as an absolute maximum, not more than 1 1/4 lbs. of clear beef per week, if you have it.

In Restaurants and Hotels

Restaurants must not serve boiled beef at more than two meals per week.

Beefsteak at not more than one meal per week.

Roast beef at not more than one meal per week.

Citizens were urged to "Plant a war garden; help win the war". The people were advised to plant a war garden for their own use. They would make more food available for shipment overseas, would reduce the transportation needs for food, and save money for themselves. The Department of Agriculture provided free leaflets instructing war gardeners. The "Women's Reserves" were called upon to fight the battle in garden and kitchen to back up the fighters in the first line.

This item appeared in a 1918 newspaper,

> *Like the tribal women of old, we have sent forth our men and children to war, and we must take up the first great task of fending for the family. Our family that must be fed is made up of the great nations whose armies are facing the enemy...every woman's real war work is to make the home pantry as independent as possible of the world pantry.*

Homemakers were urged to substitute their own products for store-bought items. For sugar, substitute sorghum syrup or honey; for candy, homemade crystallized fruits and fruit pastes; for raisins, dried cherries; for Brazil nuts, walnuts and hickory nuts; for canned meats, home canned meats; for shipped breadstuffs, locally made items and flour.

No complaining about the situation was found in any paper, so we must assume that food restrictions and shortages were coped with as the patriotic duty of all citizens.

What was the *Gaseous Ozone*?

It had nothing to do with environmental problems of that day. It was in fact a publication produced by the Vandergrift High School, which first appeared in January of 1918.

The *Ozone* contained an assortment of editorials, short stories, poems, and personals—some with humorous undertones and others on a more serious note. It gave the students a chance to express their creativity and also to voice their opinions. It displayed a unique sense of character all of its own.

One editorial in particular shows the pride the students had in their work. "Dear Readers again we take pleasure in addressing you thus. You have shown the world that the *Ozone* is not an incident, but an institution. You have made this second edition a possibility. The *Ozone* now ranks with the leading publications of the land."

The *Ozone* was short lived and folded publication after about 14 months.

Here is a small excerpt from the February 1918 issue.

BUT NOT USELESS

My Tuesdays are meatless
My Wednesdays are wheatless;
I'm getting more eatless each day.
My home it is heatless
My bed it is sheetless
They're all sent to the Y.M.C.A.
The cafes are treatless,
My coffee is sweetless;
Each day I get poorer and wiser.
My stockings are feetless,
My trousers are seatless.
My! How I do hate the Kaiser.

Snitched from The Bulletin

Courtesy of John Miniotis

Sacred Volunteer Company of Greeks, WWI

What was the town's attitude toward the war and toward those who were called to serve in the military?

The men from the valley were inducted in groups. On their designated departure day, they would gather at the Casino Theater for some words of encouragement by some local dignitary or minister. Then, led by the drum corps, the group would march to the railroad station followed by thousands of townspeople for a rousing send off that made the men proud to serve their beloved community and country.

As an immigrant, it would be natural to have some mixed feelings when the country of your origin was at war with your new country. In May 1918, the Italians left no doubt about their loyalties. They showed their firm alliance to their adopted country in a magnificent manner by holding one of the largest patriotic parades ever held in Vandergrift. They invited the Americans to join in and there was quite a turn out of Americans to show that these two great nations were allies and would stand together in spite of the prolific propaganda that was coming from the enemy. Almost every Italian in the community was in the line of march.

Rumors Of Peace

On October 13, 1918, a rumor of the war's end set off a wild celebration in Vandergrift. Quoting from the *Vandergrift News*,

> *The peace news created a big stir here. The blowing of whistles soon had the population aroused and the big end of the population climbed out of their warm beds and joined in a celebration that made the hills echo the glad tidings. Any old instrument that would make a noise was called into play, the lids of garbage cans predominating. The whistles announced the news about 4 o'clock (a.m.) and from then till midday thousands of citizens paraded the streets making the sky echo with their sounds.*

It was the liveliest Sunday morning without a doubt that Vandergrift ever experienced, and although some claim the celebration was a little premature, the news was enough to make anyone with red blood in their veins celebrate.

Little knots of people dotted the streets all morning, going over and over the news and waiting for more definite information. In the afternoon, a funeral for the Kaiser was conducted in a very fitting manner. The Phillip's hearse was decorated with appropriate signs showing that it contained the corpse of the German warlord. With bands of music followed by 200 automobiles, the pseudo-funeral passed over almost every street of the town and then to the cemetery at the top of the hill. From the cemetery, the procession proceeded to Apollo. During it all, efforts were made to sell Liberty Bonds. It was reported that $10,000 in bonds were sold during the celebration.

Hostilities finally ceased when an armistice was signed on November 11, 1918, at 11 a.m. (the eleventh hour of the eleventh day of the eleventh month.) For years to follow, at 11 o'clock, on November 11, the fire whistles and the church bells would sound off in unison prompting all the town's school students to rise and quietly reflect on the Great War and on those from their community who had paid the supreme sacrifice for their freedom.

The World War stayed in the news long after the war was over. In May 1919, a battle tank arrived in Vandergrift by rail. It was here at the same time as a war trophy train and both drew large crowds.

On Monday morning, although it rained continuously, the crew of the battle tank took courage and gave an exhibition in the hollow at the picnic grounds. The tank did everything that tanks are supposed to do. School was dismissed for the children to attend the performance. The vicinity surrounding the tank was one mass of youthful humanity.

Burgess McGeary was advised by Congressman Robbins that Vandergrift was to receive a German cannon as a memento of the great victory in the great world war and as acknowledgment of the bravery of the soldiers from Vandergrift and vicinity. There will be more on this in a later chapter.

As a show of appreciation to its brave veterans, Vandergrift conducted a welcome home day in September 1919. It became one of the biggest events in Vandergrift's history. It was estimated that 25-30,000 were in town for the Soldier's Welcome Home Celebration. More than 500 soldiers registered to participate in the celebration that began on a Friday night with a dance. The next day led off with a parade.

Five hundred veterans followed Cermonne's Military Band from Pittsburgh. The band had 40 musicians, all veterans and all wearing the uniform of their service. The local police on horseback, headed the parade followed by Stitt's Drum Corps. Then came the

Courtesy of Buttermilk Falls Publishing Company

The War Ends, Grant Avenue, 1919

veterans of the Civil War in a motor bus, the Spanish American War vets, and finally the World War veterans. "The parade was the finest ever witnessed in Vandergrift—and many eyes were wet with tears for the boys who were there in spirit only."

The celebration went on to have a great dinner (lunch) at the skating rink provided by the ladies of the Presbyterian Church. "It was some feed" the vets said. This was followed by two speakers, a boxing exhibit (it was the first real exhibit of the kind ever witnessed here), a greased pig race, and a water fight between the two local fire departments (ended in a draw.)

The veterans then had a supper at the rink. At seven o'clock, they proceeded to a community dance on Columbia Avenue to music furnished by the Vandergrift Liberty Band. The street was almost too small for the crowd. The dance was interrupted at nine o'clock for fireworks, said to be the best ever.

Many soldiers who had attended celebrations in other towns said that Vandergrift's Welcome Home Day was "the best of them all."

With the war behind, Vandergrift was ready to enter a new decade of opportunities and challenges. Designed and led by men of vision, and built of people who measured up to what George McMurtry believed they could be if given a chance, Vandergrift had a good foundation for was ahead.

Founder McMurtry, now deceased, had lived only long enough to see his ideas and dreams begin, but his spirit of investment and hard work carried on in this place created to be "Better Than The Best."

Reflections Of The Times

Stories of the Day

Meatless

Vandergrift citizens were encouraged to make sacrifices to help American soldiers overseas, as evidenced by this cartoon appearing on the front page of the Vandergrift News, *February 28, 1918.*

GOVERNMENT DEMANDS FLOUR SUPPLY REPORTS

All Householders Must Report Flour Supply at Once—Card Printed in Newspapers Must be Used.

All householders in Pennsylvania have been ordered by the United States Food Administration to report the quantity of flour in their possession on a flour supply card issued by the Federal Food Administrator for this County and printed below in this paper. The card will not be issued in other form than that found printed in the newspapers so that if you are affected by the order you must cut out the clipping and mail it to the Federal Food Administrator for your County.

The following statement was issued by Mr. Heinz, Federal Food Administrator for Pennsylvania, in commenting on the above rule:

"The flour supply card issued by the Food Administration is the first step in a campaign to learn how much wheat flour is stored away in the homes. Householders are given the opportunity to report on the flour supply card the number in their households, the amount of wheat flour on hand (including whole wheat and graham flour) and the amount they consider their thirty days' requirement. Those who fail to report will run the risk of prosecution and the penalty for hoarding—$5000 fine and two years' imprisonment or both. If any persons fail to report, the Food Administration can promise them no leniency, if found guilty of hoarding.

"By directing the public to state their flour holdings on the flour supply card the Food Administration is taking the step necessary to prevent a possible flour famine. Hoarders hasten famine. If next May, June or July we find ourselves without wheat flour, it will be because thousands of tons are stored away in cellars by unpatriotic householders who banish any consideration of the soldiers in their greed to have their own desire satisfied. The flour supply card is a government action which will meet with the approval of all those who have taken the time to study food conditions abroad and who know therefore that food is probably the foremost factor

How Much Flour Do You Have?

With flour in great demand on the war front, Vandergrift citizens were asked to report how much flour they had, as well as to conserve it. A report form was included with this article found in the March 7, 1918 Vandergrift News.

Both Items in this Reflection of the Times Courtesy of Buttermilk Falls Publishing Company

"Well—that settles it!
"Time and strength and muss and—
"Old Tub—here's where we part.
"Me for an ELECTRIC Washer—
T-O-O-O-O-D-A-Y!"

A frail little woman can turn out a great big wash with no more effort than transferring the clothes and hanging them out.

And don't forget too, that the old tub always leaves a trail behind it—slop and muss and fuss and cleaning up; other household duties delayed, neglect of children (say nothing about the husband) and—oh, goodness—you know them all.

Just as sure as you are living, some day you are going to have an Electric Washer. What is the use of putting off that happy moment!

Just make up your mind and tell us that you have done so—'phone, postal or call.

Next Monday—9 a. m. on the line for you.

Vandergrift Electric Light and Power Co.

135-137 Washington Avenue.

Courtesy of Buttermilk Falls Publishing Company

Why should the housewife labor all day? From an edition of the Vandergrift News, circa 1920.

Chapter Seven

Bettering Ourselves

Moving from one decade to the next should be a relatively simple thing, turn the calendar, and life goes on as before. Not so with America, as it moved from the Teens into the Twenties. Authors have given the first 20 years of our 20th century titles such as, "The Age of Innocence" or "The Moral Crusades." People saw the nation as a place where they had a common destiny, where their fortunes were interlocked, where wise planning and statesmanship could devise new ways to improve mankind. They worked together to improve the nation and the world.

Unions struggled to improve the lot of working men and women; child labor laws ended the abuse of children in the workplace. Women struggled for years in the Woman's Suffrage movement to get the right to vote. The Constitution of the United States was amended to prohibit the manufacture and sale of alcoholic beverages (Prohibition) and end the scourge of alcoholism (it was thought.) The rich aided all manner of good works; and the really big crusade—the war to make the world safe for democracy—World War I—topped them all.

Then, as though drained by the war effort, the impulse to make over the nation and the world faded away. During the three or four years following World War I, the emotional climate changed. The torch of idealism seemed to have burned itself out. The people were tired; in particular, their public spirit, their consciences, and their hopes were weary. They felt it was time to relax, to look after themselves rather than after other people and the world—and especially it was time to cast off puritan moral restraint and have a good time. Those who abandoned the old standards became known as "The Lost Generation."

The Post-War Economy

After World War I, as might be expected, economic activity dropped as the needs of the war effort ended. The nation was in a depression through 1922, but McMurtry's Vandergrift, as in past declines, bucked the national economic decline and roared ahead with the roaring twenties. This was due in part to the diversity of the economic base created alongside McMurtry's steel industry. The spirit of capitalist freedom that McMurtry built into his town was to prove invaluable through many trying times.

In 1921, the *Vandergrift News* reported under the headline, "Glove Company Never Shuts Down," that the new factory building on Columbia Avenue was almost ready for 100 percent production. When completed, this company would have one of the most modern factories of its kind in the United States and the quality of the gloves manufactured would keep the factory in constant operation. From the article:

> *When other factories of this kind are shut down or are only working part time, this plant is operating at increased capacity. The company kept in mind the comfort of its employees by installing sanitary toilet rooms and giving special attention to heating, lighting, and ventilation. A large electric percolator gives a plentiful supply of hot coffee at all times. The new sewing machines are a wonder. They are all run by power and the speed at which they sew is almost beyond belief. Good wages are paid for an 8-hour day.*

During 1922 many men in the mill and foundry struggled on reduced wages because of limited work. A rumor was circulated that as many as 75 families had been ordered out of their homes because they were unable to pay the rent. But an investigation conducted by the *Vandergrift News* proved the rumor to be unfounded. The report stated that, "Vandergrift landlords were not in the habit of throwing tenants

Courtesy of Vandergrift: First 75 Years

Hyde Park Glove Company in the 1920s

out during business downturns." Not one case was found and none were likely to be found as business conditions were improving.

By October 1922, the Citizens National Bank of Vandergrift announced that the Federal Reserve Board had granted a new 99-year charter increasing their capital from $50,000 to $125,000 and giving them right to greatly expand their services—a sure sign of improving conditions.

Even in the midst of trying economic times, Vandergrift's residents and their civic pride suffered little. In 1922 the town had its most successful Christmas Seal charity drive ever and doubled the previous year's donations. And then, as if by divine reward, 1923 brought a period of great prosperity for the town. Mass production of the automobile, appliances, and food cans skyrocketed and thus the demand for rolled steel from the Vandergrift mill. As the need for more rolled steel increased so did the demand for bigger and better rolling mill equipment components which were, fortuitously, produced at the Vandergrift foundry. With the steel mill and the foundry in full swing again, the town was booming. This opened another era of opportunity for the town and the new postwar immigrants arriving from Europe.

The Road to Change

Easy credit (a creation of the 1920s) changed owning an automobile from a luxury to an affordable convenience. As with many changes, it meant good times for some and trying times for others. To some it meant the end of their businesses or jobs. Soon to be forgotten would be the livery stables, harness and buggy whip makers, ferriers (a person who shoes

The Generous Millman

Claude Duvall France was a millman and a good one. Moving from his position in the Apollo mill to a top job in the new Vandergrift mill, France was a roller, accountable for the even thickness of the steel as it moved through a series of flattening rollers. More importantly to his fellow man, he was a kindhearted, generous man.

"Peck," as he was called, liked to help others. He once hired a hobo off the street, and gave him a home until he died, and then buried him in the France family plot. He also sponsored several immigrants, guaranteeing the government that he could provide jobs for the men when they got to Vandergrift. The descendants of these immigrants live in Vandergrift to this day.

Claude's generosity and kindness continued until 1922, when, while helping his mill crew prepare for a Fourth of July parade float, he became ill. He died unexpectedly a few days later of a ruptured appendix.

No one in his family, including his wife, Esther, realized the impact Claude's generosity had upon others until after his death when men began giving Mrs. France money. When she inquired of the reason, the men, often speaking broken English, explained, "Mr. France lent me money to bring my family from old country," or "Mr. France help me start my business." For years the money kept coming, from honest men paying tribute to a kindhearted, generous millman.

Courtesy of Leonard C. Elswick

Len Elswick, with new Railway Express truck in the early 1920s

Courtesy of Merle Yerty

Yerty Garage on Washington Avenue - 1920

SOMETHING NEW IN VANDERGRIFT
DIAMONDS, WATCHES, SILVERWARE, OTHER JEWELRY ON THE NEW CREDIT PLAN
Pay us as you get paid, We have faith in you
Protech Credit Jeweler, 152 Farragut Ave

Advertisement in Vandergrift News, *July 27, 1922*

horses) and the blacksmith. (Gone also were the stable smells, droppings on the streets and flies, especially the horse flies.)

But with the changes came many more new businesses and employment opportunities to support the automobile industry—auto dealerships, filling stations, repair shops, parts stores, and used car lots. To support auto travel, a numbering system for highways was established; roads were paved; tourist homes, cabins, roadside diners were built; and hot dog, peanut, fruit and vegetable roadside stands came on the scene. The Sunday drive with the family became the national custom. Vandergrift had its fair share in these developments.

By October 9, 1924, the completion of Vandergrift's 14th auto sales and service was announced in the local paper. Located on Columbia Avenue, it was a 2-story brick structure that conformed to the most modern conception of garage architecture. It had storage space for 90 cars on the second floor, which was accessed from the alley; the ground floor held the show room and service area. This new facility became the Studebaker dealership. Imagine the competition! 14 dealerships, compared with 2 today, seems incredible.

Along with the automobile came gas stations. At one time more than 7 stations were located within a mile of each other throughout the area. All these stations did auto servicing such as oil changes and lube jobs and some repair work. With so much competition, service was a big selling point. There were no self-serve pumps. Your gas was pumped, windshield

Courtesy of Buttermilk Falls Publishing Company
W. H. George Garage on Hancock Avenue, 1912

Courtesy of Buttermilk Falls Publishing Company
Narrow Grant Avenue in the 1920s

washed, oil and water checked during each stop. Many stations offered premiums for customers. In 1924, the Vandergrift Commercial College added a course entitled Garage and Automobile Accounting. The automobile reached into every aspect of life during the Twenties.

Other alterations in the fabric of the town had to be made when the automobile arrived. The main shopping streets downtown were not nearly as wide as they are now, because a wide sidewalk fronted each building. With cars parking on Grant Avenue, travel on the street became hazardous. In March 1923, the Council proposed that no parking be permitted on Grant Avenue; this was not well received by the merchants, who claimed it would hurt business. It was suggested that parking be allowed on only one side of the street. This, too, was not well received. A proposal to widen the street was dismissed because of lack of funds. So the traffic jam continued till the street was finally widened to accommodate the increased automobile traffic.

In the "Some Things Never Change department," the October 1924 *Vandergrift News* carried this item on the front page, "The hole making a bad bump in the macadam surface of the road at the corner of Grant and Washington has been repaired." Potholes were receiving notoriety even back then.

In a 1921 editorial, the *News* reported on the dissatisfaction of the area residents about the condition of the roads in and around the Kiski Valley. It claimed that Vandergrift had more cars for a town of its size than any other town in Pennsylvania, yet the town had only one paved road out of town (the Hancock extension.) The other roads were impassable in winter. Because it seemed the Kiski Valley was being neglected by both county seats (Westmoreland and Armstrong), consideration was given

Courtesy of Buttermilk Falls Publishing Company and Charles Kingirski
Charles & Honey Kingirski on Hancock Avenue near Cemetery Hill, 1926

to forming a new county with Vandergrift as its seat. (It seems the proposal got no further than the newspaper.)

Even the best of dreams cannot always foresee the needs of the future. As well as McMurtry had planned, he never imagined the streets of his town being made inadequate by a fire-driven buggy. In his day his street widths would have been considered extravagantly generous.

In fact, architect Frederick Olmsted's original designs called for even wider streets. But economic considerations forced McMurtry to trim the size of the planned wide boulevards, much to the dismay of the Olmsted firm. Today, they barely accommodate traffic moving alongside the cars parked the length of Vandergrift's streets.

New Technologies

Automobiles were not the only thing changing lifestyles in Vandergrift. Advances made in communications during the war began to reach the general public. That wonder of wonders, the ability to send words and music through the air, had arrived. In 1920, KDKA radio, in Pittsburgh, made its first regularly scheduled broadcasts of news, church services, and music. By the end of the decade, the nation had 618 stations. Sales of radios and ancillary equipment soared from $2 million to $600 million a year during the 1920s.

A 1922 syndicated column appearing in the *Vandergrift News* described radio as follows:

> *Radio telephony is a great modern miracle, a dream more fantastic*

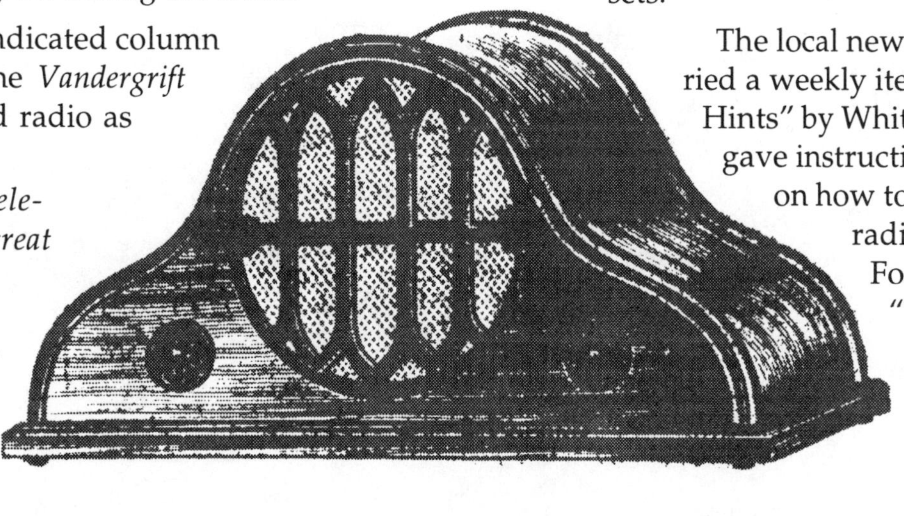

ATWATER KENT RADIO - SUPER PERFORMANCE ELECTRIC, 7 TUBES AND ONE RECTIFYING TUBE $106 - WITHOUT TUBES SPEAKERS IN THREE SIZES $20 EASY TERMS L. PETERS, 154 WASHINGTON AVENUE

Advertisement for a Radio, Vandergrift News, *1928*

> *and fairy-like than the Arabian Nights. Best of all, it is within the reach of everyone as the 'music of the air' is free to all who care to tune in. Prediction: Within a few years, there will be great advances in radio. No antennas or aerials will be required and the sending and receiving instruments will be made small enough to put in your pocket.*

A very good prediction.

Maybe the "music of the air" was free, but the means of receiving it certainly were not. Radios were quite expensive for those days, although kits could be purchased, and you could build your own. The Electric Shop on Columbia Avenue offered prizes for the best wireless sets constructed by amateurs. The owners of the Pioneer Radio Shop, Roy Stitt and W. W. Shoop, were amateur radio builders who were receiving loud and clear broadcasts from France, England, and Mexico City on homemade sets.

The local newspaper carried a weekly item, "Radio Hints" by Whit Hadley, that gave instructions and hints on how to improve radio reception. For example: "Tighten all screws and nuts in your set from time to time" or "Different ways to insure a tight aerial."

Mrs. Elizabeth Heckman, a long-time resident of Vandergrift, tells a story about her brother, Elmer, and his adventures in radio. It seems that as a young man Elmer got a radio kit apparently from one of those stores here in Vandergrift. He quickly constructed his very own radio set, with his very own aerial hooked up to the top of the Baptist Church steeple. The only problem was that he lived at 302 Franklin Avenue, ***diagonally across*** *the street from the church. A wire, acting as an aerial, went through the air, across the street, hooked on to the roof of his house, ran down into the living room where the radio was and was grounded by the cellar window.*

One day, during an electrical storm, lightening struck the Baptist Church steeple. The charge traveled across the aerial, sent a ball of fire rolling into the living room, and then continued down into the cellar, where Elmer's father was getting fruit stored in the fruit cellar. The jolt struck his father, spun him around three times, and sent him flying into a heap on the cellar steps. He was shocked, to say the least. The effects of this experience left him with poor coordination for weeks.

Despite this experience, Elmer could still listen to his favorite programs on his radio (as it was not ruined) by looking in the *Vandergrift News* for program listings. Front page coverage was given to the upcoming programs, such as this 1923 "Radio News" - "Listen in on the banquet of 600 managers of Metropolitan Life Insurance Company from the Hotel Aster in New York City. It will be a great opportunity to hear great men speak."

It would not be long till families would be glued to their radios every evening to listen to favorite programs such as Fibber McGee and Molly, Jack Benny, and serials, such as The Shadow ("Who knows what evil lurks in the hearts of men? The Shadow knows"), The Lone Ranger, and others.

Words and music were not the only things coming through the air. In 1928 aviation arrived in the Kiski Valley. In 1927 Gerald E. (Red) Lindenmuth learned to fly at Dayton, Ohio, and he acquired a World War I trainer, the Curtis Jenny (JN4-D) powered by an OX5, 90-horsepower engine. Lindenmuth took delivery of the plane at Latrobe and flew it to Vandergrift. For two years, he flew it from Mrs. Knabb's field (where

Kiski Area Senior High School is now located) during the summer and stored it at Latrobe during the winter. This was the small beginning of a growing activity on Mrs. Knabb's pasture (Allegheny Township) where Vandergrift's aviation history would be made.

Although aviation had little effect on Vandergrift during this period, newspapers, movies, and radio kept people's interest high as cash prizes were offered to those air pioneers who broke new records such as the fastest cross-country flight, longest time in the air without landing (with in-flight refueling, no less), and highest flights. The most famous of all was Charles Lindbergh's flight from Long Island, NY, to Paris on May 20-21, 1927, for a $25,000 prize. His 3,610 mile flight in 33 1/2 hours made him the most famous man of the 1920s.

Back home, mom wasn't exactly flying in the kitchen, but her life was being made easier (the advertisement said) by new appliances. Washing machines and sweepers powered by the magic of electricity were available along with electric toasters, irons, and modern gas stoves. And instead of the "iceman cometh," the iceman "goeth" as electrical refrigerators replaced the familiar icebox. The square signs to tell the iceman how many pounds of ice was needed, and the opportunity for the children to scavenge the ice chips from the back of the iceman's truck while he carried the ice into the homes, all melted away into history.

Most importantly though, all these new technologies, advantages, and luxuries created new markets for steel. A tremendous atmosphere of prosperity prevailed as did new opportunities for the workers. In 1928, 25 men from Vandergrift pooled $100 each to provide the capital for the Vandergrift Building and Loan Association, which provided much-needed home loans to the growing population of McMurtry's "Workingman's Paradise."

Double Boom Town

Although the bordering town of Vandergrift Heights was annexed into the borough of Vandergrift in 1915, it still retained much of its own flavor into the 1920s. But very much like Vandergrift, it was in itself prospering from the exploding economic conditions. With its own business district, the Heights became a second boom town within a boom town.

Mrs. Marie Milie Pugliese, a resident of the Heights during those days, recounts her memories of this second business district this way;

> *In the 1920s, Longfellow Street was a microcosm five blocks long, where the people of Vandergrift Heights could shop for almost every need, and all within walking distance—a definite little world that typified wholesome living in a small community. This was a world in sharp contrast to the present, like the daily delivery of fresh whole milk to one's own kitchen door, or shopping for meat that was cut as you watched and as you requested, and then wrapped and carried home without warning of*

contamination. One stop at Ramer's Department Store could outfit a family for the beginning of school, for Christmas and the Easter Parade.

A variety of businesses flourished in the early life of the Street. There was Wilcox's Meat Market, at the corner of Hancock and Longfellow, Crawford's Wallpaper and Paint Shop, Steele's Hardware, McNutt's Market, and Ramer's Dry Goods and Notions. The Economy Store advertised wares from 5 cents to a dollar.

Manganello's Fruit Market was a wonder of delightful aromas. The storefront was a grilled work that resembled a large bird cage and allowed one to see as well as experience the fragrance. If Salvatore, the proprietor, wasn't busy, he would be sitting near the entrance, and you didn't pass by without answering questions about the well-being of your grandmother and grandfather. Just down the street from him was Maxwell's Shoe Store and the office of Squire Bair, who was responsible for law and order.

At the hub of activity, where Longfellow and Wallace Streets cross was Ross's Pharmacy (formerly Burns'), where one could purchase pure drugs, patent medicines, toilet articles, candy, cigars, ice cream and of course, prescriptions were a specialty. There was Milie Brothers' Real Estate and Insurance, and Joseph Calderazzo, a fine tailor in the Italian tradition. (Angelo Donghia was trained under him and later occupied the corner shop that became the longtime home of Donghia Formal Wear and Tailoring.) Behind the Calderazzo shop was a Chinese laundry.

If you had a sweet tooth, William's Ice Cream Parlor and Confectionery sold magazines, newspapers and Eskimo pies, a new treat that was foil wrapped, like a present, and measured about 1 inch by 2 inches of the most delectable chocolate-coated vanilla ice cream. It cost a dime and displaced the popular 2-cent strawberry ice cream cone.

There was Donahey's Hardware Store. One step up on a broad front porch and was a display of shiny tubs, washboards, copper boilers, and all sorts of interesting stuff destined to regale the antique shopper of a few generations down the road. Next door was the beautiful red brick home of Dr. John Boale, who was one of three physicians in residence who brought comfort to those who they visited. The practice of medicine was a simple matter then; there was no government entanglement, no escalating insurance premiums, or astronomical drug costs, just a relationship between a doctor, who was your friend and a patient, who was able to pay for his or her care.

Further on down the street was Thomas's Barber Shop and Shoe Store, and Patterson's Auto Parts. Across Hawthorne Street was Pugliese's Meat Market, L. Sciullo's Drygoods Store, Shutt Brothers Meat Market (The Pugliese brothers had an alliance with the Shutt brothers where each would supply whatever the other didn't have in order to accommodate a customer—a gesture indicative of hometown friendliness.)

Buccieri's Confectionery was conveniently placed next to the Arcadia Theater (a stop one made before going in to watch the cowboys ride apace over the barren West), Pompei Bucci's very necessary Shoe

Repair Shop was on the way to the U. S. Post Office. (Mail was delivered twice daily.) There was the big brick building that housed Copelman's Men's Store, then the Great Atlantic and Pacific Tea Company. (Apartments were on the second floor, and in the basement were several bowling lanes where young men hung out.)

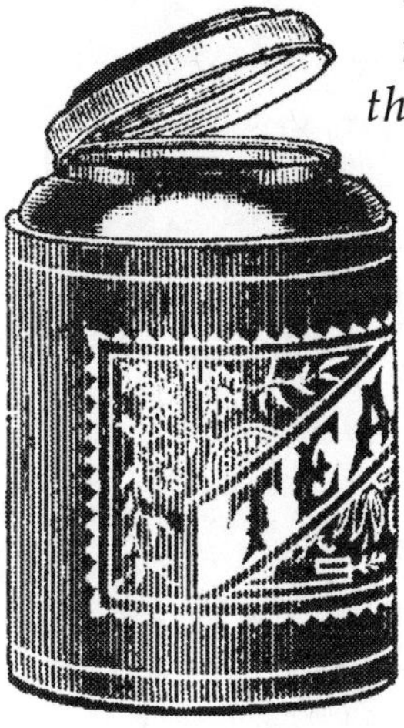

Along Longfellow Street were two elementary school buildings, the Longfellow and the Wilson Schools, with a wide area where recess brought the joyful sounds of children at play. Wehn's Peoples Pharmacy was next to the schools and beside it, Ceraso's Amusement Parlor that advertised "Bowling, Billiards, Lunch, Drinks, and Smokes."

Having lived once upon a time in the midst of this, these treasured memories will remain with me, happily ever after.

SHOPPING AROUND

What would Mom spend if she went shopping in Vandergrift during the 1920s? Here are some 1924 prices found in a 1924 edition of the Vandergrift News:

Hamburger	$ .20 lb.
Pork Chops	$ .23 lb
Ham	$ .23 lb
Sirloin Steak	$ .30 lb
Eggs	$. 25 doz
Butter	$ .53 lb
Basketball Shoes	$1.35 to $3.45
Ladies Pumps	$5.35 to $7.35
Child's Haircut	$ .25

Mill Waste Becomes New Opportunity

Mill production was at full steam. The volume of slag and ash coming out of the mill was huge. Slowly but surely this solid waste began to fill the Grove, which was a sloping valley cutting south to north from near the Heights to just above the river in the valley below. In a 1921 meeting of the Chamber of Commerce, Mr. Armstrong of the borough council advised the members that the ground in the picnic hollow (see sidebar Beautiful Grove, chapter 4) could be used anytime as a playground—IF—businessmen and others would give a helping hand in leveling out the area. The proposition was met with hearty applause and the construction of present-day Kennedy Park and Davis Field began.

In addition to the solid waste of the steel mill, the foundry also produced large volumes of unusable solid waste. In 1920 the council also granted permission for the foundry to dump slag and ash to fill the railroad cut between Franklin and Custer Avenues. The Vandergrift Land and Improvement Company turned the land over to the borough. By 1924 that huge hole had been filled. An effort to turn this new area over to the adjacent property owners was defeated, and on June 5, 1924, the council voted to accept plans for a playground and recreation park on the site. The plans included a cement wading pool and three clay tennis courts. One month later, the local newspaper announced that the tennis courts were open!

The practice of creating waste disposal fills continued in other areas of the community as well. In 1924, the mill proposed to fill Frozen Hollow (behind Holland Street); it was estimated that it would take 25 years to fill this area. The American Sheet and Tin Plate Company requested and gained the council's approval for a railroad track

S. A. Davis and Davis Field

Stewart Archibald Davis was a pioneer in the development of Vandergrift and one of the most admired of the American Sheet and Tin Plate Company executives. The Vandergrift Council saw fit to have their new athletic field carry on his name, S. A. Davis Field.

Friends and those who worked with Mr. Davis knew him as "Archie." He was known among all as a friendly man with a kindly attitude. Along with his pleasant bearing, he was a man of industry and accomplishments, as noted in a newspaper article of September 1930:

Mr. Davis first became acquainted with Vandergrift as one of the assistants of Mr. George G. McMurtry in the project of moving Apollo Iron and Steel Company down the Kiski river to the "Townsend Farm." He was also instrumental in the development of this "Model Town" that was beginning to take form. Within a few short years, Davis became the first district manager of the new plant in Vandergrift.

Davis was born in Blairsville on July 21, 1867. He began his career at the age of 17, as an employee of the great Pennsylvania Railroad. In a course of a few years he became assistant to the station agent at Apollo, PA. There is where he attracted the attention of Mr. McMurtry, who gave him a position in the electrical department of the Apollo Iron and Steel Company.

After the American Sheet and Tin Plating Company became affiliated with the United States Steel Corporation, Mr. Davis rose to be assistant to the Vice-President, Second Vice-President, then First Vice President, which rank he held until his sudden death in 1925.

The then-recently published *Encyclopedia of American Biography:* said of him: "Foremost among the executives of the steel industry in the United States...Generally regarded as an authority in the many ramifications of that essential, was Stewart Archibald Davis, Vice-President of the American Sheet and Tin Plate Company...Years of experience with one of the largest companies in the industry, in whose growth Mr. Davis has played a significant part, in a measure won for him his pre-eminence...His own character and intelligence were his main support, however...He saw far, judged wisely, and acted promptly."

From an article in the Vandergrift News:

September 1930: Vandergrift's new athletic field along Jackson Avenue will be dedicated the "S. A. Davis Athletic Field" during the Legion Bugle and Drum Corps competition.

"Davis Field" was named by council in the honor of the late "Archie" Davis, one of the town's civic leaders, whose efforts were largely responsible for the building of the athletic grounds.

The suggestion that the grounds be named "Davis Field" was made by A. R. Goodhue, councilman from the third ward of Vandergrift, and his motion was seconded by Lloyd Leighty, and passed council unanimously.

The field is now complete, the grandstand and steel bleachers are finished, making it the best athletic field in this part of the state.

Courtesy of Buttermilk Falls Publishing Company

Davis Field, circa mid-1920s, from near present-day Linden St. Note railroad tracks in foreground, used to dump slag as fill, and in background, the Custer and Lincoln schools.

on Custer Avenue from Poplar Street to the Frozen Hollow site to accommodate hauling of the waste. A narrow-gauge steam train was used to haul the waste.

In the meantime, the foundry received permission from the council to fill the gully behind Ninth Alley (behind Franklin and Sherman Avenues.) They estimated that it would take 50 years to fill this area with one million tons of slag and ash.

The increasing landfill work also opened new housing lots for the community. The American Sheet & Tin Plate Company presented plans to the council for 10 new lots on Custer Avenue and 30 on Jackson Avenue. Each lot was to have a 32-foot front.

Maintaining "Better Than The Best"

With major changes to the landscape of the town in full swing, the town leaders were careful to uphold the integrity of the community's elegant design and modern facilities. In the spring of 1921, the council awarded a contract to the Vandergrift Greenhouse to plant flower beds in the small parks. Sewers were being laid on Linden Street from Spruce to Elm Streets. Mr. Barrett deeded land to the borough for sidewalks and steps along Spruce Street and Spruce Place, and plans were made to pave Holmes Street. The council also constructed a garbage incinerator in Frozen Hollow at the intersection of

Jack F. McIntire, Sr.

The first of a line of three McIntires to serve as burgess for the town of Vandergrift, Jack F. McIntire (with the F. standing for either Frank or "Fix," as was his nickname) came to Vandergrift in 1905 from Apollo. He held the distinct honor of being the last man to produce a roll from the Apollo Iron and Steel Company, as well as being the first man to produce a finished sheet in the Vandergrift mill.

Jack was born on a farm near Vandergrift, September 6, 1867, and died December 8, 1931, at his home in Vandergrift (on Hamilton Avenue.) He served four terms as burgess of Vandergrift. His first term ran from 1914 to 1917; he later served three terms starting in 1922 until his death.

Before his public service, he became head superintendent at Vandergrift's American Sheet and Tin Plate Company, with 75 men under his direct supervision. George McMurtry held high esteem of McIntire and when the dedication ceremony of the first piece of structural steel was to be placed, he insisted that Jack be present.

Burgess Jack F. McIntire became foundational to many civic interest groups and community functions. He started the tradition of the municipal Christmas Tree in Vandergrift.

Custer and Poplar Streets (a very large incinerator). The large red brick building with its tall chimney functioned for years serving the increasing disposal needs of a booming citizenry and became a familiar landmark in town.

In March 1925, the borough took a big step by hiring W. T. Smith, the council secretary, as the new borough manager. The manager would carry on the business of the borough under direction of the council. In his position, he functioned under the direction of the council as secretary to the council, street commissioner, and aide to Burgess Jack McIntire, Sr. (town representative). Smith's duties included the charge of plumbing and sewers, and supervision of borough expenditures. His office was located in a small room west of the lobby in the front of the Casino, and his annual salary was $3000.

Reflections Of The Times

Stories of the Day

Early Vandergrift Bus Transportation

In the 1920s, when the automobile was not a common item, bus service and taxi service were a very important part of town life. Vandergrift's bus and taxi service had its company building at the corner of Grant and Sumner Avenues. In the 1930s , the company was owned by O. B. Doak and Joe Levindowsky, who had purchased it from Bird Byers and Bob Lear. Although no records have been found, it is believed that the Vandergrift Bus Company was started in 1924.

In addition to nearby sites in the valley, the bus route, by way of transfers, carried travelers as far as Greensburg or New Kensington. The Vandergrift bus made this trip 6 times a day beginning at 6:10 am and running to 6 p.m. The bus would stop for passengers anywhere along the road. A bus service also connected Vandergrift, Apollo, and Leechburg. In the late 1930s the fare was 10 cents to Apollo and 15 cents to Leechburg.

Nora Long Richey, a resident of the Poke Run area told of riding the bus to Vandergrift High School. She thought her father paid $1.50 a month. The bus would drop the students off near the school in the mornings. After school, the students would walk to the bus garage to board the bus home. The bus doors were left open so the children could wait on the bus for the return trip.

Mill and foundry bus runs were made at shift changes. The bus went through Oklahoma to Blairton, then down Paulton Hill to the West Apollo Railroad Station, then back to Vandergrift over the same route.

In 1938, the Vandergrift bus service was taken over by Eugene Weimer and in 1940 by the Vandergrift Motor Coach Company. These later buses ran through downtown and the Heights and were especially used by mill and foundry workers at shift changes. In 1947, service was discontinued because private autos displaced the need for bus service.

The buses were big International and Studebaker models. Some of the early bus and taxi drivers were Kitty and Bill Aicorn, Ping and Lefty Rollinger, Link Callen, and Curtis McDermott.

Our Own Nightingale

Most women in Vandergrift who sought work outside of the home had limited opportunities. Generally they labored as store clerks, domestic help, clerical assistants, and production workers. Melissa Snyder Knowles reached for more.

Mrs. Knowles was born in Vandergrift on January 10, 1901, to Christopher and Nellie Snyder. Her father was a roller at the mill; her mother had been a school teacher in Indiana County.

Mrs. Knowles attended school in Vandergrift and graduated in 1919. During her school years, she became noted for the quality of her singing voice. After graduation, her parents sent her to the New England Conservatory of Music in Boston to study voice and piano. Upon graduation from the conservatory, she accepted a position at the University of Alabama where she taught voice, piano, stage presence, and sight reading for a few years. In 1925, she was asked to sing at the homecoming program at Penn State University. The following summer she taught voice and piano at Penn State.

While a student in Boston, Melissa met and became engaged to a Tufts University dentistry student, Robert Knowles, who moved to Vandergrift and married Melissa in 1926. Giving up her university teaching career, Mrs. Knowles maintained a high interest in music, teaching voice and piano in her home.

She was a member of the KDKA staff band and chorus, where she sang in the chorus and was a soloist for more than 10 years from the late 1920s till the early 1940s. This group broadcast Tuesday evenings from the William Penn Hotel in Pittsburgh and was sponsored by the Philadelphia Gas Company. The chorus also performed in Indianapolis at the Kiwanis National Convention.

Locally, she sang at weddings, the Scot's Robert Burnes banquets, and at the First Presbyterian Church where she became the organist and the choir director.

She also sang at the First Methodist Church in Pittsburgh for several years and at the Sampson Funeral Home in Pittsburgh . She received $20 for each performance, very good pay for that time.

Hot Idea

This elevated oven was the latest model sold by Boyd Steele. From an early edition of the Vandergrift News.

Courtesy of Buttermilk Falls Publishing Company

WISE TURKEYS TRAINING DOWN FOR THANKSGIVING

IF only turkey birds were wise they'd read the sporting pages,
Discovering there the secret rare of lengthening out their ages.
By training down instead of up they'd so reduce their meat
That when Thanksgiving day comes round they'd not be fit to eat,
And when the buyer came along to talk with Farmer Jones
He'd say, "Why, I these birds can't buy---they're only skin and bones!"

Courtesy of Buttermilk Falls Publishing Company

Holiday Tradition

Even in the early days of Vandergrift's history, people ate turkey on Thanksgiving. Here turkeys are advised to be smart. From the Vandergrift News, *November 30, 1911.*

Courtesy of *Vandergrift: First 75 Years*

Civil War Cannon at Columbia and Grant Avenues

Chapter Eight

People and Culture in the Twenties

Remember the cannon promised to Vandergrift by Congressman Robbins mentioned previously (Chapter 6)? Well, it finally arrived by train on January 20, 1929. The 3-inch light artillery field gun was addressed to the Burgess of Vandergrift, and that is where it was delivered. It was placed right outside Burgess McGeary's office door and drew crowds of curiosity seekers. Some of the local jokers had questions as to why it was here: "Is it here to enforce prohibition?" or "Are we expecting an invasion from East Vandergrift?"

The gun was on loan from the United States Government for ornamental or memorial purposes. It was complete and ready for action. All that was needed was ammunition. It was reportedly suggested that blanks be obtained, and it could be used to fire salutes on special occasions.

By May 1921, the cannon had been mounted on a pedestal at the head of Washington Avenue near the Honor Roll Tablet where it was dedicated with great fanfare on May 8. On that day, all residents were asked to display flags. The Liberty Band led a parade of veterans and bands through town. One of the highlights of the parade were the remaining Veterans of the Civil War. The parade ended at the site where the cannon was mounted, and the cannon was presented to the American Legion in a speech by Judge James S. Beacom.

Not to be outdone by the upstarts from World War I, the Civil War Veterans asked permission of the council to place a Civil War cannon in the center of the street at Columbia and Grant Avenue. No record of a dedication program is known, but the group must have gotten permission because residents remember the cannon barrel mounted on a cement pedestal at this location for years. The present location of the cannon is unknown, but one resident thinks it is buried under what is now the parking lot of the American Legion.

A humorous little story, found in an old *Vandergrift News* article, about another cannon is also part of the town's history. Debi Shupe retells the account.

> *It has come to our attention, that yet another creative mind has been hard at work. As the story appeared*

in the Vandergrift News, a local man was busy the last few days before the celebration of the Fourth of July. He had made a cannon from a piece of pipe and placed in it "some" dynamite. He then proceeded to point the cannon skyward, like a rocket, then he applied a flame.

Boom! The cannon, powder and all left the ground. It soared through the air about 150 yards and crashed into the second floor of a home on Longfellow Street. The cannon tore through the roof and struck a bed in an upstairs bedroom, ripping a two feet square hole in the bed. One of Vandergrift's motorcycle patrolmen investigated the incident and ordered the "producer" of the cannon to appear at a hearing before the local Burgess. Upon listening to the case, the Burgess ordered the young man to repay the homeowners for the damages amounting to $250. This Fourth of July enthusiast was also discouraged highly from reproducing any further such cannons.

Extra! Extra! Read All About It!

Vandergrift had two newspapers until 1919 when the *Vandergrift Citizen* went out of business for lack of help due to the war. In March 1925, the *Citizen* was reestablished on a weekly publication. The publisher's reason for starting the paper again is worth reading:

Vandergrift's Newspapers

Two newspapers published at various times in Vandergrift's early history. The earliest, the *Vandergrift Citizen*, reported local news weekly. In 1898 it was brought from Apollo by *Apollo Herald* editor and owner, Mrs. H. M. Cochran. She sold it to Edward Welsh, of Welsh Printing Company in 1904, who edited and published the *Vandergrift Citizen* weekly until 1926 except for a 6 year suspension between 1919 and 1925.

The *Vandergrift News* was shortly thereafter founded and owned by a local man, Otto Lindquist. It too was printed by Welsh Printing Company. *The News'* second owner/editor, George A. Hunger, a former mayor of Vandergrift, purchased and installed a complete shop in Vandergrift in what is now the Masonic Temple on Washington Avenue.

As reported in the *Vandergrift News*, November 17, 1930, in conjunction with the paper's Silver Anniversary, the first weekly *Vandergrift News* issue, November 16,1905, reported local events, minor accidents, weddings and society news.

In 1909 the *Vandergrift News* was purchased by O. H. Cochran, and continued its weekly reports for 17 years under Cochran's leadership. In 1919, the subscription list from the *Vandergrift Citizen* was acquired and combined, giving the *News* the largest circulation in the area at the time. A New York City newspaper broker, J. B. Shale, in 1926 purchased the holdings of the *Vandergrift News*, which included the *Vandergrift Citizen*, and a year later, sold to R. E. Stough who renamed the two, the *Vandergrift News.* He then combined it with a third local weekly publication called *The Vandergrift Economist.* The *Economist* was the product of the work of two men, Charles Sobers and Jack Sayles. R. E. Stough is credited with changing from a weekly to a daily paper. Its first issue was published November 13, 1927.

The following June, Herbert D. Brauff purchased and began publications.

As has been its [Vandergrift's] history in years past, it has suffered less from the period of depression through which we have been passing than most manufacturing towns. Then Vandergrift has grown in size, not in boom fashion but steadily until it has now practically used up its available desirable lots in the original area and has reached far out over the hills and into the valleys beyond in one direction at least until we now practically continuous to Blairton on the Greensburg Road. A town the size and quality of Vandergrift needs more than one industry, so we feel it needs more than one newspaper and this we propose to give to the citizens.

And give, they did. The paper was to be delivered free to every home for an indefinite period. When they did start selling subscriptions for $2.00 a year, they made an arrangement with the fire companies to sell subscriptions. The fire companies received $1.00 for every one sold.

The Hi-Newsette

The publication of the high school newspaper was started in December 1926 and became a regular activity of the school under the sponsorship of Miss Esther McDowell and Mr. Kenneth Thompson. *The High Newsette* was raised to the same status as the athletic and music programs. It was published by the journalism class supervised by Miss Evelyn Love. This outstanding newspaper linked the school and the town in patronization, financial support, and participation in school and municipal events. It served the school and community till 1962.

The Lost Generation

While the town was moving ahead, so were the people. How were Vandergrift citizens adjusting to the turmoil of the 1920s? The era was most notably a youth rebellion. Once boys had tried to be paragons of gallantry, industry, and idealism. Girls had aspired to seem modest and maidenly. For those joining the "lost generation", all this would change. The noted writer F. Scott Fitzgerald suggested that, "America was going on the greatest, gaudiest spree in history." All, of course, to the dismay of their elders.

There was a prevailing desire to shake off the restraints of puritanism, to upset the long-standing conventions of decorum. Young women seemed to lead the way. The long petticoat dresses of the early 1920s gave way to clinging dresses reaching to just above the knee, stockings were rolled down to below the knee and horror of horrors, women gave up wearing corsets. Hair was cut above the ears, and large hats were not in fashion.

The change in appearance was matched by a change in decorum. As women took up smoking cigarettes and drinking alcohol, they felt free to join the men at the bar in the speakeasies for a cigarette and a shot of moonshine. Young men felt free to appear in public without a coat. They delighted in the change in women's fashions

> **Terms to Know**
>
> *Bootleg*—alcoholic liquor secretly and unlawfully made, sold and transported
>
> *Booze*—alcoholic liquor; a drinking bout
>
> *Flapper*—a young woman, often one who tries to appear sophisticated in style
>
> *Moonshine*—smuggled or illicitly distilled liquor
>
> *Speakeasy*—a place where intoxicating liquors are sold without a license or otherwise contrary to law
>
> *Still*—a distilling apparatus used to make liquor

and in new freedoms provided by the automobile, such as "parking" and necking.

The demure waltz and two-step gave way to scandalous dances such as the Charleston, Blackbottom, and Shimmy. It was the era of bathtub gin, mahjongg, Freud, jazz babies, and flappers. Writer H. L. Menchen suggested that America was like a zoo!

For those who joined in, it was a rebellion against the religious and moral code of their parents. In their rebellion, they found only disillusionment and behind it all, a sense of futility. The axiom of the decade was surely "Eat, drink, and be merry", with the corollary, "For tomorrow we die." The theme song of the Lost Generation was, "In the mean time, in between time, ain't we got fun."

Vandergrift and the Lost Generation

Although these dramatic changes were centered in the big cities, small towns like Vandergrift mirrored the current trends. But not everyone joined the "rebellion," and for the most part, those things that undergirded our society remained in place. Vandergrift's churches, fraternal organizations, civic and veterans groups continued on course undaunted by the new turmoil effecting the nation.

A November 1924 news item headed, "Vandergrift Successfully Invaded By Salvation Army" announced the results of a successful fund drive to raise $3,000 to establish a permanent Salvation Army presence in the town. A large crowd gathered at the opening of the new headquarters at 128 Columbia Avenue to welcome Captain Reif, the first local Salvation Army commander.

The Army went right to work. Just 1 month later, it was reported that on Thanksgiving 173 needy persons were helped with food and clothing gathered by school children for the Salvation Army. They also announced that they had arranged through their representative at the North Pole for Santa to visit Vandergrift every Saturday afternoon and evening till Christmas arrived. They opened an employment bureau at their headquarters. It appears the new trends had not changed the idea we should help one another.

In the meantime, in East Vandergrift, two immigrant groups were once again able to worship with the songs, hymns, and liturgy of their homelands and continue

> **Woman Lawyer**
>
> The first woman lawyer admitted to practice in Cambria County was from Vandergrift. Helen Ivory was admitted on January 2, 1922. She was a graduate of Vandergrift High School and the University of Pittsburgh Law School. She received her B.S. Degree in 1919 and was the first woman graduate of the School of Economics at the University of Pittsburgh.

their centuries-old customs and devotion to the church; St. Casimir's Lithuanian Roman Catholic Church was opened in 1922, and the All Saints Polish Roman Catholic Church was opened in 1924. Obviously, the church was still alive and well also.

The Protestant churches were not sitting on their hands either. In a show of ecumenical cooperation, they began combined union services in July 1924 in the high school auditorium with a large crowd.

The Vandergrift Commercial College upgraded its courses in line with changing events. In 1924, the fall opening announced a new technical program that included mathematics, mechanical drawing, electrical courses, and a college preparatory course. They also added a garage and automobile accounting course.

The Fire Companies

The fire companies continued their outstanding service to the community. To show off their pride and community spirit, Vandergrift fire companies hosted the 13th Annual Western Pennsylvania's Convention in 1923—an honor for the young town. Both companies expanded their membership by organizing the ladies auxiliaries. In consideration of one another, the two companies joined to form the Vandergrift Fireman's Relief Association to provide insurance for its members in case of accident or death. This action formed a lasting bond between the two companies.

The companies worked hard to raise funds to purchase new modern equipment to keep abreast of the rapid advances in

Courtesy of Buttermilk Falls Publishing Company and Charles Kingirski

Ahrens-Fox Pumper Truck, 1925. Burgess McIntire is seated opposite the driver. The truck has recently (1995) been restored by members of the No. 1 Fire Department.

firefighting techniques. In 1925, the town council purchased an Ahrens Fox 1000-Gallon Pumper, the most modern fire truck available, for the George G. McMurtry Fire Department for $13,550. The fire company then decided to raise the money to purchase a Seagrave Double-Banked Ladder Truck for $9,500. The Heights Fire Department obtained an Ahrens Fox in 1927 in addition to its 2 other motor firetrucks. The George G. McMurtry Fire Department still has and maintains its Ahrens Fox Pumper as a collector's item—this nationally famous model fire truck can be seen at the Number One Fire Hall.

To assure proper maintenance and care of the new Ahrens Fox Pumper, the council appointed Eugene Frank Yaley "to full charge of the new fire pumper at a salary of $150 per month. Mr. Yaley will have full jurisdiction over the machine and all assistants will be chosen by the fire chief and himself."

The firemen loved a parade, and when each company appeared decked out in uniform (to include the ladies) along with their modern equipment, they won many prizes as they traveled about the area. In 1925, the Heights Fire Department made the members of the Liberty Band honorary members of the department. For the next 10 years, the Liberty Band led the Heights Fire Department in parades to win many prizes.

Courtesy of Buttermilk Falls Publishing Company

1923 Fireman's Convention Parade on Grant Avenue

The firemen especially denied the call to the individualism of the 1920s by continuing to serve their fellow citizens in their dangerous tasks. They made the town proud of them in every respect.

The Fraternal Organizations

The fraternal organizations likewise continued to thrive during the 1920s.

The Masons set up a lodge in Vandergrift in January 1925. In March, the newly organized group held "the social event of the season with a reception, banquet, and dance at the Italian Hall in Vandergrift. The hall was tastefully decorated in subdued lighting effects by many floor and table lamps. All ladies were given fancy colored fezzes which with the beautiful colored gowns blended with the red fezzes of the nobles, making a wonderful scene."

In 1928, the Twin County Lodge of Elks No. 838 was established at 108 Washington Avenue. Under the leadership of Henton Herron, this African American Elks lodge continued to thrive during the Depression and became known as the "Biggest Little Lodge in Western Pennsylvania."

The Civil War is not generally considered to be a part of Vandergrift's history because the town did not exist at that time. Yet, almost every parade mentioned the participation of Civil War Veterans. The Grand Army of the Republic (G.A.R.) was a veteran's organization of that great war. By the 1920s, most of these vets were quite elderly and their numbers decreasing. To counter this, the Patriotic Society was formed. It was a lodge made up of sons and grandsons of the Civil War veterans. The daughters of the veterans also worked with this group to sustain the work of the G.A.R.

On May 27, 1922, the Victor Emanuel III Lodge of the Sons of Italy dedicated their new lodge hall at the corner of Franklin and

Courtesy of Harold Doutt

The Sons of Italy Lodge

Garfield (Walnut) Street. This remains as one of the landmark buildings in town because it not only served the Sons of Italy members, but the community as a place of recreation and entertainment.

Sure evidence of this, and of some breaking down of ethnic barriers, was the notice in the news on January 25, 1925, that the Robert Burns banquet held to honor the Scottish poet by that name would be held in the Sons of Italy Hall. A Scottish banquet in an Italian hall—some advance from the early days of the town. The lodge hall became more affectionately known as the "Sons."

Courtesy of Dr. Joseph O' Brien

American Legion Drum and Bugle Corps, 1920s

The Drum and Bugle Corps

During the 1920s, the American Legion formed a drum and bugle corps made up of veterans of World War I. It was an outstanding musical marching organization. Wearing their distinctive silver WWI-type helmets, they performed all over the area. On one occasion, a special train carried Legion members and the drum and corps to Louisville, Kentucky where the corps performed at the national convention of the American Legion.

The drum and bugle corps included many community leaders among its members. Because of the quality and demeanor of the corps, its members became role models for other young men in the community. Wherever they performed, the corps left a favorable impression of Vandergrift and its residents. A feature of the corps in 1927 was its 5-year-old bugle playing mascot, complete with uniform. That mascot was Joseph C. O' Brien, who in the 1950s became the director of Vandergrift's famous Thunderers Drum and Bugle Corps.

The American Legion Drum and Bugle Corps would continue to appear in parades until the 1940s. Too often they were seen coming from the railroad station with black drapes over their muffled drums, as they escorted the returned remains of some local soldier who had been killed in action in World War II.

This drum and bugle corps was another outstanding group of volunteers that put forth a great effort and displayed a great pride in their organization and their town.

Other Mainstays of the Community

The Red Cross carried on its important functions. Vandergrift had an annual Red Cross Day. In November 1924 the local newspaper reported:

> *Next Sabbath afternoon beginning at 2:00 o'clock has been set as the time when the great privilege will be offered the people of our community to renew their membership in the Red Cross through the Vandergrift chapter. The homes of the community will be visited by duly authorized persons to solicit your membership for another year.*

The idea of promoting fellowship even extended outside the usual lodges and fraternities as the various departments in the steel mill began having annual banquets in 1925. By March, the Bricklayers, the Electrical Department, and the Open Hearth Department had banquets "for the purpose of stimulating a personal friendship of one for the other in the departments."

The Roaring Twenties had minimal effect on the mainline institutions that governed Vandergrift's society. People still banded together to help one another. Van-

Courtesy of Buttermilk Falls Publishing Company

Cartoon From Vandergrift News, January 9, 1919

dergrift did, however, seem to join in more readily in one aspect of the times: Prohibition.

No Booze!—But Not Really

On January 16, 1920, the Constitution of the United States was revised by the 18th Amendment enforced by the National Prohibition Act. This new law made the manufacture and sale of beer, wine, and liquor illegal.

This law created a phenomenon that became the centerpiece of the moral rebellion of the 1920s. The public demand for action against the use of alcohol was so great, our Constitution was changed. Yet, upon its being made law, its restrictions were flaunted right and left. Previously law abiding, respectable citizens began to regularly and unremorsefully violate the law by patronizing bootleggers and speakeasies, by making home brew and bathtub gin, and by carrying hip and pocket flasks to parties. The consumption of alcohol was higher than ever. Moonshining became big business, often protected by corrupt police and judges.

As you may recall, Vandergrift was already a dry town. "No alcohol allowed for 99 years" according to the town charter. With the loss of legal sources of alcohol outside the town, the illegal making of alcohol increased. A few news items from the times will illustrate this.

"Booze Dens Raided," March 1923. State police raided 18 places in the Valley where they found a large supply of moonshine, stills and barrels of mash. In East Vandergrift, police netted 4 men, 5 stills, 9 barrels of mash, and 7 gallons of moonshine liquor. Those arrested were given a hearing and released on $1,000 bail each.

"Speakeasy," January 1924. Constable John Klingensmith arrested a man in North Vandergrift for manufacturing and possessing intoxicating liquor. A quantity of beer and wine was confiscated. After a hearing, he was admitted to Armstrong County jail.

"Raid," November 27, 1924. Chief of Police Karl Kruppa and Constable Spang of East Vandergrift raided 6 homes. 7 arrests were made including 2 women. 5 stills were found along with quantities of mash and moonshine. The squire gave them bond for their appearance in court.

Although no raids in Vandergrift are mentioned in this sampling, you can be sure these same activities were going on in town. In fact, Nate Roberto, retired barber, told of the police coming to his family's home and carrying out a barrel of wine that his father had made for their own consumption. They dumped it in the street.

The Prohibition Act was said to be the final product of the American conscience

Circumventing the "Spirit" of the Law

As much as 1 million gallons of alcohol were produced legally each year for medicinal purposes. Doctors prescribed liberal doses!

A special grape juice from California, when placed in the cellar for 60 days, would produce a 15 percent alcohol content wine. Vineyards boomed with government loan assistance!

Near beer was a legal, half of one percent alcohol beer that never became popular. More in demand was WORT, half-brewed beer. Just add yeast and in due course, you had real beer.

Vandergrift Speakeasies Raided

Booze production was big business in the Vandergrift area, but not legally. During the early part of the century, alcoholic beverages were produced in the basements of more than a few local homes. In particular, the Park Plan and Heights sections of town seemed the largest producers. These two sections of Vandergrift were not yet annexed into the main borough of Vandergrift, leaving them out of the jurisdiction of local authorities and affording a safe haven for such establishments. In one 1915 newspaper account of a small police raid, an officer was quoted as saying that there was enough booze stored up in some of the houses to start a wholesale liquor distributorship.

These home-based entrepreneurs continued unchecked until a July evening in 1916. On July 16 of that year, the district attorney, armed with a stack of search warrants and a small army of State Police troopers, county detectives, and local authorities descended on the Park Plan and Vandergrift Heights.

Working from the tips given by local residents, the authorities swept through home after home arresting more than 19 local residents. They also found more than illegal liquor production. Apparently many of the booze producers had moved up into bigger and better things since the smaller raid of 1915. Many of the homes now ran fully equipped speakeasies, and several offered prostitution services, complete with rooms available for their customers.

The newspaper account of the event not only listed the names of those arrested in the raid but, as was the common practice of the day, listed their known nationalities; 3 Italians, 1 Spaniard and 1 Lithuanian.

that had prevailed before to the 1920s. The attitude of the 1920s would have none of it, and prohibition soon became a very strange episode in our history.

The Good, the Bad, and the Ugly

Vandergrift was not free of other types of law breaking either. The town witnessed the whole range of illegal activity from minor to major crime.

A December 1921 *Vandergrift News* item reported that Vandergrift was infected with shoplifters who were causing a great loss to the businesses. In the past, many who were caught, including members of prominent families, were not charged when the stolen items were returned. The businesses warned that henceforth, all cases would be pushed to the limit of the law.

Mystery surrounded the shooting of a former Vandergrift barber in Arnold in March, 1923. Police believe the victim may have been a member of the Black Hand Society, and they theorized that the shooting was the work of the Society. Reliable information was that two major factions of the Black Hand Society existed; one in Sharpsburg and one in Vandergrift. The Society had been formed by a lawless band of the lower class.

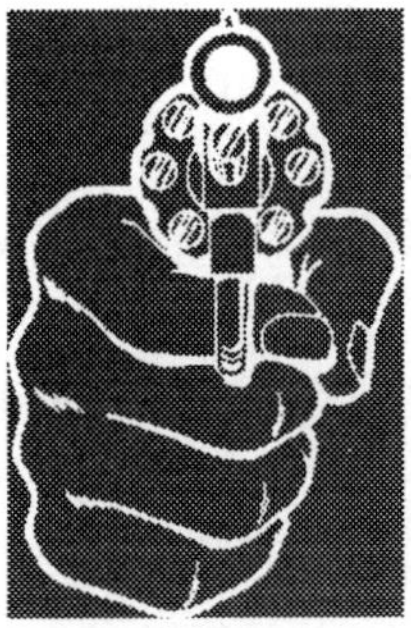

A major crime of the era was a bank holdup on November 4, 1925.

Lawrence Walthour left the Vandergrift Savings and Trust Company carrying $75,000 to be transported to Pittsburgh. James Coward stood across the street near the mill office, took a white handkerchief from his pocket that was the signal to three men who were waiting in a car near the old

Vandergrift Block. When Walthour came by, one man stepped out with drawn gun. Walthour immediately kicked the gun from his hand. Another man who was behind Walthour hit him several times with a gun, knocked him unconscious, and took the satchel containing the money.

The third man was in the car with the engine running, so the getaway was quick. They had a well-planned route: out the Serpentine Road, through Leechburg, to Schenley to the Vota Farm, where some of the money was divided and the men scattered. Guided by people who had seen the speeding car, some men from Vandergrift arrived at the Vota Farm and found the abandoned get away car. (The Vandergrift Chief of Police, Garver, directed the pursuit by way of Oklahoma, away from the direction of the getaway.)

The State Police were brought in on the case, and after some astute detective work arrested a group of known criminals from Monongahela City. They were James Coward, Andrew Lucas, Vincent Isenberg, Joseph Masterrano, John Vota, Albin Anderson, and Alex Zeberick. All received fines and jail sentences up to 20 years except for John Vota who claimed his life had been threatened if he did not cooperate. Although still at large, Zeberick was found guilty.

Of the $75,000 stolen, $60,000 was found hidden near the West Virginia border. James Coward gave $3,140 to Police Chief Garver and asked him to keep it for a few days. Garver was never officially implicated in the holdup, but the suspicious nature of his actions caused the council to suspend him on December 3, 1926.

The business district area at Columbia Avenue was also a challenge for local police. This item appeared in the January 5, 1924 *Vandergrift News* under the heading, "Disorderly Conduct for Benefit of Church."

> *When the police force invaded the scene of carousing Sunday evening at the shop of Tony Baze, 136 Columbia Avenue, the proprietor protested. He declared that the singing and Punch and Judy show going on was a charity benefit for his church. The officers arrested Baze and his partner "Squeak" and fined them the limit.*
>
> *When the officers had completed this job they crossed the street and closed the shop at 135 Columbia Avenue, also the scene of dancing and singing. The proprietors were fined.*

(The Sunday Blue Laws placed severe restrictions on Sunday activities.)

During the first half of the 1920s, a secret organization thought by many to exist only in the South made an appearance in the communities of the Kiski Valley; it was the Ku Klux Klan (KKK). Strangely enough, the "new" KKK was organized to combat the excesses of the Lost Generation of the Roaring Twenties. They saw themselves as the guardians of religion, morality, and patriotism as well as white supremacy. Although the Klan existed in Vandergrift, it was much more active in Apollo and Leechburg. The newspaper indicated that several bootleggers had "folded their tents" in a hurry and left town at the urging of the Klan.

On October 9, 1924, it was reported that 7,500 Klansmen gathered at the Apollo fairgrounds. They arrived by rail and streetcar and in 1,600 automobiles. The main speaker was Judge Gilbert L. Nations, the presidential candidate of the American Party. An airplane circled again and again over Apollo and Vandergrift showing a huge cross of electric lights on the bottom of the plane. The meeting included one hour of fireworks. "The final cars left the grounds at 3:50 a. m. All that remained were the ashes of three burned crosses and memories of Armstrong County's largest Konclave."

A November 1924 news item reported in part,

> *In full regalia; hooded and masked, 200 members of the Ku Klux Klan filed into Vandergrift's First Presbyterian Church just as the service began Sunday evening, November 16, and sat through the sermon and services. Their appearance was in appreciation for a series of sermons favorable to the Klan that Reverend W. A. Roulston, pastor of the church, had given. Their appearance caused a sensation. All were unaware of plans for the Klansmen's visit. It was a fitting climax to sermons on the Klan—though a surprise.*

Although there were cross burnings on a hillside overlooking the town, no large demonstrations occurred in Vandergrift.

Days of Fun

Instead of problems to solve, Americans craved excitement. Almost anything in the news, no matter how trivial, gave it to them; gangland crimes, world championship boxing, royal visits, Lindburgh's Atlantic flight. What excitement they could not get in

Swimming Holes in the Days Gone By

The sultry days of August have not changed in the past 100 years. Today the Vandergrift Area Pool provides for a cool dip on a blazing hot summer day. Here is how they did it in days gone by:

The River. This was a natural spot for swimming holes, and there were, in fact, two popular places on the river for recreation. One was on the north side of the river toward Apollo, at the bend in the river just before Allison Park (North Apollo). The other was also on the north side of the river, below the present Vandergrift bridge, "just below the icehouse" about halfway to the Keppel Farm (Riverview).

Wagner's. Situated in the general area of the present Vandergrift Area Pool, Wagner's was a pond formed by the damming of the small stream that ran down the hollow from the cemetery.

Pine Run. There was a popular swimming spot on Pine Run just below West Vandergrift.

Griftlo Park. Griftlo Park, across the river in Armstrong County, had a real swimming pool and a lake.

B. A. B. The river and Pine Run have both been mentioned as B. A. B.s, or places where in certain situations, bathing attire was optional at best. And they talk about kids today!

the news, they sought through sports and movies.

Sports, for participants and for spectators, occupied a great part of the citizen's leisure time. Baseball and basketball predominated with a several of teams in Vandergrift and throughout the valley providing virtual year-round sports opportunities. Teams came from the mill and foundry, churches, and fraternal and veterans organizations. A sportswriter suggested in 1923 that the best players be selected from each team to form a team to play the similarly made-up team from other towns on Saturdays. "This ought to furnish plenty of good sport for the summer." It could not be determined if this was ever done. In any case, sports provided a wholesome outlet for the people.

The high school provided sports opportunities for the younger set. In 1925, Vandergrift High School hosted the first countywide basketball tournament in Westmoreland County. 8 teams participated: Jeanette, Irwin, Scottsdale, Monessen, West Newton, Greensburg, and Vandergrift. The tournament was won by Scottsdale; Vandergrift placed third. Players on the VHS team were Hammer, Kirkiewski, Paul, Lash (Capt.), Mitchell, subs: McCoy, Williams, and Marley.

A 1921 news item of interest to hunters indicated that deer seen on the Jackson Farm in Apollo were evidence that the state's game policy was working. Several years earlier, deer had been released in Westmoreland County, and there had been recent sightings at Roaring Run and at Rearick's Fording as well. The last deer was killed in this area in 1820, when Owen Jones clubbed a deer with an oar as it attempted to swim the river at the old Warren Ferry above the Apollo bridge.

(This suggests that there were no deer seen in this area for 100 years; 1820-1921. The disappearance of the white tail deer occurred across the state due in large to the uncontrolled commercial hunting practices of the 19th century. Efforts by the Pennsylvania Game Commission and the state's sportsmen have since restored deer populations to current record numbers.)

Tennis was a popular sport. In 1923, the public courts on Franklin Avenue were occupied every day by more players than could be suitably taken care of and for this reason, an additional court was being laid out. The players were asked to help with the new court, and upon completion, a city tournament would be held with junior and senior divisions, in singles and doubles and with men's and women's divisions—all to play for the Vandergrift championships.

The boxing game in Vandergrift was gaining popularity in 1922 as evidenced by the large crowd that attended the night's show at the skating rink when five of the speediest bouts ever staged in the town were presented. Every bout was fast and furious, and the patrons who went for action got it at every go. Two local fighters in the contest were "Battling Pete" and "K. O. Baustert."

On With The Show

In Hollywood, the fantasies of the 1920s galloped unchecked in the movies. In 1927, not only images would be projected from the screen, but sound also, as the first "talky" was produced in 1927 with Al Jolson in the "Jazz Singer." The great passion for this type of entertainment continued locally through the decade.

The big news for the Casino Building was that the borough purchased the building from the Casino Corporation for $30,000

Courtesy of Gertrude Keirn

Courtesy of Jean and Mary Panza

The Rise of the Hemline

The changes in the lengths of dresses are easily seen in these two photos. *Above* Raymond and Rosella Keirn, 1912. *Right* Rose Panza, 1925.

Courtesy of Buttermilk Falls Publishing Company

Big Sale

Check out those prices! Rubin's Store on Grant Avenue was holding a sale to close out its entire summer stock back in 1927. Isadore Rubin is standing in front of the store.

in February of 1921. With this purchase, "the borough acquires the best property in Vandergrift or in the valley for that matter." The lease for the theater was put out for bid and was won by Wister Elliot, the owner of the Star Theater. He acquired a lease at $450 per month. The theater had been newly renovated with new wiring, plaster and paint. Elliot planned to operate a combination vaudeville and motion picture concern.

Mr. Elliot also purchased the Kiski Theater from Leonard Elswick in May 1922. This later became the Manos Theater (where Fontana's Casa della Pasta is now located at 115 Grant Avenue).

The Vandergrift area produced its own movie star in this era. In November 1922, Ward McCallister, the son of Morrow McCallister of Oklahoma, had the leading role in the movie, "A Woman of No Importance" then showing at the Star Theater. The theme of the movie was that girls seldom marry the men they flirt with. Many thought it was one of the most interesting pictures ever seen in Vandergrift.

On the Heights, the Arcadia Theater opened on January 20, 1923, on Longfellow Street. The people were exceptionally pleased as Mr. Buck, the owner and manager, had booked exceptional pictures and had a good orchestra each evening. The first movie was "Fast Mail," a topnotch film shown in one of "the most modern structures outside the large cities. It was built for safety and comfort." Later, this theater would show mainly double-feature western films and serials and became affectionately known as the "Ranch House" by moviegoers.

In February 1924, Elliot purchased the Stoughton Building at 129 Grant Avenue (where Tees N' Tops is now located), which contained the Star Theater. He planned to enlarge the theater that was on the first floor of this building.

The borough minutes of August 2, 1926, record plans to issue bonds in the amount of $100,000 to improve the Casino Building. On September 22, 1926, the minutes report leasing of the theater to the Indiana Theater Company for 10-years with an additional 5-year option.

In addition to the movies, there was vaudeville at the Casino, which included such acts as 3 dancing bears and other live

The New Casino

Vandergrift will undoubtedly have one of the finest theaters in Western Pennsylvania when the Casino is remodeled. Mr. W. M. Elliot is sparing no expense in making the Casino a modern and comfortable playhouse. All the features of the large playhouse will be incorporated into the new Casino. The stage will be enlarged to accommodate large productions, the orchestra pit is being rearranged, placing the new organ on the extreme left thus facilitating correct rendering of the different scores, the floors will be covered with heavy plush carpet, new diffused lighting effects will be installed, comfort rooms grace the mezzanine floor—in fact nothing is left out for the comfort of the patrons. It is well to mention the fact that the new organ is a manifold type, the arrangement of pipes around the proscenium being conducive to correct acoustical elements. Vandergrift should be proud of its new show house.

from the Vandergrift News, *December 11, 1924*

WHY NOT HAVE DINNER AT THE PENN -GRANT HOTEL THIS SUNDAY?

Music by Margaret Hamilton, Margaret Cline, and Noris Swenk

MENU—$1.25

Mock Turtle Soup
Olives
Celery
Roast Young Turkey, Cranberry Sauce
Roast Leg of Lamb, Mint Jelly
Fried Spring Chicken, Corn Fritters
Fillet of Beef, Larded, Mushrooms
Creamed New Spinach   Green Beans
Mashed Potatoes   Stuffed Baked Potatoes
Sherbet
Pineapple Salad
Hot Raisin Muffins
Green Apple, Hot Mince and Cocoanut Custard Pie
Ice Cream   Cake
Coffee   Mints

Music—12:30 to 2:00
Dinner—12:00 to 2:00; 5:30 to 7:30

Penn-Grant Hotel Menu
from an advertisement in the December 15, 1928 edition of the Vandergrift News

entertainment. The Chatauquas (discussed in an earlier chapter) still came to town, as did the Lyceum programs and plays and operettas by the students at the high school.

The Lyceum programs (the name is from a sacred enclosure in Athens where Aristotle lectured) were originally meant to be adult education programs in the natural sciences. By the 1920s, they had become more entertainment than educational. In 1924, Vandergrift's Lyceum series included 10 programs and were held in the high school auditorium. One of the "world's greatest lecturers" returned to Vandergrift for the second time. William J. Bryan, a nationally known statesmen, appeared at the high school auditorium on November 3, 1924. His lecture was entitled "The World's Greatest Need." The last program of the year was Elsie Baker, the noted American contralto singer star of the "Victrola." The series of 10 programs could be purchased for only $3.00, while individual programs would cost $1.00 at the door.

By the late 1920s and 1930s, the competition of radio, movies, and the automobile tended to kill the Lyceum and the Chatauquas.

The Kiski Valley also had a complete amusement park at this time. Founded in 1922, Griftlo Park was a popular recreation area with its wooded picnic areas, rides, dance pavilion, boating lake and large swimming pool. The park drew large crowds all summer long (Its name comes from the last syllable of Vander**grift** and Apol**lo**: *grift - lo.*)

In July each year, the Kiski Valley Fair at the Apollo Fair Grounds was a big draw for the people of Vandergrift. In 1921, the fair featured horse races (including 100 horses,) vaudeville, automobile polo, and more. In Vandergrift all the stores closed so everyone could attend the fair.

In January 1924, the Kiski Valley Kennel Club solicited members in Vandergrift to help boost the American Kennel Club Dog Show to be held here in the spring. Reportedly chicken shows were also an annual event in the earlier days of the town.

Vandergrift seemed to go all out in whatever it did in the way of recreation. Halloween was no exception, especially in 1924. The council appointed a committee to plan the activities and Burgess Jack McIntire scheduled the festivities for Saturday, November 1, so the mill men could participate in the parade and the street dance to follow. The celebration was, as the local paper read,

> *to be as big and every bit as good as any year previous and a whole lot better than some of the parades in other towns. Case after case of red fire has been handed over to the red fire committee for distribution and the line of march will be brightly lighted.*

> ["Red fire" was apparently a hand-held torch-like flare that cast a red flame when lit.]

Music for the street dance was provided by Olin Zack's Synkopators, one of the best bands in Armstrong County. A number of generous cash prizes were offered for the best costumes. The burgess declared that the "police force will give way to the hordes of ghosts and spooks for that night only and the merriment will cease at eleven o'clock."

As the end of the Roaring Twenties approached, the diversity of activities in Vandergrift seems ample evidence that the revolt of the American conscience had little serious effect on the citizens of McMurtry's town. People still cared about and for one another. They worked for and donated generously to worthy causes. These were people who held firm to their values and worked hard to make Vandergrift a grand place to work and live.

Courtesy of Buttermilk Falls Publishing Company

This picture of the Ive Fiscus Orchestra, which was based in and operated from Vandergrift, was taken in 1927. They played for many a flapper doing the Charleston.

Shown from left to right are Fiscus, Wendy Harmon, Red Moore, Paul Alcorn, Bob Parsons, Kenny Frew, Howard Cline, Bill Hodge and John Patterson.

A Visit To

Once upon a time, there was a beautiful local park where Vandergrift residents could go for an afternoon picnic, a boat ride, or an evening of music and dancing.

As early as 1911, a parcel of land in North Apollo was made into a park, at that time named Allison Park, where picnics and Sunday band concerts were held. Later, in 1915, Hays Dancing School gave instruction on Friday evenings in standard and modern dance at the park. Ladies and gentlemen could learn the fine art of dance for as little as 25 to 30 cents.

Henry St. Peter, a glassblower from Jeannette, who also worked as a policeman in Oakford Park, purchased Allison Park in 1922. Over the next few years, he developed it into a popular attraction for those of all ages.

Henry added some concession stands that he acquired from Oakford Park. A merry-go-round, aerial swings, and a swimming pool were installed. With two dance pavilions, ballfields, a small fishing pond, and a pond large enough to hold a dozen rowboats and a family or two of ducks, it was a pleasant place to spend a summer afternoon.

In July 1922, the American Natural Gas Company held their annual Basket Picnic at the park. Among the days events were various contests for children and adults, including a Horseshoe contest, 50 to 100 Yard Dash, Tug-of-War, Three-Legged Race, Running Broad Jump, Ball Throwing contest, a Cracker Contest for the ladies, a Fat Men's Race, and a Monster Kiddie Kar Race.

Courtesy of Eugene A. St. Peter

Automobile Entrance to Griftlo Park

Griftlo Park

Prizes were awarded, some unique to the time period—a mechanical doll to girls under ten; silk hose, lingerie clasps, and a Dorrine Case to the ladies. Men might win more traditional prizes, such as a Gillette razor or a silk tie; boys, a ball and bat or Boy Scout knife. Dancing was programmed for the afternoon, as were baseball games, and a group photograph was taken. The gas company provided free ice cream, coffee or lemonade; and Playground Girls were available to romp and play with the children present.

Henry St. Peter continued to make improvements. A large concrete fountain was built in the park in 1923 and 3,500 feet of water pipe installed to supply the kitchen. By May 1924, the park featured new tables, better lighting, and a 75-foot long building, housing a shooting gallery with moving targets to test the skill of local sharpshooters.

About 1925, to avoid confusion with Allison Park in Pittsburgh, a contest was held that resulted in the park's name being changed to Griftlo—being the second syllable of Vandergrift and the last two letters of Apollo. The park was located along the river between the two towns.

Streetcars from the Pittsburgh and Allegheny Valley Traction Line transported folks to Griftlo Park from Apollo, Leechburg, and Vandergrift. Jess Richard of North Apollo remembers performing at the Griftlo dance hall. He described the dance hall as at least 50 feet square, with seats around the edge of the polished hardwood floor and a small stage. Jess picked his mandolin, playing what he calls "hillbilly" music, along with

Courtesy of Eugene A. St. Peter

The Swimming Pool at Griftlo Park

two friends, one playing guitar and the other a fiddle. They rode the trolley car to Griftlo on Saturday nights and strummed out polka's, waltzes, and square dance music, without payment, to those who came to dance and listen.

Special lights mounted in the dance hall let patrons know when the streetcars were coming in. When the last car of the evening came, everyone scrambled to get their ride home.

Starting in 1926 and continuing until at least 1930, the *Vandergrift News* and Griftlo Park management sponsored an annual Kiski Valley Kiddie Day. Aimed at giving all area children a day of fun before they returned to school in September, Kiddie Day became a huge success. Coupons were published each day in the newspaper, a week or so in advance, for free rides on the merry-go-round and swings. Attendants at the park gave out popcorn, lemonade, and ice cream along with favors. Water sports, games, and races lured young participants from as far away as Hyde Park, Avonmore, and Weinel's Crossroads.

In 1930, the motto became "Biggest day in the history of the park," with a goal of 10,000 children and adults attending from all the small towns in the valley. Two evening dances entertained adults with the Vagabond Orchestra of Vandergrift playing at the park pavilion and Ament's Orchestra of Apollo performing at the square dance pavilion.

Griftlo Park attracted people from all over the valley; the Salvation Army, community churches, factories, and mills all held picnics and outings there. Family reunions were commonplace. Mrs. Gifford Pinchot campaigned for her husband, who was later elected governor of Pennsylvania by

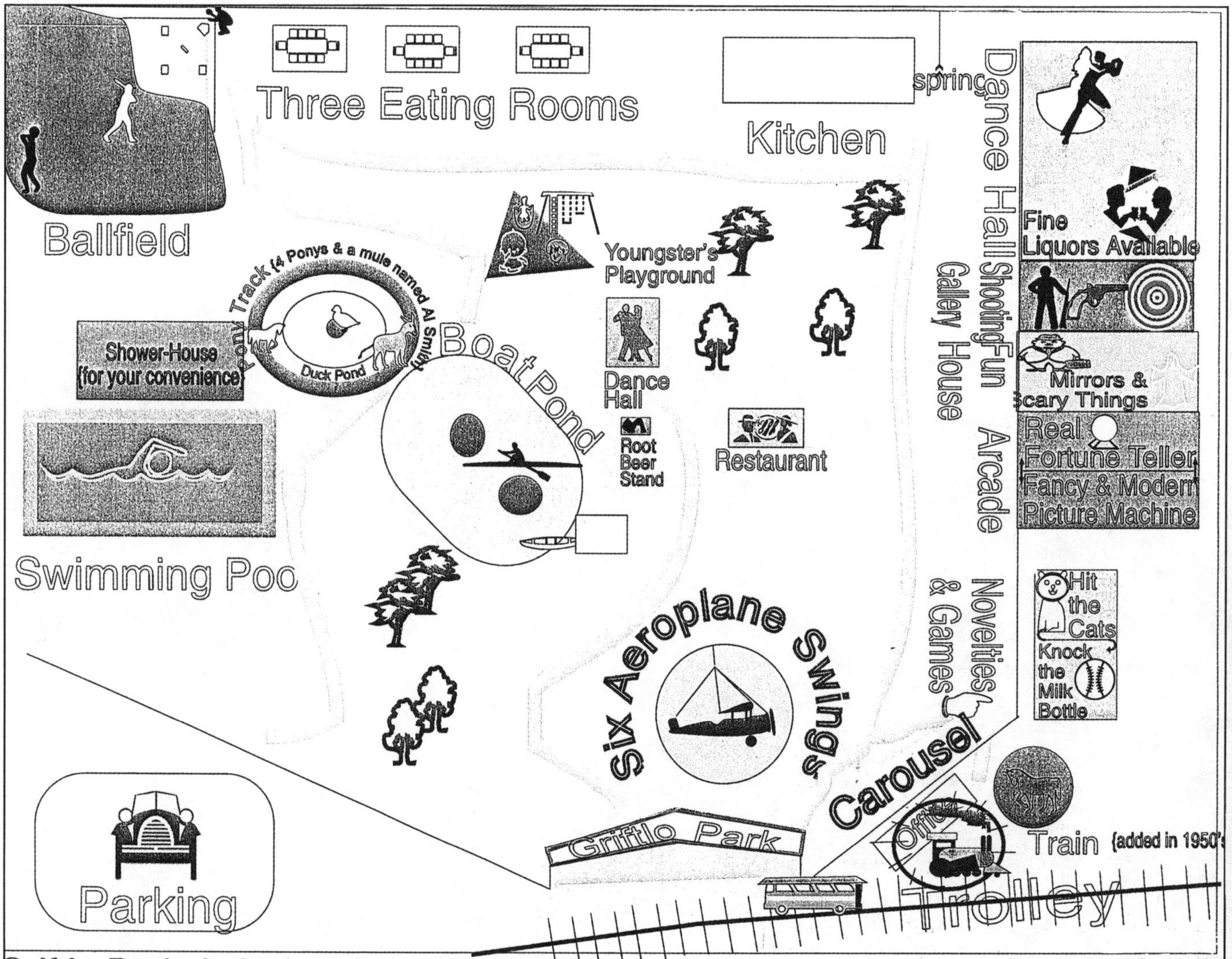

Griftlo Park, in its heydav, circa 1929.

giving a speech at Griftlo Park around 1930. Henry St. Peter's grandson, Eugene, recounted that many people came to the political function, and many local and State Police on motorcycles controlled the crowd.

Griftlo Park flourished until March 18, 1936 when floodwaters from the Kiskiminetas River came raging through the park. Boats, merry-go-round horses, bath houses, and buildings floated away. Even the streetcar rails were washed out during the flood. When the water receded, restoration began. One of the buildings was relocated and housed a restaurant and office. Carnival rides were replaced, and Eugene St. Peter put a new hardwood floor in what was once a merry-go-round, making it a dance floor.

Sometime after 1936, Henry St. Peter died, and thereafter Griftlo Park was leased to different individuals. At one time the park was leased to a Mr. George Baustert, who offered pony rides to the children.

During WWII, 3 men from Monesson planned a fireworks display which was left uncovered and somehow became ignited, setting off all the fireworks at once. Apparently, this was the topic of conversation around the valley for some time!

The Griftlo Park swimming pool was closed in 1948, partly because of problems with the water system. Also, Crooked Creek State Park was becoming a popular place to picnic and swim, because it had no admission fee.

Still, Griftlo Park remained open. Jess Richard told of going there in 1949 or 1950 to a circus, where cages lined up along the ballfield held monkeys and tigers.

In the 1950s and later, square dances and auctions continued to be held in the dance hall. The picnic area remained open until the mid-1960s, when Griftlo Park closed completely, ending more than 5 decades of enjoyment for residents of Vandergrift and surrounding communities.

Courtesy of Eugene A. St. Peter

Aerial View of Griftlo Park, circa 1929

Reflections Of The Times

Stories of the Day

One of the First Black Football Players in Vandergrift: Chuck Miles

In 1929, football in Vandergrift was just about the same as any other year—pep rallies, bonfires, and cheering crowds, not to mention a few teenage scuffles and fistfights outside the field. But there was one thing that was different—Chuck Miles tried out for the Vandergrift High School football team and earned the position of guard. That made him the first black player to ever wear a Vandergrift uniform. He played in the 1929 and 1930 seasons.

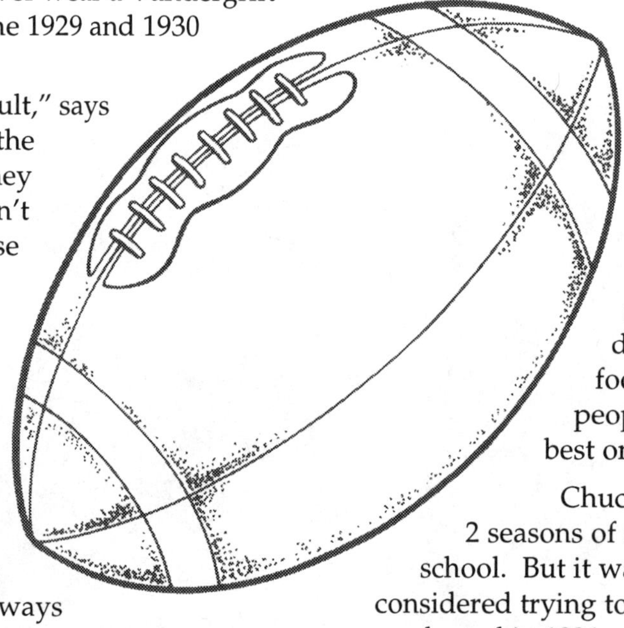

"Yes, it was difficult," says Miles. "But it was more the fans than the players. They made remarks, but it didn't bother me at all. I was use to that. I heard it on the streets all the time. I guess they just weren't ready for me."

Miles, who is now 86, still lives in Vandergrift with his wife, Lois. In the years when they were growing up, Vandergrift wasn't always a friendly place for blacks.

"People more or less tolerated you," says Lois. "When I was a child, I might be walking along and people would say, 'Here comes a cloud down the street.' They wouldn't come after you at all, just call you names and things like that."

Chuck remembers walking into stores in town and being ignored while white customers were waited on.

"They'd hardly want to wait on you, even if it was your turn," adds Lois.

But Chuck says he blocked such indignities and racist comments out of his mind when he played football. And he credits the rest of the team with respecting him and never joining in.

"There wasn't too many blacks playing at all then, in any of the schools," he says. "Most of them never went to high school. As they got old enough to get a job, they quit school and started to work."

Lois was 10 years behind Chuck in school and never saw him play a game. "I didn't even know what football was. But I still hear people say he was one of the best on the team," she says.

Chuck says he loved playing the 2 seasons of football while he was in school. But it wasn't something he considered trying to continue after he graduated in 1931.

"I got a job in the mill and stayed there for 42 years."

He might occasionally show up at a local high school football game, but says he hasn't made it to any recently. Some of his former teammates are still in town and stop him on the street to catch up on old times every once in awhile.

"There's still some of us hanging around," he says with a laugh.

Disastrous Results

Vandergrift was not without its share of accidents and mishaps. With more than 12,000 people in Vandergrift alone, and another several thousand in the adjoining vicinities, accidents were bound to happen. The following is a short synopsis of area disasters from the Vandergrift News *that help to give a clearer picture of what Vandergrift life was like in the first half of the 20th century.*

On April 18, 1912, a Vandergrift resident filed suit to recover damages in the sum of $25,000 from the Kiski Valley Laundry Company. On October 23, 1911, she had been operating a mangle, at $6.00 a week, when her fingers became caught in the roll, and she called to the manager for help. She alleged that the manager threw the power on, and her hand was drawn in between the rolls and remained there for 20 minutes. She alleged she "sustained grievous, severe, painful and permanent injuries to her left hand." The first, second, and third fingers had to be amputated, and the remaining fingers are stiff, causing her to be crippled for life and unable to earn a livelihood.

On April 30, 1913, 2 streetcars collided. The Vandergrift-Apollo trolley car smashed into the rear end of the regular car to Leechburg when it stopped to discharge passengers at Hyde Park. No one was injured, but all received a good shaking up. Both cars remained on the track and were towed to the barn after the passengers were transferred to another car.

A Vandergrift resident lost his wife and 5-year-old daughter on the Lusitania when it sank off the coast of Ireland May 7, 1915.

On May 30, 1913, a local stonemason, F. M. Moore, died in a Pittsburgh hospital of injuries he received while walking along the railroad tracks on East Vandergrift, earlier in the day. It was thought that he had been walking along the railroad tracks and stepped out of the way of a west-bound train and was struck by an east-bound train, possibly the Bummer (the midnight train); his severed legs were found inside the rails of the east-bound track, a distance away from where his body was found between the tracks. His brother-in-law was summoned and he flagged the first freight train going west, which took the injured man to Allegheny General Hospital in Pittsburgh, where he died the same afternoon. Today he would have been life-flighted from the scene and in a trauma unit in less than an hour. Moore was well known in Vandergrift as because he had done the stone work on some of the first houses built in town and continued to work here until his untimely death at age 36.

The loss of life from walking on the railroad tracks was so prevalent that campaigns were begun to teach the dangers of using the tracks as a shortcut or playing on the tracks. In November 1916, the Pennsylvania Railroad issued an illustrated calendar which was distributed to schools on the east and west lines in an effort to prevent this needless loss of life. On the Pennsylvania Railroad alone, there was "a man, woman, or child killed, while trespassing, for nearly every day of the year." In the United States as a whole, an average of 15 persons were killed each day while walking on the tracks, where they had no right to walk.

On September 9, 1915, a 3-story building fire claimed the lives of the pool room proprietor, Lugi Cucci, and one of the female employees.

A North Vandergrift child lost his life July 20, 1924, after eating glass from a china doll, which broke while he was playing with it.

October 17, 1947, was a sad day in Vandergrift. Robert E. Fitzgerald, a 16-year-old Vandergrift High School football player died of injuries suffered in practice and aggravated in the local school's game with Baldwin Township. The funeral procession was thought to be the largest in Vandergrift history. 8 members of the Boy Scout Troop were on duty at the church as a guard of honor. 6 members of the football team served as pallbearers, while the other 30 served as honorary ones.

Jean and Mary Panza
Voices From Another Era

Jean G. Panza was born in 1909 at his family home on Columbia Avenue. He recalled stories of his father, Louis Panza, who voyaged from Italy in 1905 and journeyed straight to the town of Vandergrift. Jean's father operated a shoe shop in a building that was demolished for the installation of the Columbia Avenue Parking lot. There was a special smile on Jean's face as he spoke of his father. You could see by his expression the recollection of special memories from times that were truly dear to him. Jean said, "My father was a good man. He worked hard. He didn't just repair and shine shoes, he made shoes! I still have some of the shoe forms and the shoemaker tool he used with a screwdriver, pliers, and cutter all made into one. You just flipped it over to use each tool, instead of wasting time fetching one of everything."

Mr. Panza reminisced, "When I was 5 years old, my father took me on the boat to Italy. I still have a vivid image of the town's hilly terrain. I remember groups of bunk beds pushed up against the wall. You understand, this was done so they could fit a large number of family members in a very small place. When my father and I returned from Italy, we got to Ellis Island, I saw the great lady, the Statue of Liberty. I hadn't been vaccinated and they insisted I have this done before I got off the boat, even though I was born here, they were afraid I brought back some disease with me from Italy."

In remembering his father, Jean said, "My father was also a musician. He was the band leader. He played the clarinet and the mandolin. He'd get 4 or 5 people together, and they would go from house to house and serenade people. They played for weddings, engagements, showers, and even while you were having a baby. My father's life was filled with family and work, but, most of his spare time was spent with these groups."

"I lost my father when I was 9. 9 years old was too soon to lose your father," Jean spoke slowly. After a long pause, he continued, "My mother remarried in 1925. He was a butcher and the shop was at the front of the house right here where we still live today on Linden Street. The butcher shop was here until the 1950s."

"Mary and I have been married 53 years," Jean continued.

"We remember many of things that were here, but are now gone." Mary said, " I remember when there were 5 grocery stores just on Linden Street. There were 2 lumber companies, Donghia and Gross."

"Kaste's Bottled Milk on Grant Avenue," Jean interjected. "The town had 12,000 people at one time. 5-6,000 worked at the mill. The money supported a lot of the businesses. Besides the small grocery stores and butcher shops, we had an A&P, Kroger... I remember when the train track ran where Kennedy Park is today. The train would run

Courtesy of Amy Myers

Jean and Mary Panza. On the table is the original radio that Panza used to listen to baseball games in the late 1930s. He would chart the games on butcher paper. In front of the radio are 2 of those charts, including 1 from a World Series featuring Babe Ruth.

up there from the mill and dump slag. That's how they filled it in, you know," said Jean, "that's why they never built any permanent buildings on that property, they were afraid the slag might sink, so they just used it as a park. And there were 4 or more shoemakers. We also rode the trolley from North Vandergrift to Leechburg and Apollo to shop. It cost a nickel to ride the trolley. We all went to Griftlo Park."

Mary smiled and recalled, "Oh it was beautiful—especially the lake."

Jean exclaimed, "There was a swimming pool and rides, too! People took picnic lunches. All the churches used to hold outings at the park. When the automobile got popular, folks started to lose interest....they went farther away to other places and parks."

Mary explained, "Everyone spent more time with their families and neighbors back then. We used to have Sunday picnics at Pine Run. After the picnic was over, we all carried home some of the vegetables from the gardens my father and our neighbors grew down there."

Jean continued by conveying the same kind of examples, "My family had their garden just below where St. Gertrude's Cemetery is today. I remember helping my uncle carry bushels of tomatoes to my car, a 1937 Plymouth, then we'd ride home."

While remembering the holidays, Jean recalled, "We had great holiday feasts on Christmas Eve and also the day before Lent started. On the day before Lent, we had huge parties and loads of food, just like the Mardi Gras in New Orleans—everyone came. The family had 33 different food items served on Christmas Eve, 7 of which were types of fish. We still practice this tradition today."

Jean remarked on the entertainment of the day, "I remember we used to go to the Casino Theater for free. I got complimentary tickets for hanging up movie advertisements."

Mr. Panza worked for 28 years as an accounting auditor for the H. J. Heinz, Co. in Pittsburgh. He declared, "They were good people to work for! In fact, even though I am retired, they still remember me every Christmas."

Ending their reflections of the past, Jean rolled out a delightful rendition of the Warsaw Concerto on his 75-year-old piano. Neither piano nor pianist seemed to be a day over twenty. In conclusion, Jean said kindly, "There are no strangers here. Make sure you come back again!"

Miss McComb and Music in Vandergrift

Miss Mabel McComb gave piano lessons in her home at 104 Custer Avenue, Vandergrift for many years—from at least the 1920s through 1950 and probably much longer. But she did more than just teach Vandergrift children how to play the piano.

She formed a Musical Theory Club and, endeavored to inspire children through understanding the classics. She instructed her pupils in piano basics through strict practice schedules (at least half an hour per day and preferably more). But whether piano students achieved skill was often beside the point.

Miss McComb, through the Vandergrift Junior Music Club, also gave students social and music appreciation lessons, enhancing what Vandergrift public schools were trying to instill via classroom and extracurricular musical activities. Miss McComb's recital programs, her rhythm band, and her "musical teas" inspired continually.

Courtesy of Vandergrift: First 75 Years

Hancock Avenue, circa early 1930s

Chapter Nine

Depression and Disaster Test the "Best"

From the high roll of prosperity to the low roll of depression—what a difference a year made! Bootleggers offered to accept script, and somewhere in the State of Washington someone made wooden nickels. It was not a pretty picture. The rich transferred fortunes into gold and some even buried it in the woods, never to be found or seen again. Others decided to ship their fortunes to Switzerland where it would be safe. Yet others set up shop with machine guns mounted under the eaves of their country estates, awaiting the inevitable revolution. There was not enough money in the United States Treasury to meet payroll; food supplies were falling, and laborers were fainting from hunger while holding on to paychecks that couldn't be cashed. This was the year people knew as *the year that the money stopped.*

The Great Depression would be the most powerful influence on American life since the Civil War. The effects were felt on business, professions, government, education, entertainment, and most of all, the political ideal. This was a decade of economic standstill, and it packed a bigger punch than anything in history to this point. It was far more reaching than even World War I. America stopped growing. Standstill was unfamiliar and very frightening, it was not the *American Way*. America did not pull out of this and get back on her feet again until after the attack at Pearl Harbor in December 1941.

Vandergrift however, remained insulated from the immediate impact of the crash that rocked the nation during the last week in October 1929. In fact, the news of the stock market crash did not even show up in the local newspaper until the middle of November. Very fortuitously for the town, this national economic disaster occurred at a time when Vandergrift was swimming in prosperity. From community life to town expansion projects, the town showed little or no sign of financial ruin or distress. The continuing growth of local businesses was recorded in the newspapers

Signs of Prosperity

Some things you might have read about during this time:

Girls Form Baseball League! Women to Play with "Mushball"

On a day in August 1932, Vandergrift's men would no longer be the only ones to appear on the local "diamond." The formation of a girl's baseball team was announced by the Young People's Council of Westmoreland County Sabbath School Association.

At the first practice of the team, 13 girls showed up for try-outs. When the team selection was completed, a schedule was made; Hyde Park's team was their first opponent. The only thing that made the women's league different from the men's was the type of ball used. The women chose to go with a "mushball" rather than the nasty hardball of the men's league.

Community Picnic Nears: Help Needed

On May 18, 1929 People from Vandergrift, East Vandergrift, North Vandergrift, and Oklahoma are getting ready for the Annual Community Picnic at nearby Griftlo Park. Those to attend the gala event are expected to exceed 10,000 in number.

Food and ride tickets will be passed out to the children during school hours next Wednesday morning. Ride tickets will include the Merry-Go-Round and Slide.

The need for transportation has not been met. The paper is reporting that at least 500 automobiles are needed to transport those wishing to attend. Some 5,000 of those needing a ride to the park are children. As Vandergrift is hosting the event, and most of the autos needed are in the community of Vandergrift, it is expected that residents will meet this need as they have in the past.

Events include allowing time for lunch at the lunch stands located in the park, band concerts, school drills, races and other games for the children; and perhaps "a fat man" race for the adults. There will also be dancing for the adults. Departure for the children is scheduled to begin at 5:00 p.m. Drivers are encouraged to meet the youngsters at the pool parking area.

As in the past, merchants have donated prizes for the children. All that attend are expected to have a very enjoyable day.

Football League to Tackle Vandergrift

The Pittsburgh Conference Football League will make a debut appearance in Vandergrift this season. The Vandergrift Independents have joined a six-team loop under the auspices of the Pittsburgh body. Monessen, Export, Fayette City, Westmoreland (Jeannette), and the Pittsburgh Beltzhoovers or the J. J. Veronas are the other teams to complete this section of the league.

The promoter of this league is Steve Cox, and he will be heading up a meeting soon to decide forfeits, and schedules, and rules that will govern the league. This meeting is to take place in Pittsburgh.

Vandergrift is scheduled to open its loop game on September 24, 1932, using the high school's football field. The local school's team will be playing in Butler that week, freeing-up-the field. The conference league teams will play all their games on Saturday while the Pittsburgh League will play on Sundays.

Joe Butch will manage the local team and represent it at all meetings. Such managers would decide districts so as to keep the "loops" close together in area to reduce cost of operations. The Independent's first game is against Portage.

Note: The first crowd to view this new league was estimated to be nearly 2,000 people; Vandergrift lost its first game by the score of 6 to nothing.

and in council meeting records of that day. Prosperity was also evident in the cultural activities, the development of parks, the growth of schools and the burgeoning population.

The 1930 newspapers reported that the mill rebuilt most of its equipment. Machinery not being rebuilt was replaced by new equipment. New businesses were being incorporated, and those in existence were expanding. Money was appropriated to widen town streets, install new concrete street lights, and even build a new bridge. There was a new athletic field for the high school and the town, built with a major grandstand and steel bleachers, making it one of the finest fields anywhere in the state. Existing parks were improved upon, and new ones were taking shape. 1930 was one of the biggest years for road construction and improvement in our area.

At this same time the population grew by almost 2,000. Talking pictures arrived at the Arcadia Theater. A new organization for the youth of the town, the Boys Scouts of America, was introduced to the community offering new opportunities and experiences for almost 400 boys of Vandergrift.

How was prosperity maintained so well in Vandergrift, while the national economy floundered? Backlogs. Because of the backlog of orders for the mill that had spilled over from the 1920s, the town of Vandergrift did not suffer the same adversities that many other towns had to endure during the Great Depression. With almost two and one-half years of backlogged work orders, the mill and a local coal mine that fueled the mill (Hick's Mine), continued to prosper. The mill and consequently the town remained healthy, until the advance mill contracts started to dry up. The gradual decline did not begin until the first months of 1932.

When most of the larger cities and industrial areas were suffering from the 1929 Depression, it was amazing to see the article that appeared in the *Vandergrift News* on February 11, 1930:

> *Four engines running in mill, improvement continues with orders still coming in.*

This reassured the work force that when they left work on Friday, there would be work to come back to on Monday.

Also in February 1930, the newspaper went on to report that the town of Vandergrift showed expansion along with the news that its early businesses were still prospering. It went on to show that 71% of each dollar made in Vandergrift stayed in Vandergrift. In fact, the town was so prosperous that in 1930, even the town's tax collector made history. At the year's end with the closing of the books, his office showed a very low deficit of 9/10 of 1% of uncollected taxes.

The town was still expanding, and the lumber yards were still doing a booming business. In fact all the merchants of Vandergrift did well, as long as the mill was working well. As late as March 1932, they were unaware of a Depression. One auto dealership in town had expanded and remodeled twice between 1930 and 1932. His sales had increased steadily each year. The year-end records showed a growth rate of 10 to 20 additional automobiles from the year before. Other merchants had similar experiences until late in the year of 1932 and early 1933.

There were other developments in Vandergrift's industries and economic growth during this period. J. A. Farrell, finance head of United States Steel Company, visited Vandergrift's plant of American Sheet and Tin Plate Company, on more than one occasion. Inspection of the plant was the main reason behind his visits, because Vandergrift's mill was to become a subsidiary of U. S. Steel. During Mr. Farrell's visits, he frequently remarked about Vandergrift being such a beautiful, clean little town. Farrell should not have been so surprised to find the town in such condition. He was a former manager of Vandergrift's American Sheet and Tin Plate Company. Perhaps having been transferred to the Pittsburgh office made him aware of and appreciate the cleanliness of Vandergrift.

The mill also had a very fine safety record for the late 1920s and early 1930s; only 2 accidents resulting in permanent injury and two fatalities were reported to the *Vandergrift News* on February 11, 1930. The total number of injuries was reported at 73, a slight increase from the year before. New structures and the increase in building inside the mill were to blame for the rise in accidents. The mill had added a new restaurant, new warehouses, and a new annealing unit all during 1929. Not only did the new additions create hazards, but they increased the number of employees that the mill had under payroll. Added to this was an increase in the number of hours actually worked per day and per week.

A display of dedication to safety was shown each work day. At the 8 a.m. and 4 a.m. whistles, each man would raise his right hand as a sign and pledge of his oath of "safety first." It also indicated his pledge to follow the rules of safety posted within the mill. Each section of the mill had a safety committee to oversee the rules listed. This committee was changed each week, so that every man had at least one chance a year to serve on the committee.

It appeared McMurtry's "Better Than The Best" dream town had once again proved its founder's vision by surviving even the "worst of the worst" of times. But inevitably the effects of the Great Depression began to seep into the valley. As its influence progressed across the nation, its hardship finally arrived in the "Workingman's Paradise." But in the midst of this trial, the true character of those who had been drawn to McMurtry's dream was revealed, and in their fortitude, McMurtry's ideals concerning investment into his employees and community would shine true.

Hard Time in Paradise

By 1933 hard times had arrived. The Citizens Bank, located on the corner of Grant and Farragut Avenues, had closed its doors. Local residents with savings in the bank were unable to retrieve their money for several years. At the same time, the work in the mill had slowed as the back orders dwindled. Men went without work, or at best, were getting reduced hours and wages.

The Salvation Army started a soup kitchen for the needy. Charity drives for food and clothing were held by such groups as the Boy Scouts and Ladies Sunday School Classes. There were benefit sporting events, and the Fire Departments held lawn fetes to help raise money for the needy. People took turns helping those around them who were less fortunate. Those who had jobs were not making great wages, but they had

Worker Peter Piper packs
a pair o' painful peepers,
And for the boner Piper pulled
he rates a booby prize:
He put his goggles in his pocket
once too much by jeepers -
Now Peter Piper's in a pickle,
paying through his eyes!
WAR PRODUCTION DRIVE COMMITTEE

Courtesy of Ron Ankeny and Allegheny Ludlum

Safety Sign at the Mill

Odds and Ends of the Times

Nightschool became a new endeavor in the town. About 250 people enrolled to take courses in reading and English. Commercial classes were also offered. 5 local teachers volunteered their services to teach these classes and had the blessing of the school superintendent.

During the early 1930s, a new post office was built. The old post office was on Grant Avenue near the corner of Sumner Avenue. We are still using the "new" building that was built.

The new bridge in Vandergrift opened in 1932. To celebrate this opening, an ox roast was held. The ox was donated by a citizen of the town, and a group of volunteers minded the fires and spit, keeping careful watch over the feast.

Courtesy of Buttermilk Falls Publishing Company

Old Vandergrift Post Office on Grant Avenue

It was also in the early 1930s that the Homestead Grays, an African-American team, came to play baseball in our town on a semiregular schedule. The games drew a nice-sized crowd as well as the support of the town's authorities.

1932 was the start of the annual air show at the Vandergrift air field. It was also the year that a new community water supply system was installed. A new railroad span was opened over the Kiski River in July of the same year.

The Boy Scouts had made such an impact in our community that a similar group for the young women of the town was considered at this time.

A major road work project was closer to becoming a reality in 1933. A shorter route to Vandergrift from Kittanning was in the planning stages. This would introduce more traffic through the town.

Regrettably there was also the unsavory lot of the criminal element. Even in the midst of the town's spirit of pride and care, some people refused to rise to the occasion and instead opted for the quick buck by illegal gain. Fortunately most criminal activities were limited, but one criminal element did arrive, which took hold for a season: illegal gambling and slot machines. Some believe that the Depression afforded just the right climate for this vice to flourish in our area.

Courtesy of Buttermilk Falls Publishing Company and Joe Milanak

No Longer There

The above picture was taken sometime during the 1930s and it shows a ballpark you'll never be able to find. The park was in East Vandergrift where a lot of good sandlot players performed. The reason you'll have trouble finding it is that it was owned by the foundry and the park is 100 or more feet underground today.

Below is the old foot bridge across the Kiski River which served as the river crossing between Vandergrift and North Vandergrift while the new Vandergrift bridge was being constructed in 1932.

Courtesy of Buttermilk Falls Publishing Company and L. E. Swenk

their pride, and no job was too small.

The times called for unique measures in just about every walk of life. Although the direct effects of the Depression had been delayed, when hard times hit, they were sorely felt. After riding a high for so long (and even though the low was not as low as many of the larger cities experienced), it was still a big adjustment for the citizens of such a proud and successful town.

In the midst of these tough times, the people pooled their resources to help those who were not as fortunate. They supported charity basketball games, movies, plays, dances, clothing and even food drives. The small grocery stores permitted people to "run a tab" until things got better. They let families make whatever payments they could, be it weekly or monthly. Some families went back to the old system of barter and trade. But whatever means were used, the town folk helped each other in the true traditions of its founding father.

Those unemployed were given permission to dig or mine their own coal. This was to be used strictly for personal use. A few diggers had to be relocated because they were mining too close to the mill and putting other workers at risk. This seemed to be the only negative situation that arose from the free coal digging.

Those who had money were encouraged to spend, not horde their resources, so that others might be able to work. If you could afford a few extras, you would be helping your neighbor and your friends by making those purchases. It would take money to "jump-start" the success that Vandergrift merchants had known and had come to enjoy.

In 1932, ads appeared in the town paper for the spending of "Prosperity Vouchers." These were not to pay on old accounts. They were issued to purchase new merchandise. However, there were some who could not afford these vouchers; some people could not even afford much-needed medical attention.

In some homes, new recipes began surfacing, things such as "depression pot pie." Many men of Vandergrift took up hunting and fishing to supplement the meat for the table. Most often, soup was the main course, and the broth was based on bones that may have been used at least once before. Once this stock was cooked, the women devised many ways to vary this meal. Sometimes small squares of breadlike dough were dropped on the boiling broth and cooked until tender. If you were fortunate enough, a piece of pork or venison would be added for more flavor.

Recipe For Survival

Another popular, inexpensive meal of the time, still found today in many homes, was Pasta Fajoule. To make this "exotic" dish of beans and pasta:

Soak Great Northern beans, or whatever beans are available, overnight in water. The next morning, after draining and rinsing, bring to a boil and cook to desired firmness. Prepare in a separate pot any small pasta, such as thin spaghetti or ditalini. When both beans and macaroni are done, combine into one pot. For added flavor, fry a few pieces of onion in a pan, add a couple of tablespoons of tomato paste, and season with salt and pepper. Simmer for a 10-15 minutes. Combine with beans and macaroni, and simmer together. Top with grated parmesan cheese.

Not only were the mealtime habits altered, but the way people spent their recreational time was also changed. In the winter, family sledriding outings were encouraged. Several of the downtown and Heights streets were blocked off and monitored by the local patrolman. The children loved these winter evening activities, but adults had to be coaxed into venturing out in the cold with their children. Families spent more time inventing games to play outdoors and in the family's livingroom. Many card clubs and sewing clubs were organized; few of these clubs are still in existence today.

The various circuses that visited the town provided entertainment to many. Even if a family could not afford the price of admission, they always had the free circus parades. Crowds of old and young alike assembled as early as six o'clock in the morning to watch the Sparks Circus arrive at the Pennsylvania Railroad yard in town.

One interesting event that drew a large crowd and provided free entertainment was a flag pole climbing feat. A man climbed the distance of 100 feet—all in a day's work. His job was to replace a broken chain on the flag pole at the Municipal Building on Washington Avenue. Scores of people gathered to watch the 50-minute climb to the top and stayed to watch the repair job and descent, which took another 30 minutes.

When things did improve and work was good again, people who had extended that little extra for others were repaid. A man's word was valued, and few men would fall back on promises to repay debts. Most of the small storekeepers recall being left with only small amounts of bills unpaid during all their years of operation. This truly speaks well of the integrity of the citizens of Vandergrift.

No record of this era would be complete without note of the depression camps. To save money, some of the people left the city to come and stay in what would become known as their 'summer homes.' There were many "Depression Camps" showing up along the small streams in the Kiski Valley, as well as in other nearby wooded areas. In these camps, primitive environments existed. There were no electric lights, no movies, no ice cream, or

The Vandergrift Grays

The Vandergrift Grays, that were an amateur baseball team, consisted of a group of talented men from Vandergrift and North Vandergrift. Some of the members went on to play professional baseball in the Negro Leagues. Joe Preston, Sr., was one of these men. He played for the Pittsburgh Crawfords from 1932 to 1936.

In the 1920s, the Vandergrift Grays baseball team (an African American team) was the runner-up in the state championships and placed 3 players on the state all-star team (C. Johnson, C. Chestine, and J. Moore). They were judged the best sportsmen in the tournament and were awarded a trophy.

From the 1930s to the 1940s the Vandergrift Grays played such clubs as the City Club of New Kensington, the Leechburg Giants, and the Apollo Athletics. These games were played at home and away. The team traveled by bus, car and trolleys to get to the neighboring towns. The championship games were played at Yatesboro, PA.

W. T. Hutchenson and William Gray were two of the local businessmen who sponsored the Grays.

Courtesy of Buttermilk Falls Publishing Company

Drifter's Home during the Depression Years; Located Where Vandergrift Golf Course is Today

other things we might consider necessities; however, there was freedom and plenty of fresh air. Here the honor code system was in effect 24 hours a day with little infraction. Most of these camps were modestly furnished with only the bare essentials. There were a few exceptions; several of these dwellings were rather well kept and stocked with some of the comforts from better times. Regardless of the conditions of the dwellings, all of the residents seemed to share in the swimming holes and in gathering around the campfires to sing a few songs each night.

The Flood of '36

It was 1936. The economy had not improved. Work was still scarce in the mill. Trouble always seems to come in bundles. The winter of 1936 had dumped heavy snow across the region. In March the snow melted, but it melted too fast. Then the rain came; it came down in buckets. The hillsides and sloping valleys, unable to absorb the torrent, sent the water into the brooks, runs, and creeks, which in turn overflowed their gorged banks to the Kiskiminetas river. The resulting flood delivered the Kiski Valley and Vandergrift its most devastating disaster in its history. The *Vandergrift News* carried headlines that read:

THOUSANDS FLEEING FLOOD FIND REFUGE HERE

TWO DIE

KISKI FLOOD RECEDES

VANDERGRIFT RALLIES TO AID OF STRICKEN FAMILIES

FOOD, SHELTER STEM INTENSE SUFFERING

RIVER SWEEPS MAN TO DEATH AS TORRENT SPREADS HAVOC

HOMES, SPANS WASHED AWAY

To understand the tremendous force of the Kiski River on March 17-18, 1936, one must remember that the Conemaugh River, joined by the Loyalhanna Creek at Saltsburg to form the Kiskiminetas, flows downhill all the way from its source above

Courtesy of CoraBelle Walter

East Vandergrift from the Air

Courtesy of Buttermilk Falls Publishing Company

East Vandergrift

Johnstown. When high, the Kiski is one of the swiftest rivers in the country. On this St. Patrick's Day, the river showed no mercy to whatever was in its path. Houses, bridges, cars, and people all floated down the river to the new Vandergrift bridge that remained standing.

Upriver the Apollo bridge was swept off its piers at 4:25 a.m. March 18th; another stronger railroad bridge lasted until 7:00 a.m. The Avonmore bridge further upstream had gone earlier in the morning. (The Hyde Park footbridge was also destroyed.)

On the 50th anniversary of the '36 flood, John Gibson, a staff writer for the *Valley News Dispatch*, recalled a story about a dramatic rescue:

The view from Vandergrift Bridge was a heartbreaking one. The surging Kiskiminetas River lifted houses from their foundations and in the North Vandergrift district, smashed them under the bridge.

Most residents, noting the river's rapid rise, abandoned their homes, but not Andrew Earley.

W. W. 'Snake' Heddinger, a veteran Vandergrift fireman, takes up the story:

"The firemen had tried twice to get him to

Courtesy of CoraBelle Walter

North Vandergrift

Courtesy of Valley News Dispatch and F. Lloyd Earhart

leave his place," Heddinger recalls. "We could see him (Earley) looking out the attic window as the house got closer to the bridge. Then, suddenly, he was gone and before you knew it the house smashed into the bridge."

To this day, says Heddinger, he doesn't know—except that it might have been a miracle—how Earley managed to escape.

"We all rushed to the other side (the downriver side) of the bridge when his (Earley's) house went under the bridge and all we could see was what looked like tinderwood. That's all that was left of that house," says Heddinger.

"Then we heard him shouting 'I'm here!' Somehow, he must have got out of the back of the attic as the house was crushed under the bridge and he managed to grab hold of a telephone cable that was strung under the bridge. He got one arm and one leg over it."

Heddinger had the foresight to have a long rope strung out on the span "in case we needed it." The firefighter rescuers needed it.

"We looped the rope so we could put it over the bridge and swing it toward Andy," Heddinger recalls. "But I couldn't see him because he was under the bridge and I didn't want to get the rope in the water because it would get wet and make it too heavy

Courtesy of Valley News Dispatch and F. Lloyd Earhart

The Flood from the Vandergrift Bridge

Courtesy of Valley News Dispatch and F. Lloyd Earhart

The Rescue: Earley Holding on to Lifeline

to swing.

Paul Means, one of the firefighters, sprang to the rescue." 'I'll go over and direct you!' " he shouted to Heddinger and he quickly leaned from the bridge railing and shouted both words of assurance to Earley and directions to Heddinger.

"We shouted 'Andy, put your arm through the loop and make a twist in the rope and we'll haul you up,'" says Heddinger. "We tried several times and finally Paul shouted, 'He's got it! He's got it. Hang on, Andy. Pull him up, quick.'"

Earley released his hold on the telephone cable and, suspended by the rope, swing out over the river's rushing torrent.

For an agonizing second, the rescuers shared the same horrible thought: Please dear Lord, don't let

Frank Gourley, Trolley Driver

Courtesy of Harold Doutt

Street Car on Warren St. in neighboring Apollo

Frank Gourley was employed by West Penn Trolley Company in 1918 and later drove buses for the Kiski Valley for 17 years. Gourley's career with the trolley line prematurely ended with the great Saint Patrick's Day Flood of 1936.

Gourley ran the trolley from Leechburg to Apollo, making 8 roundtrips per day. He sometimes slept in the car barn in Leechburg until the first car would leave in the morning, around 5:20 a.m. taking him to his home in Apollo. On that infamous day in March when the flood of '36 hit, Mr. Gourley was running about 20 minutes late for his stop in Apollo. It was to be the last run for the day; it was also to be the last run of the trolley in the valley.

Running behind schedule as a result of the rising waters, he pressed on toward North Apollo. The water from the nearby river began to actually enter the trolley's door. His only thought and goal was that he needed to make it to North Apollo, so he could park the trolley on the highest point on the run. When he arrived in North Apollo, he picked a spot on the track near what is Eleventh Street today. It was just a few streets over from his home on Sixteenth Street.

The flood damage was devastating to all the communities along the river's path, but it ended this only form of transportation in the valley. The last of the trolley's tracks were finally removed in 1962.

Courtesy of CoraBelle Walters

Flood Waters Overtake the Foundry

the rope break.

"Before we knew it." says Heddinger, "Andy's head appeared by the bridge rail and we hauled him over the railing. I remember, he grabbed me and kissed me and said, 'Snake, you, old devil!'"

F. Lloyd Earhart was beginning his career as a photographer, and he had his camera trained on the flood to record history. He shot 80 pictures that day, and one of them was Earley being rescued.

The Red Cross coordinated the relief work in Vandergrift. The homeless were housed in homes, churches, schools, firehalls, and any other available place. Food for the flood victims was provided by individual families, the American Legion, and the Salvation Army. J. A. Grimm, Burgess of Vandergrift, placed the city's credit at the disposal of the relief workers. Truckload after truckload of food and

Courtesy of Valley News Dispatch and F. Lloyd Earhart

Flood Aftermath in North Vandergrift

clothing came rolling into Vandergrift from other communities.

A hospital was set up in Boyd M. Swank's vacant building, at 171 Washington Avenue. The hospital was under the direction of J. Lace, M.D. During the time from March 18 to April 14, 63 persons were hospitalized and 315 outpatients were treated and given medicine.

In the 1976 newspaper article (the *News-Citizen,* March 17, 1976), Mrs. Mary C. Kershner wrote:

> *Those who took flood refugees into their homes and those who were their guests became friends. If you read that the child or grandchild of someone who stayed in your home has graduated from college, attained some honor in his or her job, or in community service, you share in the pride of the family who had lost everything but had fought their way back. It seems somehow an American phenomenon.*

The flood had strained the very fabric of a town already under the gun of a devastating economic depression but again McMurtry's "best" came forth and survived. Now as life began to resettle in the valley, another challenge loomed over the far horizons. World War II was about to begin.

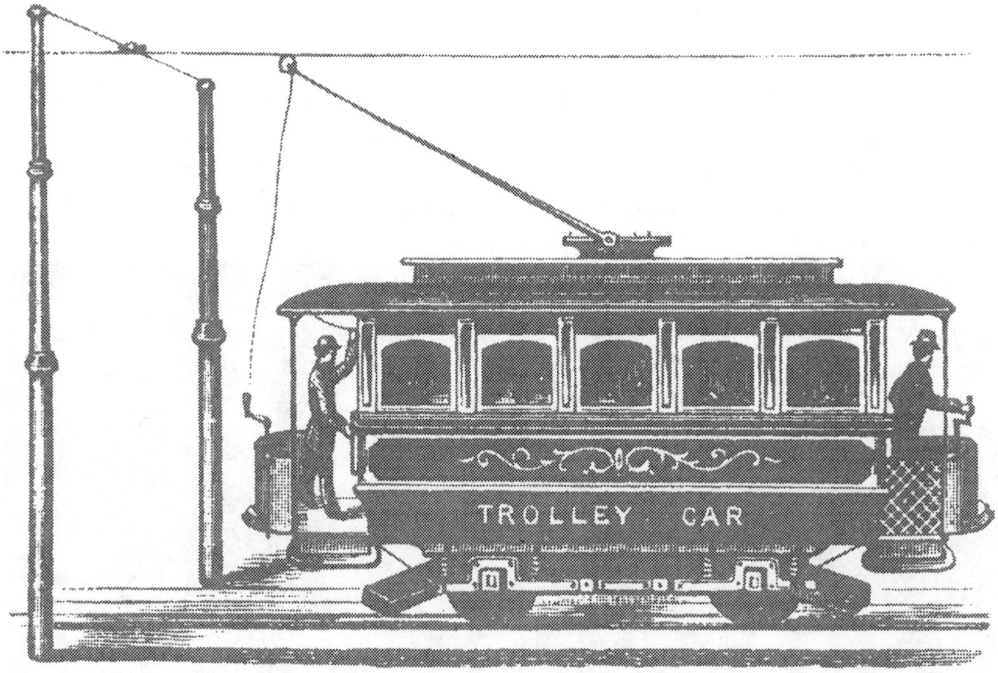

Reflections Of The Times

Stories of the Day

John Albert 'Joker' Grimm

According to his son, John Albert Grimm was always a tremendously likeable man who didn't take life too seriously and who was loved by everyone, which to a degree explained his nickname, "Joker." His popularity also helps to explain why he was elected burgess (similar to a mayor) in 1932 and served 2 terms until 1940. When he died 8 years later, his funeral was one of the largest seen in Vandergrift up to that time.

In 1932, at the height of the Depression, the whole country's political mood changed and people began voting Democrat. Vandergrift, long a Republican stronghold, was no exception, and so Democratic candidate John Grimm was elected burgess.

He gained an excellent reputation in the years he served as burgess. John often bought groceries for those who were suffering during the Depression. His wife, Margaret, would try to keep the family's bill down at the market, but every time she'd go there, she would find a big bill, courtesy of John's charitable efforts.

As an influx of hobos from the railroad came to eat at the Grimm household everyday, John often laughingly said someone must have put an "X" on their house. But in reality, he knew the plight of the men from the railroad flatcars and hobo jungles near the North Vandergrift bridge. Grimm, as many families in Vandergrift did at the time, took it upon himself to help however he could.

John Albert Grimm was born around 1882, and 20 years later he married Margaret, a woman born on the same day, of the same month, of the same year. He came with his dad to Vandergrift in 1895 from Bell Township. His dad owned Grimm's Harness Shop and Hardware Store in Apollo, the biggest of its kind in that town. When his father came to Vandergrift, he bought land in the business district and later built several buildings there and then sold them. One of his buildings, for which he retained ownership, was his bank, of which he was president. The bank, Vandergrift Savings and Trust, failed sometime after the Crash of 1929; but Grimm's father did not live to see its collapse. He died sometime before 1922.

Grimm was always civic-minded; served as chief of police for about 10 years and then later ran for county sheriff in 1942. In between his civil service opportunities, he worked at American Sheet and Tin Plating as a foreman in the open hearth. At age 20, he also became an auctioneer.

Several events marked Grimm's time in office as burgess. He organized the first ox roast at the opening of the new bridge to North Vandergrift. The event was so successful, it was held every year afterwards for more than a decade, and was later revived in the 1960s. During his administration, Vandergrift built the borough building, complete with indoor horseshoe pits. John saw several federal projects accomplished in Vandergrift, including the building of a stone wall around the old high school. In 1932, he was also responsible for the first curfew in Vandergrift; at 8:45 p.m. the whistle blew, and everyone under 18 had to be inside. Something else was also initiated during his administration, against his wishes—parking meters on the streets.

Most people remember John Albert Grimm fondly. With the Depression affecting most everyone, and with little to smile about, it was a blessing to have John "Joker" Grimm in charge.

Health Care Through the Years in Vandergrift

"Mommy, what does quarantine mean?"

"Hush, child, it means you can't go in there!"

Today we don't think about quarantine, but at one time it was the rule for contagious diseases. If you were fortunate enough to have been born with a strong constitution, and the home remedies worked, then you made it through the disease. Now antibiotics have eliminated the need for quarantine except in a few rare instances. But remember, although Alexander Fleming discovered penicillin in 1928, it wasn't until 1940 that Howard W. Florey and Ernest Chain reported on how it could be purified for use.

Quarantine is the absolute prohibition of exit or entrance from or to any apartment or building, except by those authorized by the Health Authorities and to whom permits have been issued. Violation of quarantine would be followed by prosecution. So stated the Board of Health as reported in the *Vandergrift News* on May 20, 1912.

April 25, 1912, brought a visit from the county health officer in Greensburg to examine area residents who had smallpox. The health officer had been here one week earlier and diagnosed a man, who thought he had chickenpox, as having smallpox in a mild form. The man and everyone with whom he had come in contact, were quarantined immediately for 18 days or had to be vaccinated. 2 men who had been exposed to the disease but who left town before they could be notified, were sought out by the State Troopers and when found, placed in quarantine. At 4 homes, guards maintained a vigil to assure an absolute quarantine. Council appropriated $30 to the Board of Health for fumigating public places once a week to halt the spread of this disease.

On May 9, 1912, the Vandergrift Board of Health issued an edict that any person who violated the quarantine restrictions for anyone suffering from anthrax, bubonic plague, cerebrospinal meningitis, chickenpox, Asiatic cholera, diphtheria, German measles, measles, mumps, relapsing fever, scarlet fever, smallpox, typhus fever, yellow fever, or whooping cough, upon conviction for each offense, shall, "for every such offense, ... be sentenced to pay a fine of not less than fifty dollars, or more than one hundred dollars .... or be imprisoned in the county jail for a period of not less than ten or more than thirty days, or both at the discretion of the court." This was no small sum of money during those years.

On May 20, 1915, the Board of Health of Vandergrift issued a warning that it might be necessary to close the schools or at least some of the rooms because of an epidemic of scarlet fever, diphtheria, and measles in the borough. At the time of the announcement, there were 13 cases of scarlet fever, 4 cases of diphtheria, and 40 cases of measles in Vandergrift. The citizens were asked to observe the quarantine and promptly report all cases known to exist. All persons were subject to a penalty of the law for knowingly exposing themselves to communicable disease. With no antibiotics to lighten the course of the diseases, one has to wonder just how so many survived at all.

On August 10, 1915, a 10 month old male died of Cholera infantum.

On October 18, 1928, a Diphtheria outbreak caused the closing of the North Vandergrift schools until at least October 29, 1928, while the schools were being disinfected.

In 1928, an influenza outbreak caused the Apollo Board of Health to close the churches, schools, and all public places of amusement; while Vandergrift remained undecided as to what to do.

On January 4, 1929, 2 local residents died from the influenza outbreak. By January 7, 1929, there were 34 new cases of flu in Vandergrift bringing the total to 1,000.

In 1935, a measles epidemic made 1935 an unhealthy year for Vandergrift residents. The disease averaged 6 cases a day for 2 months, for a total of 382 cases. 1 case of malaria, 1 case of whooping cough, and 1 case of diphtheria, and 3 cases of erysipelas were also reported. Sulfa drugs, although discovered accidently by Paul Gelmo in 1908, were first reported to kill bacteria by Gerhard Domagk in 1935.

The Starving Artist who Painted for his Meals

The mural over the Postmaster's Office in Vandergrift was painted by artist, Fred Hogg. It was commissioned by the U. S. Treasury Department as part of President Franklin Roosevelt's New Deal Art Projects in the 1930s and 1940s. The program was designed to restore confidence in getting people back to work and to restore the economy from the effects of the Depression. In the words of President Roosevelt, the art was painted for the people of this country by their own kind, in their own country—a sort of saying, "Act locally, think nationally."

Mr. Hogg was chosen from local competitions; he was paid $20 per square foot and had 2 years to complete it.

The program provided murals and sculptures for newly constructed federal buildings. The Vandergrift Post Office, built in 1936, qualified for the program. The murals were expected to represent local historical themes, industry or landscapes. In fact, more than 90% of Pennsylvania's Post Offices, courthouses, train stations, and public libraries, as well as various legislature offices, had murals in them.

The artist had to consult with the postmaster and other townspeople to ensure that the subject would be meaningful. At that time, the railway mail service was at its height, with about 10,000 trains moving mail into every small town across the U. S. Mr. Hogg therefore portrayed employees working at the Vandergrift train station, hauling and sorting the mail in the interior of a railroad postal car.

What was Happening in the Churches?

Successful efforts by the Slovaks to form their own church encouraged other groups to do the same. St. Gertrude's church members of Lithuanian speech formed St. Casimir's Church in l922, and the Polish Church, All Saint's, officially began with the first mass in 1924. Both congregations were in East Vandergrift.

A Salvation Army Corp was also formed in Vandergrift in 1924, and in 1932 they bought and renovated a building on Columbia Avenue for their headquarters.

There were endings as well as beginnings. Sometime in 1926, the All Saints' Episcopal Church on Sherman Avenue stopped having services. A series of mergers starting in 1925 among several Methodist congregations resulted in the "Episcopal" title being dropped from the name, and the local group was simply the First Methodist Church for many years.

The Depression affected Vandergrift's churches as incomes dropped and the economy soured. New projects were tabled, and only the most urgent repairs were made to the aging buildings. St. Gertrude's had to close its parochial school in 1932, not to reopen for almost 15 years.

It seems, however, that the mutual distress of the day caused the area ministers to come together in a gesture of unity. As the Vandergrift Ministerial Association was formed in 1932 by the new pastor of the First Church of God, Rev. J. T. Lackey. He led the organization as its first president.

1936 brought double trouble for St. Casimir's congregation. The church burned in January, and the St. Patricks Day flood carried away what was left. In spite of their personal losses to the flood, the parish rebuilt the church late in 1936.

Most of the residents of East Vandergrift and North Vandergrift also lost their homes and businesses to the flood. Many Vandergrift church people took two or three homeless families into their own homes until the floods' damage could be cleaned up and new houses built. It was a time of demonstrating "love your neighbor."

In spite of economic problems, the churches went on as they had begun—preaching and teaching the gospel of Jesus Christ, baptizing and marrying folks, and burying their dead. They continued to send their young and sometimes, not-so-young, men and women into various ministries here and elsewhere.

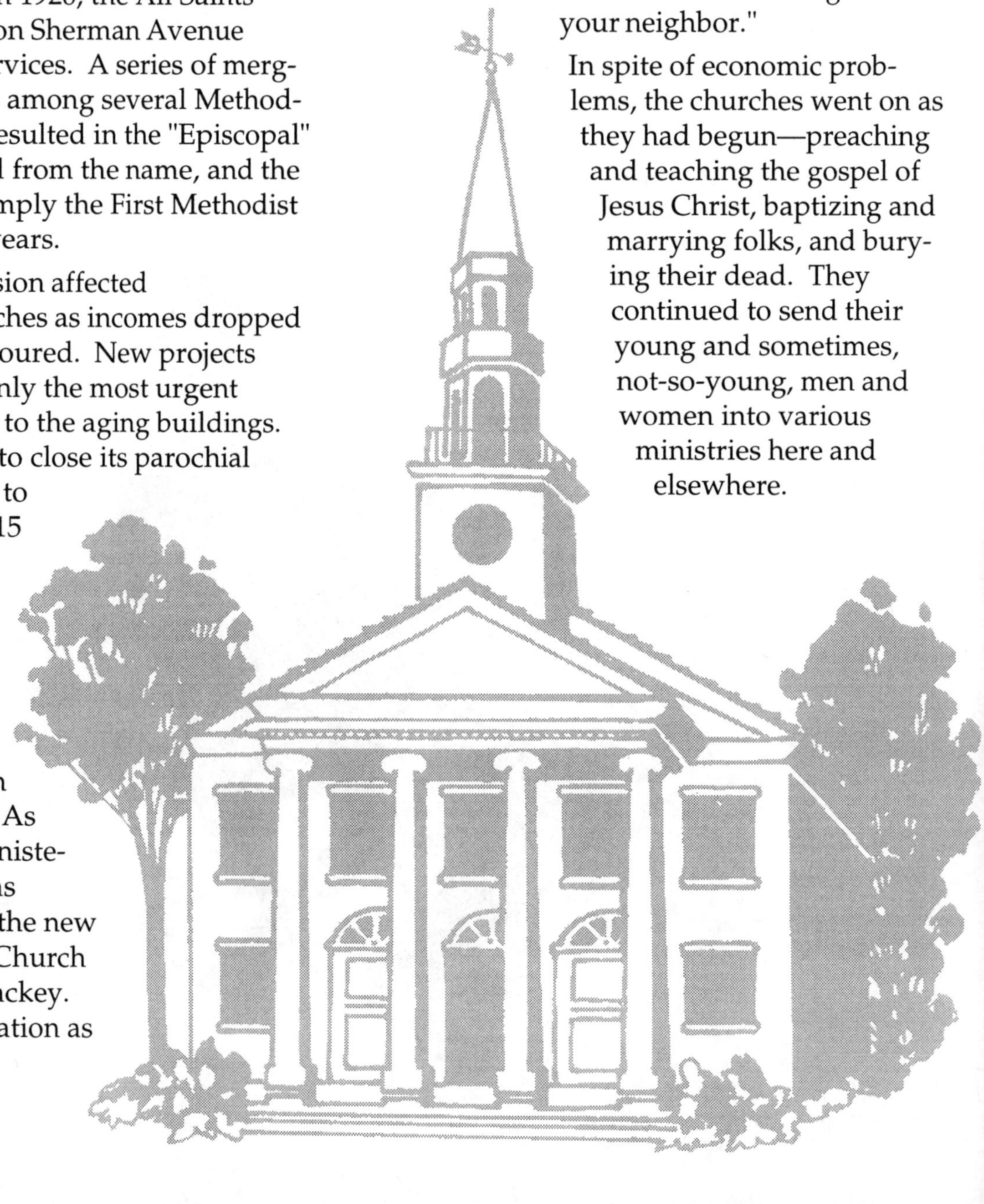

Willing hands did good works, feeding the hungry, clothing the naked, visiting the sick. Rummage sales, church dinners, concerts, the sale of all sorts of merchandise and foodstuffs from knives to strawberries, and simply reaching deep into wallets and purses funded countless projects. Counsel, encouragement, and Godly love lifted burdens and heavy hearts as church families helped one another and other people in those trying times.

The World War II years spurred new dedication to Godly matters as members were drawn to prayer for loved ones in the armed services. Ladies Circles and Societies made bandages or knitted socks for the boys and girls away from home. Childrens' classes made small gifts to be sent to hospitals for the wounded Veterans. At the conclusion of the War, every church bell in town rang out the joyful news of peace.

During the early years of Vandergrift, a person's church was often the center of social life. Sunday worship service, Sunday church school, catechism classes, children's and youth groups, men's and ladies' groups, missionary societies, and athletic-based groups such as bowling and softball teams gave people a sense of belonging and accomplishment that they needed. For a time there were also inter-church softball and bowling leagues where folks met for fun and fellowship.

Some groups also had denominational summer church camping sites for children such as Lutherlyn, and some had annual family camp meetings, notably the Methodist and Free Methodist churches of the area.

Individuals wishing to serve their churches had plenty of options. Elder, deacon, steward, trustee, teacher, usher, secretary, treasurer, sexton, choir member, choirmaster, organist, pianist, bell choir director, circle leader, cooks, committee chairpeople and members—the list went on and on. It took many hands to make the churches work.

In the years between the world wars and afterward, the zeal of the people was periodically renewed by traveling speakers and evangelists such as Mrs. Mary H. Armour, who taught at the Methodist Church in 1931. Her radio broadcasts and books made Billy Sunday a favorite of many.

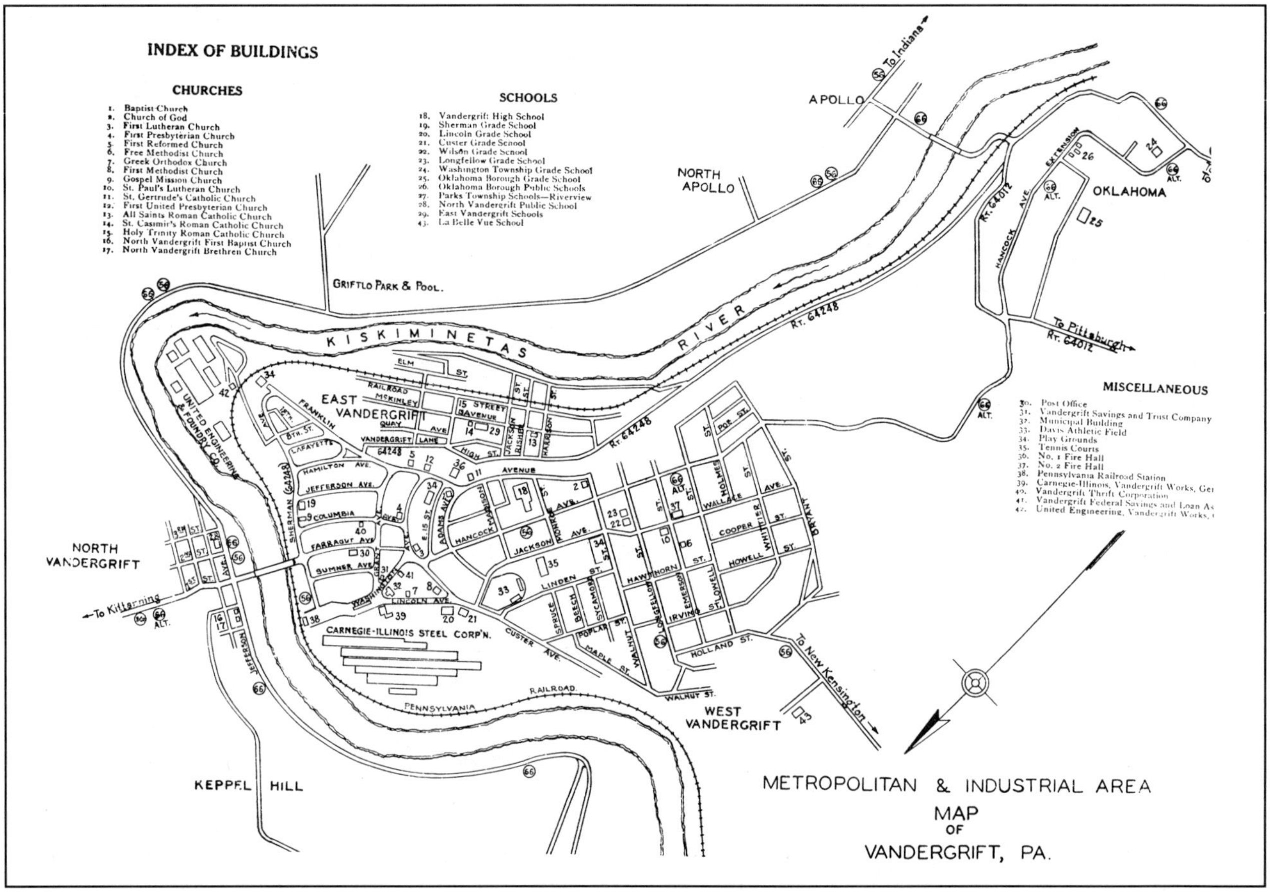

Courtesy of Welsh Printing

Vandergrift, Circa 1940

Chapter Ten

The World War Two Era

It was Sunday, December 7, 1941. The sun was just rising in the eastern sky when 350 Japanese dive-bombers, torpedo bombers, and pursuit planes left their aircraft carriers in the Pacific and headed for the American naval base at Pearl Harbor. The American Pacific Fleet was almost destroyed that morning as bombs fell everywhere. In all, 19 warships were sunk or damaged, and some 265 planes destroyed, most of them while they were still on the ground. More than 3,500 Americans were killed or wounded that morning. Pearl Harbor became the worst naval disaster in American history.

A Vandergrift native, Francis "Chich" Silvestri, was stationed at Hickam Airfield, located several miles west of Honolulu at the mouth of Pearl Harbor when the attack occurred. Here is his story, related to news reporter Judy Laurinatis, on December 4, 1991, as it appeared in the local paper,

> *Silvestri was having breakfast that morning with Stanley Romano, a Leechburg native. He remembers that the fleet was in.*
>
> *"Downtown Honolulu was a sea of white," Silvestri said, referring to naval dress whites on the men who arrived.*
>
> *At a few moments to 8, the attack hit and the men were ordered to their gunnery posts.*
>
> *Silvestri noted that technically it was peacetime so therefore they were not prepared to fight.*
>
> *They were at the gun posts, Silvestri stationed outdoors at the end of a runway—**with no ammunition.***

Back home all ears were tuned to the radio to hear news about the bombing and to find out what President Franklin Roosevelt and the Congress would do. On December 8, F. D. R. went before Congress and spoke these words that have been recorded in history:

> *Yesterday, December 7, 1941—a day which will live in infamy—the United States of America was suddenly and deliberately attacked by naval and air forces of the Empire of Japan...*

After his speech, it took the Congress only 33 minutes to declare that a state of war existed between the United States and Japan. That same day in England, both

houses of Parliament voted unanimously to declare war on Japan. 3 days later, Germany and Italy declared war on the United States, and World War II had begun in earnest. In less than a week, the United States had gone from an isolationist attitude to involvement in the world's affairs.

War Time Work

In a blink of an eye, with the explosion of the first bombs of Pearl Harbor, the Great Depression was gone. The nation mobilized for war. The factories and shipyards were swiftly geared to produce planes, tanks, ships, and weapons.

In a short time, the United States had the biggest military force in its history. At peak strength, more than 15 million men and women were serving in the armed forces. Unemployment vanished. Because of the manpower shortage, women joined the work force in large numbers. "Rosie the Riveter" became a symbol of the war effort across the nation.

The Vandergrift mills had their own version of "Rosie the Riveter." Judy Laurinatis gives us an account of one of those patriotic women:

As the men went off to fight in W. W. II, many women were called, too—to work in the metals industries in the Kiski Valley.

Anna (Logero) Vota was an electrical lab technician for U. S. Steel in Vandergrift from about 1943 to 1945, and it was her job to test the strength of steel being manufactured.

She and her helper, Esther Ceraso, worked the 8 a.m. to 4 p.m. or 4 p.m. to midnight shifts, joining the many "women all through the mill" who did all of the jobs the steelworkers-turned-soldiers once did. She said they were paid the same wages.

With her husband, John, serving in the Army overseas, Mrs. Vota was working at Schenley Distilleries in Gilpin Township when the call came.

"The mill called me and asked if I would work there. They were making the materials needed to make planes," she said.

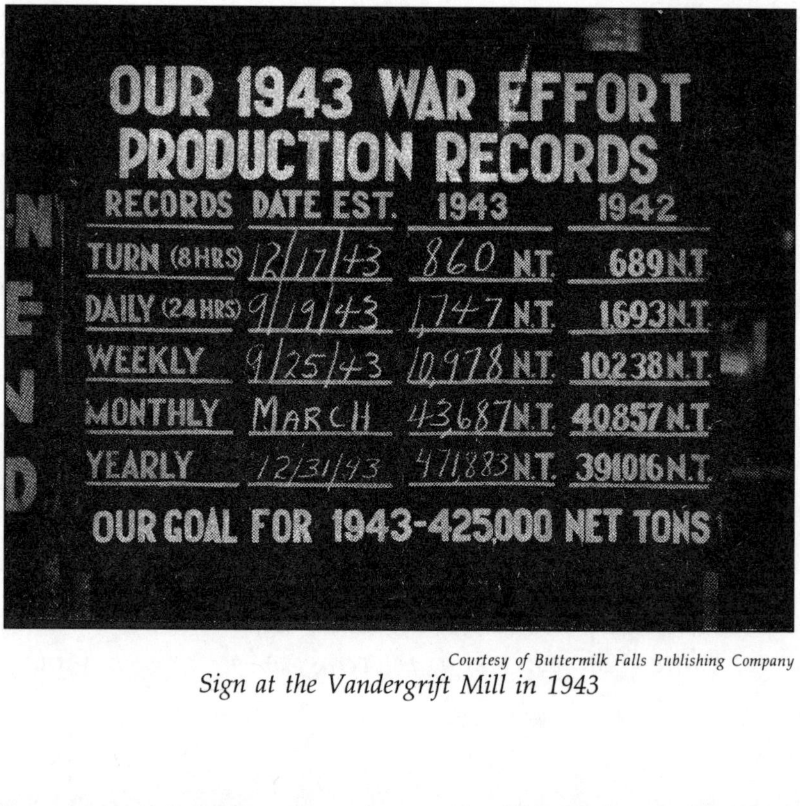

Courtesy of Buttermilk Falls Publishing Company

Sign at the Vandergrift Mill in 1943

"I asked Schenley if I could have my job back [after the war] if I went to work at the Mill, but they said 'No.' But I went anyway. I told them my husband is in the Service."

Mrs. Vota, a Vandergrift native, said that many of the women who worked at the mills had husbands who were serving in the armed forces and believed they were offered the jobs because of that fact.

As the men were discharged, the women were furloughed to make room for the returning veterans.

Mrs. Vota never joined the workforce again but said she didn't mind leaving the mill. "I was glad I had my husband back," she said.

Mrs. Vota is a perfect example of how the lifestyle in Vandergrift changed as it did in every town in the country. All able-bodied young men between the ages of 18 and 30 were enlisted in the armed services. The high school graduating classes were missing many boys. They had turned 18 and were off to war. Their diplomas were sent to their homes. The wives, mothers, and older fathers were left at home to work and pray for the safety of their loved ones.

The mill went into full swing. It was considered a patriotic duty to put out more steel production. The mill was working 24 hours a day with 3 full, 8-hour, work turns each day. By the end of 1942, the workers had put out 391,016 net tons of steel. This was not enough, more had to be done. By

Courtesy of Harold Doutt

Number 7 Hot Mill Crew, 1943

the end of 1943, the net tons were up to 471,883. Steel was being produced for victory. This was more than a job; it was the preservation of a way of life that all had learned to appreciate and love.

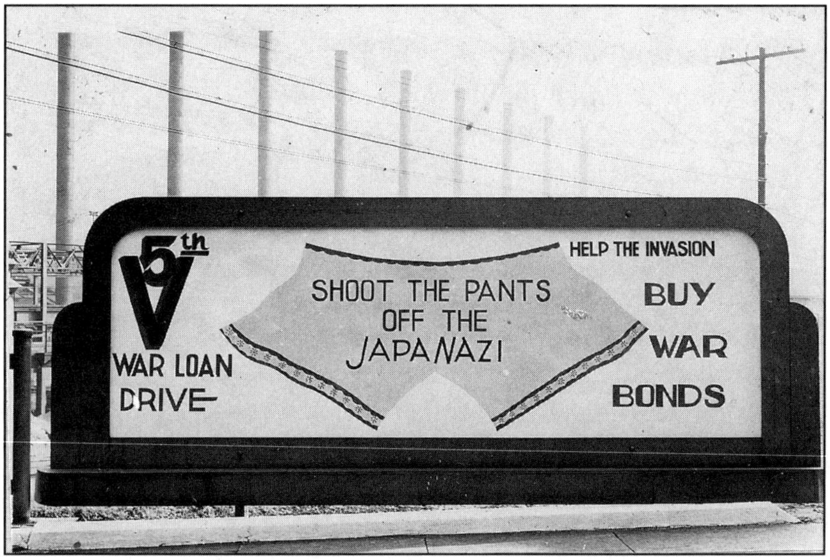

Courtesy of Ron Ankeny and Allegheny Ludlum

Sign in front of Mill Encouraged People to Buy War Bonds

A large sign was placed outside the mill to help remind the workers and the citizens what had to be done. The sign was changed regularly. Sometimes it was funny, but most of the time it was very serious. One of the signs in 1944 was a prayer:

> *Dear Lord, lest I continue my complacent way, help me to remember somewhere out there a man died for me today. As long as there be war, I then must ask an answer, am I worth dying for?*

The messages on the signs reminded the people to plant victory gardens, buy war bonds, have a good attendance record on the war job, donate blood for plasma, write regularly to the folks in the armed forces, and to have faith in the future.

President Roosevelt was also reminding us to have faith in the future. He was regularly on the radio with his "fireside chats." These were talks of optimistic determination and reporting of the war news. Once he declared,

> *No matter what our enemies in their desperation may attempt to do to us—we will say with the people of London, 'We can take it,' and what is more, we can give it back—with compound interest.*

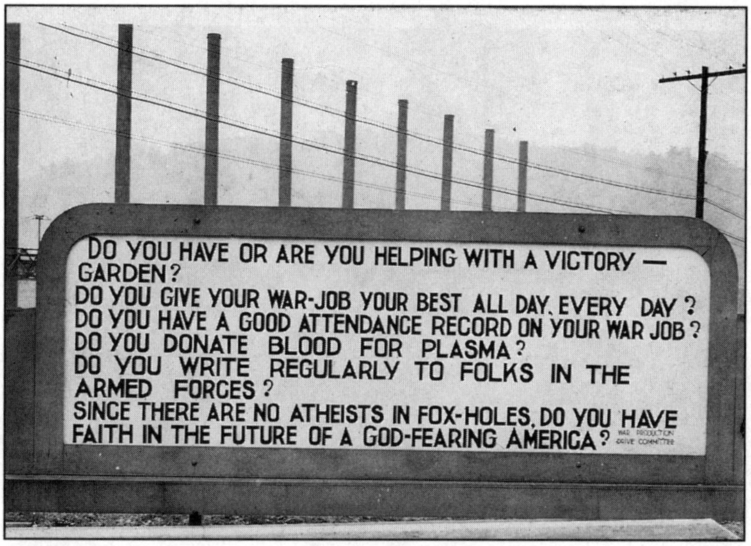

Courtesy of Ron Ankeny and Allegheny Ludlum

Sign in front of the Vandergrift Mill

Prepared for Attack

Because of the mill, Vandergrift was a prime target for enemy attack. The town organized a civil defense unit, with men as air raid wardens, older teenage boys as messengers, and young boys (Boy Scouts) to deliver war posters. The town had air raid drills and blackouts. Aircraft spotters were located on the roof of the high school (now the Vandergrift Elementary Building). When the sirens signaled an air raid drill, not even one speck of light could be seen in town, and no one was moving except the air raid wardens with their white helmets and armbands, walking the streets looking for any sign of light.

Vandergrift Museum Director Beth Caporali relates to us the spirit of

the times in her article about the aircraft spotters:

VANDERGRIFT, 1942. The Second World War is on, Vandergrift, home of a large steel mill, is considered a prime target for enemy bombers. An early warning system is needed. The solution—volunteers.

During the war, many women and teenagers serve as spotters for enemy aircraft. They attend classes to learn to identify the various types of planes, and what to do in the event of an actual sighting. As many of the spotters also serve as civil defense patrol members, they also learn the rules regarding blackouts and other safety matters.

The main spotting station in Vandergrift is the roof of the Vandergrift Elementary School (then the Vandergrift High School). Eager volunteers scan the skies with binoculars, doing their part for the war effort.

Boys form clubs dedicated to identifying the planes as well and follow along with their elders in learning the silhouettes and markings of the planes. The boys also spend many hours practicing shooting down the planes and capturing the enemy soldiers, in preparation for their turn at war.

The spotters are issued blue armbands with a gold and white patch identifying them as official Civil Defense personnel. They do not know it, but many of these armbands will still remain as family heirlooms half a century later.

All the schools had their part in the war effort too. There were air raid drills and classes on how to extinguish incendiary bombs should one hit a school or home. Schools sold "war stamps." They were 10 cents apiece. The stamps were put in a stamp book, and when the book was filled, it was exchanged for a War Bond. It was a big deal when you had enough money to get the bond. You were recognized in class and also got a letter from the Secretary of the Treasury.

There was a great emphasis on first aid. Adult classes were held in various places, and then there were small group meetings in homes all over town to practice what had been learned. The Boy Scouts and the Girl Scouts also emphasized first aid badges.

Rifle clubs became very popular during the war with girls and boys. There was an indoor range on Longfellow Street in the 100 block (it has since been torn down).

Collecting and Saving

During these war years, there were special collections of all kinds. The Arcadia Theater carried on a program to collect shortage items. Kids could get in the movie free on special days by donating such items as phonograph records, aluminum items (a lot of mothers came up missing some pots

Courtesy of Ron Ankeny and Allegheny Ludlum

A Reminder to Collect and Save

and pans), clean tin cans, and canned goods. Some youngsters collected milkweed pods in 5-lb. onion sacks. These were given to civil defense who sent them to the proper destinations where they were used as filling (kapok) for life vests. A small payment was given for each sack you could fill.

Other children were issued box traps and would set up a trap line of 10 to 20 traps in the woods and fields to snare live rabbits. The rabbits were given to sportsman's groups who turned the skins over to the government. The rabbit's fur was used as lining for pilot's flying helmets and jackets. For each fur given, a person received 25 cents.

Everyone in the community labored in some way for the war effort. Ladies knitted sweaters, gloves, socks, and scarves with wool provided by the Red Cross. Kids knitted squares, which were then sewn together to make blankets. These items were sent to service men through the Red Cross. Mothers saved grease from cooking and turned it over to the butchers and were paid a few pennies per pound. The grease was used in making soap.

This was a time of saving. Everyone in Vandergrift who had any space at all had a victory garden to save food. In fact, it was considered unpatriotic to have space and not put in a garden. The attitude was that if you did not plant a garden you were helping to starve a soldier. So like it or not, everyone became a farmer of sorts.

The government got into the saving act, and saving became mandatory. Meat, sugar, butter, shoes, and gasoline were rationed. Each family was issued a ration book with ration stamps. There were so many rations points per pound, or number of shoes in a given period. If you could not give the exact number of meat ration stamps, the butcher would give you ration tokens (small red tokens) in change. Gasoline was rationed. Each auto had a sticker, "A" or "B" or "C," depending on how essential your driving was to the war effort. Most people had an "A" (non-essential), sticker. Drivers were allotted so many

Courtesy of Ron Ankeny and Allegheny Ludlum

Victory Garden Sign in front of Vandergrift Mill

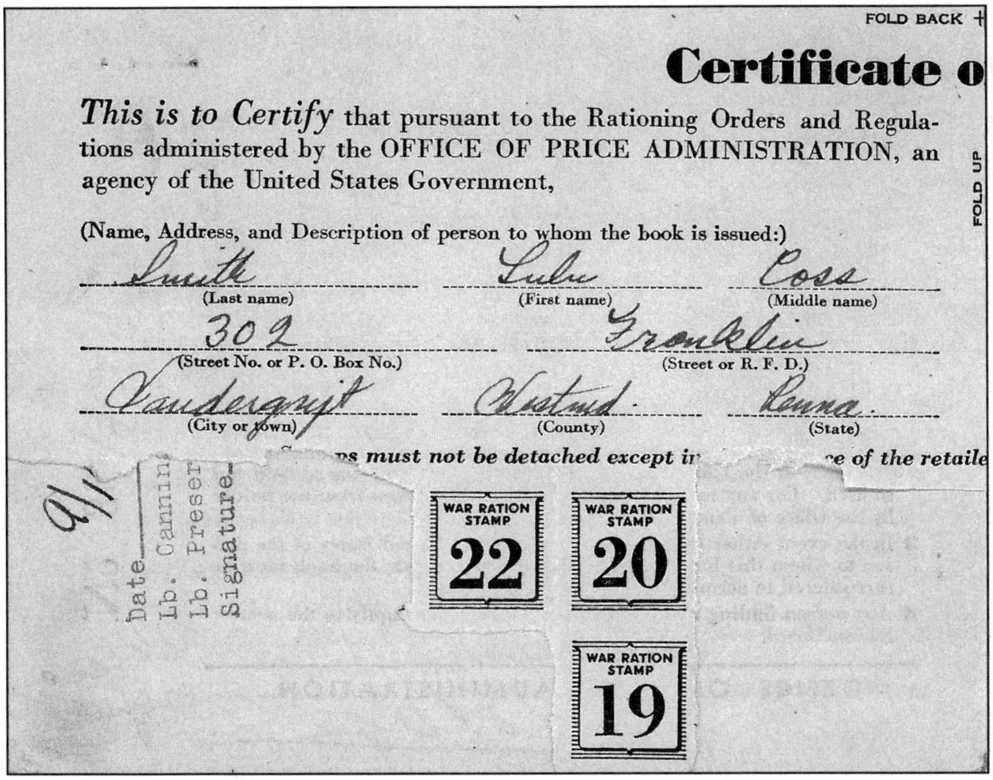
FOLD BACK

Certificate o

This is to Certify that pursuant to the Rationing Orders and Regulations administered by the OFFICE OF PRICE ADMINISTRATION, an agency of the United States Government,

FOLD UP

(Name, Address, and Description of person to whom the book is issued:)

Smith	Lulu	Coss
(Last name)	(First name)	(Middle name)

302	Franklin
(Street No. or P. O. Box No.)	(Street or R. F. D.)

Vandergrift	Westmd.	Penna.
(City or town)	(County)	(State)

...ps must not be detached except i... ...e of the retaile...

Date
Lb. Cannin...
Lb. Preser...
Signature...

WAR RATION STAMP 22

WAR RATION STAMP 20

WAR RATION STAMP 19

Courtesy of Elizabeth Heckman

Ration Coupon Book Used in Vandergrift

gallons per month. Trading, exchanging, and buying of ration coupons took place when you wanted to go on vacation. Tires were available for only essential vehicles. Needless to say, there was very little traveling at this time. But who needed to travel? Vandergrift had everything one could need within walking distance.

Families were issued a small flag to display in their window indicating that someone from the family was in the service. It was a small rectangular flag with a red border and gold fringe at the bottom with a star in the center. The star was blue if the loved one was serving in the U. S., red if serving overseas, and gold if killed in action.

Bad Things Don't Last Forever

The most dreaded thing at this time was the telegraph message. This was how the family was informed that their loved one was wounded, missing in action, or dead. Vandergrift resident Ken Blose recalls seeing a casket of a dead serviceman, arriving at the Vandergrift railroad station. "The casket was led by the Legion Drum and Bugle Corps who had their drums draped in black and [were] playing a slow, soulful beat. The procession proceeded to the funeral home."

This scene was very representative of the feelings of all when one of the hometown boys were killed. It didn't matter if you knew him personally or not. Every family was touched one way or another by this war, and one never knew when tragedy would hit.

Courtesy of Ron Ankeny and Allegheny Ludlum

Victory Sign at the Vandergrift Mill

Courtesy of Ron Ankeny and Allegheny Ludlum

Newspaper Boy in the 1940s

News of the war came mostly by newspaper. The foreign correspondents did an excellent job of reporting what had happened. Everyone waited daily for the paperboy to throw the newspaper on the porch. When something really big happened, like D-Day (the offensive invasion of Europe), V. E. Day (Victory in Europe), and V. J. Day (Victory in Japan), the paperboys hit the streets with the extra editions of the Pittsburgh papers. They carried their papers through the streets of town shouting, "Extra, extra, read all about it!" People would come out of their houses to buy the paper.

By the spring of 1945 the events for the end of the war were happening rapidly:

March 8	*American troops cross the Rhine River*
April 13	*Soviet troops capture Vienna*
April 16	*Allies begin all-out offensive in Italy*
April 22	*Soviet troops enter Berlin*
April 27	*Soviet and American troops join in Europe*
April 29	*Germans surrender in Italy*
May 2	*Berlin surrenders*
May 7	*Germany surrenders unconditionally*
August 6	*First atomic bomb is dropped on Hiroshima*
August 9	*Atomic bomb is dropped on Nagasaki*
August 10	*Japan opens peace negotiations*
August 15	*Japan accepts terms of Potsdam Declaration*
September 2	*Japan signs surrender*

In Vandergrift, excitement and anticipation rose. On V. J. Day it all broke loose—the fire whistle blew, the church bells rang, people rode through town in their cars tooting their horns, people ran from their homes jumping with excitement. The boys were coming home!

It took awhile, but families began to see their loved ones once again, and life began to go back to normal. Everyone tried to pick up life right where they left off before the war. "Rosie The Riveter" went back home as the men went back to their jobs in the mills. McMurtry's Vandergrift had passed another test. The residents had carried on the integrity of their legacy in pride and dignity. With the approach of the 1950s, attentions turned from war and death to life and entertainment.

Reflections Of The Times

Stories of the Day

Shopping in Downtown Vandergrift

"Hello! How's the family? Has your sister had her baby yet? Has your brother gone back to work at the mill? Let's go to Speer's for a coke."

These familiar words you might have heard downtown created a personal atmosphere in the Grant Avenue shopping area of Vandergrift during the 1940s and 1950s.

Here is a reflection of those times as related to Andrea Bracken by family members who remember those days:

Back during the 1940s and 1950s, many stores prospered in Vandergrift. A list of some of these stores includes: Altmeyer's Home Stores, Artley's Dress Shop, Bishop Shoe Store, Brock's Dodge and Plymouth Sales, Kroger's Store, Duppstadt's Jewelers, G. C. Murphy's Five and Dime, Geraci's Children's Clothing Store, Hilty's Drug Store, J. C. Penney's with an upstairs, Mango's Music store, McCrory's Five and Dime, Miller's Shoe Store, Peggy Ann's Clothing Store, Ruben's Department Store, Sac Shoe Repair , the Working Man Store, and Gregg's Bakery. Some of the stores that were around in the past are still here today: Isaly's, the Fashion Store, and Malcolm's Clothing. The Casino and Manos Theaters had new showings every week and they were always packed on Saturday night.

The Vandergrift business district was a very busy place. Adults as well as children were everywhere. It took a long time to get needed accessories at a store. Some register lines took as long as half an hour. Most people had trouble finding a place to park along the streets. Walking along sidewalks on a Saturday night was nearly impossible. Saturday nights were the busiest time to go "downtown" and shop. The busiest hours were anywhere between 6:30 and 9:00 p.m. You had to take your chances if you had plans to get home early.

There were several hangouts for children. Benjamin and Kuhn Drug Stores with their great soda fountains were great places to get ice cream. Sweet Lane Coffee Shop and Speer's Restaurant had cokes for $.05 and french fries for $.15. The bowling alley was also a major kid's hang out.

Business was heavy in those days, but the friendly small-town atmosphere was never lost in the hustle and bustle.

The Snakedance and The Sled

After the war, citizens of Vandergrift found many forms of recreation. Local resident, Bernice McCutcheon recounts a fond memory from her youth:

One of the more exciting events to which a teenager could look forward was the snakedance that was held before every rival football game.

The snakedance got its name from the appearance it took as it proceeded through town, with the participants—sometimes as many as 200 or 300—holding hands and being led by the cheerleaders. The participants slithered and slid like a slippery snake, and if you were at the end of the snake, the force was so great that your feet rarely touched the ground.

The Vandergrift High School Band led the group, followed by the cheerleaders and then the student body. It formed at the high school parking lot early in the evening prior to the day of the BIG game. From there we would proceed to the Heights section of town, which was then populated by several businesses. One business, in particular, was called the Village Grill, commonly known as Hiney's, which was a popular hang-out for teenagers of that era.

Our snakedance would go through the grill, around the juke box area and back out the front door while the band played fight songs and the group sang and cheered. Upon leaving the Heights, we would proceed to the downtown area, singing and cheering as we went, weaving through trees and traffic.

In the downtown section, we would stop occasionally for a cheer or song. Then we would weave through the business district, sometimes going through G. C. Murphy Five and Ten. Sometimes we would go through the Casino Theater while the movie was showing.

The event culminated in a giant bonfire at the football stadium parking lot, which resulted in a rally where the rival coach was usually burned in effigy.

As a result of our snakedance, school spirit reached a peak that carried over to the following day's football game.

And when the football season was over and snow flew, well, all the fun went downhill, literally. One gentlemen remembers:

Back in the days of fewer cars, more snow, and no road salting, Vandergrift's hills made a great place for youngsters (and some adults) to sled ride. During the winters in the 1930s and 1940s, when we had a good snowfall, the borough would close off certain streets for sled riding. Whittier Street was used in the Heights. You could slide all the way from Hancock to Wallace Street.

Downtown, they blocked Harrison and East Adams Avenues for sledding. If the snow was well packed and icy, and if you had a good sled and were a good driver, you could sometimes go down Harrison to East Adams to Hancock to Washington Avenue all the way down to the railroad station. It seemed that hundreds of kids took advantage of this opportunity, as you would have to stand in line for your turn to sled down the hill. Races and distance competitions added to the fun.

As exciting as this was, however, older Vandergrift citizens have recalled times in the 1920s that were even more thrilling. They remember riding sleds, made and donated by the mill, all the way from the top of Hancock Avenue at Cemetery Hill to the train station!

Courtesy of Ron Ankeny and Allegheny Ludlum

Sled Riding in the Forties

Pioneer Baseball

It was after the war, that Vandergrift got its professional baseball team. In 1947 the Pioneer Baseball Team and the Middle Atlantic Baseball League made its debut in Vandergrift and played here until 1950. It was a Class C farm club of the Philadelphia major league baseball team. The Pioneers played against teams from Erie, Uniontown, Johnstown, Butler, Oil City, New Castle, Niagara Falls, Greensburg, and Youngstown. Vandergrift fans saw some great baseball during this period with the local team winning the championship in 1947 and 1948. The Pioneers had the highest score ever in the league, Pioneers 25 - Butler 8. This was a delight to the fans.

Some of the players coming here had received signing bonuses of as much as $2,000 and were paid $300-350 a month by Philadelphia. All the other expenses were paid by the local club. This was good money for that time.

After a couple years of operation, the team was in financial trouble as a result of poor management practices and failure to pay federal taxes on their income. The board of directors elected Dick Hunger to be president of the club because of his past experience with promoting sports and gave him the mandate to resolve their financial problems. Dick Hunger, Joe Ceraso, and Joe Bucci went to Washington

Courtesy of Vandergrift: First 75 Years

The Vandergrift Pioneers

to talk with the Internal Revenue Service and were successful in getting the tax debt cut in half.

In the late 1940s, professional wrestling was a very popular sport on TV. Hunger felt that a wrestling match here in Vandergrift would be a great fundraiser to pay off the team's tax debts. To do this, someone had to have a Pennsylvania State wrestling promoter's license, so Dick applied and received a license to promote wrestling matches. He arranged a wrestling show at Davis Field that would feature Primo Canero (the ex-world champion), Eagle (the world champion), Mike Mazurki (a movie star), the Baron out of Germany, and others. The wrestlers came by bus to Davis Field and a large crowd; enough money was raised to pay the baseball club's debt.

Courtesy of Buttermilk Falls Publishing Company

Home of the Vandergrift Pioneers: Davis Field in the late 1940s

Al Burdis, superintendent of the mill at that time, was on the board of directors and arranged for the mill to pick up many of the club's expenses. This included travel expenses by car for Dick Hunger and Brute Kramer, the team's manager, to go to away games. Sometimes, according to William Hays, a longtime resident, the mill would even cover payroll during lean times. The mill had found it was to their advantage to have the team in town—production actually went up the day after a game!

"Brute" Kramer, the general manager of the Pioneers, was a very small man despite the nickname "Brute." He later went on the management positions at the Johnstown ball club and then to St. Vincent College sports department.

From the 1947 and 1948 championship teams, Jack Mayor, a centerfielder, and Mike Goliat, a Slickville native, went on to play in the major leagues. Bill Smith, who is now a resident in the area, had an 11-2 pitching record with this club and finished his career pitching for Toronto, a Triple A League team, a step from the majors. Rudy Minarcin, a North Vandergrift resident, also played for the Pioneers and went on to play major league ball.

Rudy Minarcin, Pioneer

One of Vandergrift's best-known personalities is Rudy Minarcin. Rudy is a former major league baseball player whose name is sure to be recognized by any true baseball fan. He pitched for numerous teams in his career and gained national recognition. He played alongside such greats as Jackie Robinson, Stan Musial, and Satchel Paige.

Rudy played ball most of his life. While in high school, he kept maintained a busy sports schedule as a pitcher during baseball season and as quarterback through the football season. In addition to his baseball opportunities after high school, Rudy was offered approximately 30 football scholarships from various colleges and universities, including Notre Dame. But, an offer to make money right out of school and an attractive signing bonus ultimately enticed him to begin his professional baseball career. After graduating from Vandergrift High School, Rudy signed a contract with the Vandergrift Pioneers, Vandergrift's minor league ball club. Later on in his career, Minarcin went on to play with the Cincinnati Reds and the Boston Red Sox.

Minarcin's tremendous pitching skills were demonstrated in what he says are 2 of his favorite moments in the sport, successfully pitching a one-hitter against the Pirates and his pitching victory against the Brooklyn Dodgers, when the Dodgers were in their prime.

Despite Rudy's many travels and the tempting allure of major cities, he moved back to Vandergrift where he now owns a food market. Rudy holds a sincere love of Vandergrift and remembers fondly the old hustle and bustle of Vandergrift streets.

Following the days of his baseball career, Rudy has directed his energies to his family and grandchildren.

William Hays
Seeing News Happen

William Hays was born in Pittsburgh in 1904. His father worked in the Homestead Mills. William was quite familiar with smokey mill towns. Here he brings us his memories of those days, and what Vandergrift was like in the 1930s and 1940s.

I remember many times when noon seemed like twilight, because of all the smokey haze from the factories. You could wipe the soot off your window sills and wash your curtains every month. It didn't matter. Everything was still dirty.

I left school when I was not quite 13 years old. I applied and was accepted at the Ralston Trade School on 15th and Penn Avenues in Pittsburgh. This is where I learned the printing trade. After that, I enlisted in the Navy for four years.

In March of 1928, when I first got off the train in Vandergrift, I thought to myself, "My this is a dirty little town." That's because as I walked up the street from the train station, I could see nothing but smoke coming from the stacks at the mill. But much to my surprise as I made my way up town, everyone I passed warmly spoke, "Hello!..How are you?..Nice day." I said to myself, "Well it might be a dirty little town, but it's a friendly town."

I came to town for a job opening at the *Vandergrift News-Citizen*. Mr. [Herbert] Brauff owned the paper at that time. $49 a week was the union scale wage at that time, however, he only wanted to pay me $45 a week. I told him that it wasn't enough, but I'd stay and help for a week till he could find someone else. On Saturday, payday, I decided to take the train home to Pittsburgh. Back then, they used to pay you in cash. They put it in a little brown envelope. I opened mine on the train only to discover it contained one single $50 bill. I didn't know what to do. I pondered it all weekend and decided to catch the earliest train to Vandergrift Monday morning.

I went into the paper, sat down, never said anything about the pay and just did my work. Years later I finally mentioned it to Mr. Brauff. He laughed and said, "Well Bill, it wasn't that I didn't want to pay you the $49, it was that my editor, advertising editor and shop foreman were all making $45 then, and I figured it wouldn't be fair to pay you more. However, after I saw your work that week, I decided the best thing to do was pay all of you $50 a week."

You know what people liked to read best in the newspaper? The scandal column! We'd put good things and bad things in too! We never named the actual names when we told the bad deed stories, like the time we told about the business man in the big black car who'd pick up a certain young lady everyday at noon and be gone for an hour. We didn't have to tell...town talk was so good everybody knew who we meant anyway.

The newspaper business was good to me. I even worked during the depression. When Mr. Brauff bought another newspaper in North Carolina he asked if I thought I could run the Vandergrift paper. "Sure, I said." So from 1928 until 1945, I was composing room

Courtesy of William Hayes

The Vandergrift News *Shop, 1936. From front: Helen Engel, William Hayes, Josephine Hoffman, Stella Hartzell, and at right, Forrest Eckstrandt*

foreman. I did everything at the paper. I ordered the paper, worked on mechanics, composed stories, you name it—I did it! One day the Eastern United States Vice President of the United Press stopped by the paper for a visit. He said I was the only manager he knew who actually did hands on work in the shop. He said there was nothing wrong with that; it was great!

Back in the early years it was real dangerous to work at the steel mill. Every week all the men contributed a part of their pay to a death benefit fund. That was real tough money to give away, because some of them were making only 15¢ a week, but they knew it might be their family that needed the money if something happened to them.

Joe Bragg was a friend and editor at the paper for a few years, before he left to work for a Catholic paper in Cleveland and eventually wrote 7 books. I asked him one day, "What was the best story you ever got to cover?" He thought it over and said, "I don't know, but I can tell you the worst one! I had to go out and cover a story on a death. The deceased was a woman, of quite large size. The family had a kind of rickety old outhouse. She went out to use it, and it collapsed, and she fell in the hole and suffocated, 'cause there was no one to get her out. It was hard to think of a polite way to cover this in the paper," Joe said.

On Route 56 where it meets 356 going toward Greensburg on the right at one time was an airport. I can't recall the year. Someone realized, this one evening, that a small plane kept circling over and over in the dark. Well there was no landing lights back then, so they spread the word around until a bunch of folks showed up with their automobiles. They lined up the cars and the plane used our car headlights to land the plane safely.

We made more than steel in Vandergrift. There was a box factory, a glove factory and a milk bottling company, and more. There were company coal mines, also. Some people even dug coal mines on their own property to supply themselves with coal and to sell a little to others who needed it. This helped earn extra money.

There were 6 trains a day that arrived and departed from Vandergrift. The last one at 11 p.m. was nicknamed, "the Bummer." Since there was a no alcohol ordinance in the town at that time, men used to ride the earlier train to the Hyde Park Hotel to drink and then return home on the "Bummer." Entertainment abounded; there was always something to do! We had movie theaters. Card and bingo clubs were very popular back then. Scrabble was all the rage, and everybody loved to play. There was a dinner every Saturday evening at one of the churches in town. Loads of people also rode the trolley to Griftlo Park. It was a nice place. The St. Peter's family owned it. They still own the property today. Everyone enjoyed the lake, swimming pool, picnic areas, and rides. It died out though, like a lot of things. When folks got cars, they went to parks farther away like Oakford Park in Jeannette. The damage done by the 1936 flood also took its toll.

At one time, the Chamber of Commerce had a merchant's division. They had a member who owned a restaurant on Columbia Avenue. The owner's name was Mr. Greg. Mr. Greg belonged for years to the group and paid his yearly dues faithfully, but he never came to a meeting. The Chamber finally sent someone to see him to ask "Why?" Mr. Greg relayed back to the members, "Because I don't like something that you do." Well it was suggested that he attend the next meeting and let everyone know what the problem was and maybe it could be fixed.

The meeting date rolled around, and of course everyone showed up just to see what Mr. Greg had to say. Once the regular meeting business was completed, Mr. Greg was given the floor. Mr. Greg requested that five members fetch their hats. He then asked them to look inside at the band and tell him where they were purchased. Well, it turned out only one of the five's hat was purchased in town. (Red Malcolm, who owned the local men's clothing store was the only Vandergrift hat.) Mr. Greg then asked if they understood his problem. They replied that they did not understand. So he requested that all the hats be fetched. Mr. Greg then asked, "What is the motto of your association?" The reply was, "Buy at Home!" "Well," he said, "that's the problem....you don't practice what you preach. Only 5 of the 40 hats here were bought in Vandergrift. Supporting your local community is something that we all should practice."

The Rabbi Follows His Dream

Not everyone who came to Vandergrift stayed here. Some followed their dreams to other places. Just one example is Rabbi Reubin Y. Rubinowitz, of Vasiliski, Lithuania.

Highly educated in the Conservative traditions of Judaism, he never-the-less suffered great loss and tragedy during WWI in his homeland of Lithuania. As different armies marched back and forth across his tiny country, he lost his wife 3 days after she gave birth to his youngest son, Milton, in 1914. 2 years later his only daughter, 16, died of TB and malnutrition, without medical attention because there were no doctors.

In 1921, he and 4 of his 6 sons came to the United States. Son Isadore Rubin had already settled in Vandergrift. Max, Milton, and Jack also, eventually, would live in or near the valley. The Rabbi served congregations in Braddock, PA and Chicago, Illinois, before coming to live with Isadore in Vandergrift.

He sometimes led the Vandergrift congregation in holy day worship. In 1947, Israel was about to become a nation again, and Rabbi Rubinowitz didn't want to miss a thing. He left Vandergrift at age 85 and traveled alone to Jerusalem. He lived there until he was 96. When he died his family buried him in the sacred soil of Israel, as he wished.

A Window on Vandergrift High School in the 1940s

Education in the 1940s and 1950s keynoted personalized attention. Howard Young, who is now a college professor and a former student of Vandergrift High (class of '44) recounts how this disciplined, personal approach to education made a lasting difference in his life.

As someone involved in higher education for 50 years, beginning as a college teacher in 1950, doing literary criticism and research, helping develop Spanish language examinations for Educational Testing Service, and participating in the introduction of proficiency standards in foreign language teaching, I have come over time to view my 4 years at Vandergrift High School (1940-44) with considerable respect and appreciation for the excellent education it afforded during those years of World War II.

Children of mill and foundry workers made up the bulk of the student body, and their ethnicity included large groups of Italian Americans, plus cadres of Slavic and Polish families, many students of German descent, and those with a sprinkling of Irish names. This 1940s' example of a diverse student body, so arduously sought for in the 1990s, followed a curriculum secure in its assumption that literature, history, science, mathematics, and Latin (French was also offered with Spanish soon to follow) were part of a well-educated person's needs. In short, it was a public school with a sense of discipline and content of the kind that suddenly went out of favor around the country in the 1960s and now struggles to come back. Colleges did not need to set up remedial classes for graduates from Vandergrift High School.

The war helped add to the general air of seriousness that pervaded the halls of VHS. Many of the houses in the town of winding streets had flags in the windows and a star alongside indicating a son or daughter in the service. As a contribution to the war effort, VHS allowed its seniors to leave at the end of the first semester for the service of their choice and still be granted a diploma in May. In the 1944 *Spectator*, the class historian Clodagh Hunger captures the sense of a graduating class truncated by the war, and Fran Grimes's drawings show how the war reached into all routines.

Everyone's memories of teachers will differ, and each student will have a favorite for personal reasons. I acknowledge Miss Evelyn Love, *Hi-Newsette* advisor and teacher of journalism, who gave me self-confidence, showed me I could write, and firmly steered an insecure and befuddled young man into a career of writing and education. It was she who persuaded Herbert Brauff, the publisher of the *Vandergrift News*, whose sports editor had just been drafted, to take a chance on a sophomore. I became what was surely one of the youngest sports editors of a daily newspaper in the country. To her and the many like her who meant something decisive in the lives of VHS students, this belated but enduring thank you.

Freshmen Initiation

Ken Blose relates his memories about the annual "Freshmen Initiation" ritual of the 1940s:

The upperclassmen at Vandergrift High School would gang up on the freshmen every year. They would steal the freshmen's slacks, and make them walk around town in their underpants (being sure to follow them and make lots of noise to draw attention). The upperclassmen would then throw the freshmen's pants onto a girl's porch and ring the doorbell. The freshmen would then have to retrieve their pants from her porch.

After all of that, the freshmen would then have to make their way through a "paddle line." It was all basically done in good fun, though it was a little embarrassing for the freshmen.

Dr. Benjamin Franklin Lear

Although this story centers on Dr. Benjamin Franklin Lear, a Vandergrift physician, it offers a glimpse of the town during this era through the work of Dr. Lear's general medical practice. Dorothy Lear, Dr. Lear's wife, relates his story:

Dr. Lear had his medical education at the University of Pittsburgh School of Medicine in the 1930s and began his medical practice in Vandergrift in 1939 in partnership with his father, Dr. Isaac Newton Lear. Together, Isaac and Benjamin practiced medicine in the Kiski Valley for 100 years. One of their proudest achievements was founding the Well Baby Clinic in Vandergrift. When Dr. Benjamin Lear started his practice, there were 14 physicians in Vandergrift.

General practitioners often had their offices in their homes or in locations near their homes. Emergency rooms were not as common as they are today; poor roads made the nearby hospitals less accessible than now; and of course there were no helicopters to evacuate patients. Doctors' offices became emergency rooms in small towns where no hospital existed. Having a medical office in your home made it a popular choice due to the availability of the doctor. In reality, the doctor with an office in his home was on call 24 hours a day.

The police brought traffic victims, stabbing victims, alcoholics, and all kinds of broken bodies to the office. The doctor would roll up his sleeves, suture the wounds or put a splint on a simple fracture, and send them on their way. In more serious cases, after emergency treatment, an ambulance would rush the patient to the hospital for further care.

In Dr. Lear's case, his wife Dorothy was often called on to assist with nursing duties and to clean up the bloody messes so the office would be ready for regular patients. Of course, these incidents happened at any time of the day or night.

Sometimes it was an asthmatic person who couldn't get his breath or a distraught parent with a very ill child, who banged on the doctor's door. Early in Dr. Lear's practice, while his father could assist him with the anesthetic, he would remove tonsils in his office. The patient would come in the morning and be put to sleep with ether dripped through a strainer with gauze. His wife would use the electric suction to keep the field of surgery clear of blood. The patient would recuperate all day in a back office and be discharged that night.

Most early general practitioners had a large obstetrics business, delivering babies in the mothers' homes. In the 1940s the charge was $50 for a delivery. In one 5-day period, Dr. Lear delivered 9 babies. On one occasion, his wife had to borrow a neighbor's car to go into the country to a farm house where Dr. Lear was delivering a baby to tell him that a patient in North Vandergrift was ready to deliver. Dr. Lear answered the door of the farmer's house with his gloves on and forceps in his hand and said "She'll just have to wait." When a baby was born, he would place his hand over the baby's heart and ask God's blessing on the child.

Like many small-town physicians, Dr. Lear was called away for World War II where he served as a medical officer aboard ship and ashore from 1942 to 1946. His pay was $300 a month. When a doctor was called away like this, his patient load fell on the remaining doctors in town and put a real strain on their practices.

Until after the war, there were no antibiotics or wonder drugs for doctors to use; patients were treated with aspirin, paregoric, poultices, other simple remedies, and many housecalls to check on progress. So much was learned during the war that medicine improved 100 percent.

House calls: For young readers, believe it or not, you could call a doctor to come to your home when you felt unable to go to the office. Of course, the charge for this was double. In October 1952, Dr. Lear's charge for an office call was $3 and a housecall was $6. Even at these prices, doctors often accepted pies, jelly, eggs, or other produce in lieu of money; Dr. Lear was especially generous in this respect. Dr. Lear made house calls in Vandergrift up to the day before he died in 1989.

This description of Dr. Lear would probably apply to most general practitioners in those days. Doctors were much more to their patients than a medical doctor.

"He [Dr. Lear] listened quietly for hours, to those suffering, with a patience he never learned in medical school. He was one who left his warm bed many, many nights to go to the bedside of the sick; he was a strong shoulder for many couples who had a variety of problems; he practiced a special brand of psychology with his dry sense of humor and always had time to sit and hold a patient's hand while they talked it out together."

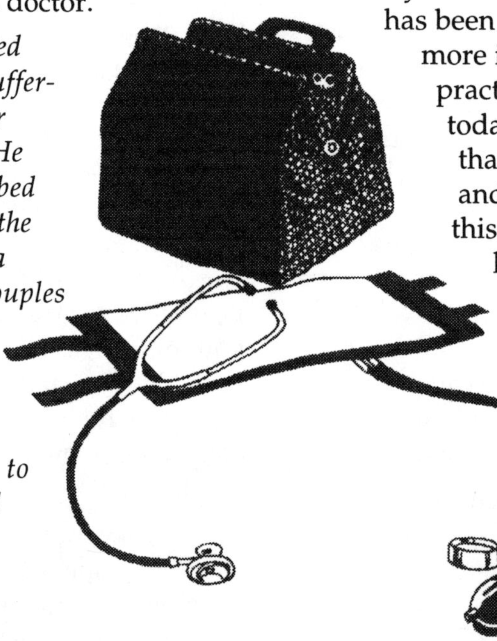

In January 1983, the *Pittsburgh Press* wanted to profile a family doctor and selected Dr. Lear for their story. Patients' comments about him indicate the type of relationship people felt with their family doctor. *"He always dispenses the right advice. I don't know how he does it. I'd be lost without him." "His office is often a confessional for patients with troubles other than physical. His shoulders carry the weight of everybody's problems. It seems he counsels as many people as he treats."* Dr. Lear said that his father taught him to show affection and concern for patients. *"He really loved people. I guess I inherited that love."*

Dr. Lear was a great supporter of high school athletics, helping out as the team doctor. He was also the mill doctor for a time.

The practice of medicine has made many advances in recent years. But something has been lost in the high-tech, high-speed, more impersonal, highly specialized practice of medicine that we have today. Lost is the loving relationship that developed between the family and the family doctor. Dr. Lear put it this way, "I want to treat my patients like family; they are family to me."

Medicine in the 1940s and 1950s may not have been as advanced as it is today, but those who experienced the doctor-patient relationship that existed then will always remember those dedicated, caring doctors with great respect and affection.

America Takes to the Air

From its modest beginnings in 1928 as a pasture land with one airplane, the Vandergrift Airport enlarged to become the local Air Mail service. Leonard C. Elswick vividly remembers the Vandergrift Airport. Here are 2 stories which he related:

One day in November 1940, Dad [Leonard G. Elswick] came home from his job at the Railway Express and told us that he had been given an additional job to do. Air mail pickup was coming to Vandergrift, and the Railway Express Company would be in the new business of air express. The pickup station would be located at Vandergrift Airport. So my dad now had the additional job of delivering and picking up the airmail and air express at the airport. This included setting up the pickup system.

Near the end of the runway at Vandergrift Airport, two 12-foot poles were set up 20 feet apart. A long rope made into a large circle was attached to each pole and to the airmail or express bag lying on the ground. The airmail plane would come in low at about 120 miles per hour; as it neared the pick-up point, the pilot would release the incoming mail bag while a hook trailing below the plane would snag the rope stretched between the two poles and off would go the return airmail to be pulled into the plane by the mechanic.

The bags for pickup were limited to 50 pounds. My dad used a large strip of white cloth to communicate with the pilot, since he had no radio. If there was more than one bag to be picked up, he would lay the white cloth between the two poles. This signaled the pilot to come around and make a second pickup. If packages were too large to fit into the pickup bag, the white cloth would be laid the opposite direction. In this case, the pilot would land the plane and pick up the oversized item. This could not be done at all pickup points because not all were located at airports. Eventually, a radio was installed in the airmail delivery vehicle to provide direct communication with the pilot. The first airmail pickup at Vandergrift was made on December 2, 1940; the first Air Express pickup on January 6, 1941.

Courtesy of Leonard G. Elswick

Airmail Pickup

The All American Aviation Company (AAA) operating out of Allegheny County Airport provided the air service for this operation. AAA was the parent company of today's US Air. Vandergrift was on Airmail Route 49E. Route 49E left the county airport and made pickups at Pitcairn, Vandergrift, Indiana, Punxsutawney, Dubois, Clearfield, Philipsburg, State College, Bellefonte, Lock Haven, Jersey Shore, and finally Williamsport. At Williamsport, the mail and express would be unloaded, return bags were taken aboard, and the aircraft serviced. A return flight was then made over the same route. Initially, Vandergrift had 2 pickups and deliveries each day. During World War II, the use of Air Express and Airmail greatly increased, and a second round trip was added to route 49E in 1943. Lawrence McCune, who also worked at Railway Express, delivered and picked up the airmail on the evening flight.

The airmail planes flew in all kinds of weather: rain, fog, and snow. Very seldom was a flight canceled for bad weather. Sometimes they would bypass a station because they could not locate it in the fog. On several occasions, the mail plane had to land at Vandergrift on its return trip to Pittsburgh because of bad weather at the county airport. It took courageous pilots and flight mechanics to operate under such extreme conditions.

One of those pilots was Gerald (Red) Lindenmuth of Vandergrift. He often flew the 49E Route. One day while flying a different route in bad weather, he crashed after hitting trees in Yorkville, Ohio, just north of Wheeling, West Virginia, after making a pickup in heavy fog. Red and his flight mechanic survived the crash, but the plane and most of the mail were destroyed by fire. Both of Red's ankles were broken in the crash, and he did not return to flying the mail.

The airmail planes seldom flew higher than 1,000 feet above the ground because the pickup points were so close together. When upper level visibility was poor, they would fly in the valleys between the hills and mountains. On one occasion when I was in North Vandergrift, I saw the plane come very low down the river from Apollo. It was so low, it had to climb to make it over the Vandergrift bridge.

Courtesy of Vandergrift: First 75 Years

Red Lindenmuth and son Jerry beside American Eagle biplane, 1931

In 1941, a mail bag fell prematurely from the mail plane as it approached Vandergrift Airport, landing on a nearby farm. My dad came back to town and went to the schools and asked for Boy Scout volunteers to search for the lost mail bag. Ralph Culp, Jr., found the bag, and I believe he received a reward of $5 for his effort.

After World War II, Railway Express eliminated the Air Express part of their business. Mr. Gourley of Riverview, Parks Township, was hired to take the airmail from the post office to the airport. He continued in this capacity until this type of airmail pickup and delivery was discontinued in 1949. The last airmail pickup in Vandergrift was made on May 28, 1949.

In this story, Mr. Elswick recalls a special time from his youth:

In the late 1930s and early 1940s, the operators of the Vandergrift Airport would attract large crowds by having parachute jumps a few times during the summer and by selling airplanes rides. Flying was still somewhat of a novelty to most people, so a Sunday outing to the airport was an exciting event.

In 1941, my dad had come to know some of the pilots at the airport through operating the airmail pickup station. One day in late spring, 2 pilots were repairing torn fabric on the bottom wing of a Waco biplane. The plane's owner explained that a lady disembarking from a sight-seeing flight had stepped off the wing walk and put her foot through the wing fabric. He said he could use a kid to help passengers get on and off the plane to make sure this did not happen again, and to ensure that the 2 passengers had their seat belts fastened. My dad said he had just the right kid: me.

The next Sunday I reported for work at noon. I was 12 years old. Every Sunday through the summer and fall of 1941, I was there. I would help push the plane out of the hangar. Since they only flew the plane on Sundays, it was parked in the rear of the hangar. We had to move 7 planes to get to the Waco.

After fueling and safety checks, the pilot would take it up for a test flight before hauling passengers. I got to go up one every test flight as part of my pay, which was 50 cents for the day, plus all the pop I wanted to drink.

At the Vandergrift Airport, the ground sloped up from the north side of the runway; a perfect vantage point for people to watch the airport activity from their cars. The whole hillside would be full of cars as people watched the planes take off and land. The owner of the Waco biplane would park his Chevrolet coupe by the fence with his airplane on the other side of the fence. He had a public announcement system in his car with a large speaker mounted on the trunk. It was part of my job to play 78 rpm records over the system. There was a whole stack of records to choose from. My favorite was Glenn Miller's "String of Pearls." As the "disc jockey," I was to keep records playing all afternoon till dark except for announcements for airplane rides.

Carl Fletcher, the plane's owner would sell tickets from his car while Joe Hollyoak would pilot the plane. If business got slow, I had to go up on the hill to the parked cars and try to sell plane ride tickets. If they could only get one passenger to go, I would hop in for a ride. Small babies that went up in their mother's arms would, 9 out of 10 times, come back after a flight sound asleep—keep in mind that this was an open cockpit plane!

This was the best summer of my life, and I couldn't wait for next summer to come, but all of this came to an end with the beginning of World War II. The Waco biplane was sold to a Southern flight school for cadet flight training, and the owner joined the Army Air Corps.

Courtesy of Ron Ankeny and Allegheny Ludlum

The Dismantling of the Open Hearths. The dust settling is from the stack (center) that just fell. Note the size of the smoke stacks (center, and right) in comparison to the men in the center of the picture.

Chapter Eleven

The Turbulent 1950s and 1960s

The 1950s and 1960s brought an economic roller coaster ride to McMurtry's town. Technological and scientific advances in every field of endeavor were changing the face of the workplace. Television ushered in a dramatic change in social life. Rock and roll, civil disobedience, and an explosion in automobile ownership, all created new and challenging problems for society.

All of these factors combined to produce serious challenges for McMurtry's Vandergrift. It was a time of change in the "Workingman's Paradise" and the Vandergrift mill.

The Open Hearth Shut Down

As McMurtry's town evolved through time so did his mill. The following is a capsulated history of the Vandergrift mill leading up to the closure of its open hearth.

Over the years, the Vandergrift plant had seen many changes. Originally it was part of Apollo Steel. By 1900 the American Sheet Steel Company had acquired the Vandergrift Works, and the Apollo rolling mills were permanently shut down in June and dismantled in October 1903.

In 1901 the American Tin Plate Company and the American Sheet Steel Company were consolidated in the new firm, and by 1902 the 2 companies were themselves merged into a single U. S. Steel subsidiary to form the American Sheet and Tin Plate Company. Further organizational changes saw the American Sheet and Tin Plate Company become a part of the Carnegie Illinois Steel Corporation in June 1936. In 1939 the Vandergrift Plant was placed under the management of Irvin Works.

Originally, the major units in the Vandergrift plant included open hearths, a blooming mill, a bar mill, double sheet mills, and cold mills. By 1906 there were 37 sheet mills, making it the largest sheet steel mill in the world at that time.

In the years between World War I and II, galvanized and terne plate stands and

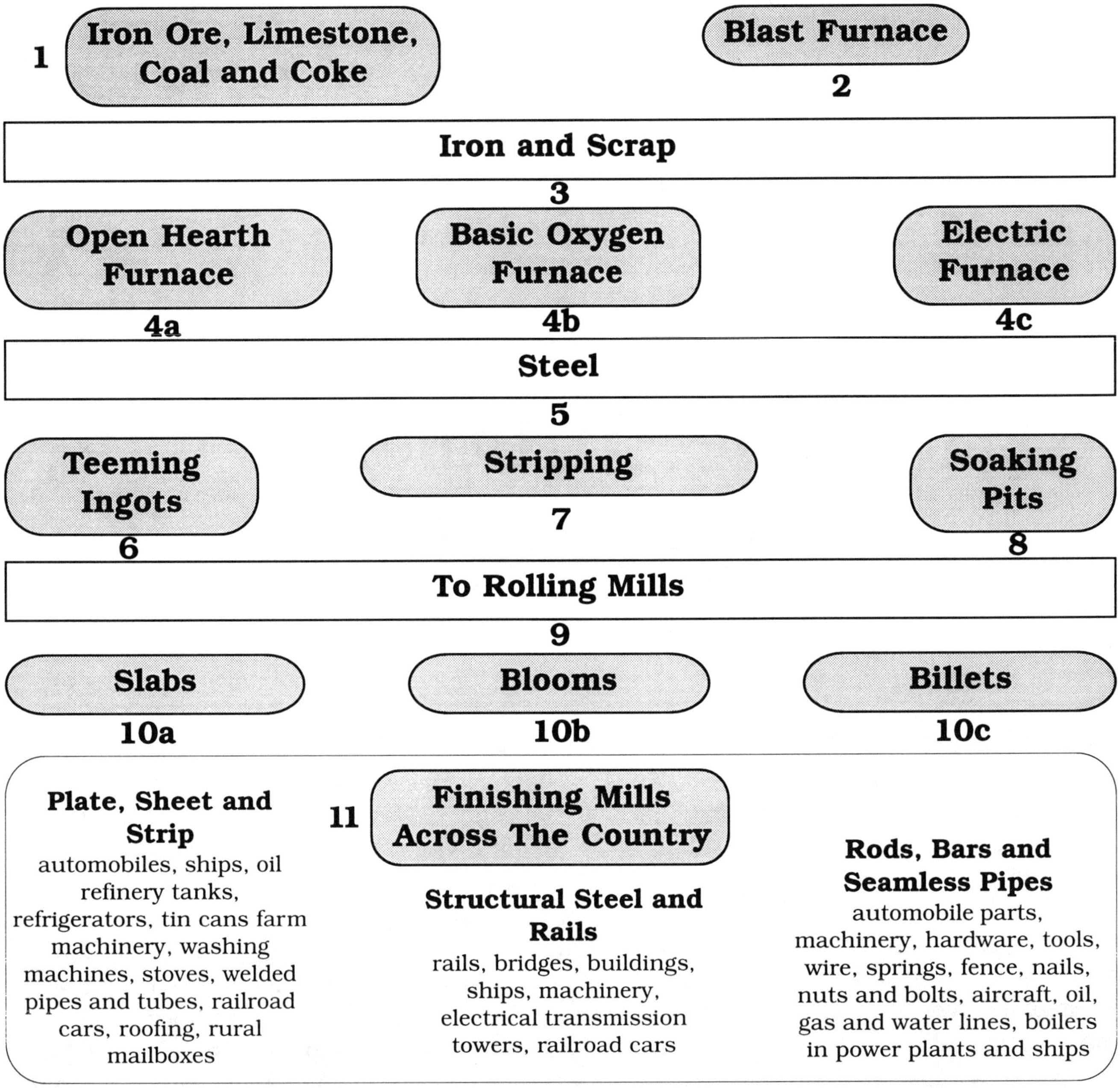

Steel Making in Vandergrift Before 1950

1) Raw materials such as iron ore, limestone and coal are dumped into the top of 2) the Blast Furnace. Hot air is blown into the furnace. The ore is changed into drops of iron, which settle to the bottom of the furnace, while the limestone joins with the impurities to form slag, which floats on top of the melted iron. The molten iron is run into a huge ladle, and then it and 3) steel scrap are put into 1 of 3 kinds of furnaces, where impurities are burned off. 4a) The open hearth furnace changes the material into purified molten steel after 8 to 12 hours of intense heat, while 4b) the basic oxygen furnace can change 80 tons of scrap and molten iron into steel in just 40 to 60 minutes. 4c) The electric furnace makes alloy steels when powerful electric currents melt the scrap and chromium, tungsten, or nickel are added. The liquid steel (5) is poured into each mold (6). After the steel has solidified into ingots, the molds are (7) stripped (lifted) from the ingots by a pair of tongs. The ingots are placed in soaking pits (8) until the center of the ingot is brought to the same temperature as the outside of the ingot. The still hot steel is placed in different rolling mills (9) where it is passed between powerful steel rolls and squeezed (somewhat like a clothes wringer) into blooms (10a), slabs (10b), and billets (10c). These are shipped to finishing mills (11) and manufactured into products.

Courtesy of Ron Ankeny and Allegheny Ludlum

The Vandergrift Mill: Rebuilding and Changing in the Late 1940s

gas and electric box annealing facilities were added.

After World War II, equipment for the processing of silicon steel strips was installed. On January 1, 1951, the Vandergrift plant was taken over by United States Steel Company, and the plant became the electrical sheet capital of the United States Steel Corporation. The electrical sheet was an alloy sheet that was high in silicon content and was used by producers of electrical equipment. The Vandergrift plant was now a specialty mill.

The open hearth was outdated and no longer needed. On October 31, 1954, operations of the open hearths and slab mill were discontinued, completing the evolution from a primarily rolling and steel-producing plant that produced such products as galvanized and terne plate, tack plate and automobile sheets to specialty finishing of stainless steel and silicon sheets.

The Open Hearth Closing Leaves Its Mark

Modern rolling equipment was installed when the open hearth was closed. The plant now only finished steel shipped in from the Irvin Works. Mill employment had dropped from an average of 3,000 to 1,000 by 1964.

All this meant major changes to the lives of local families. Part of the work force not tied to the hearth were able to remain, but men working in the open hearth, soaking pits, and slab mill had few options. Some were eligible for early retirement. Younger employees had opportunity to transfer to the Fairless Works in Philadelphia or to a plant in the Monongahela Valley.

The opportunity to transfer was an honor extended to these workers as a result of their labor history. Vandergrift steelworkers were known throughout the steel industry as a different breed of workers. There was a unique team spirit between management and labor that was a direct legacy of McMurtry's original town planning. Management and labor grew up together in the same small town. McMurtry's provision of workers owning their own home had ensured a close work force.

These men also displayed unusual pride in their work. The ideal of "something better than the best" was not just an empty quote by a big corporation to these men. McMurtry had built it into their very lives in the creation of their town nearly 60 years earlier.

The New Mill

Steel was now made in Homestead, Duquesne, and Clairton. It was shipped to the Irvin works to hot-roll, then on to Van-

Ralph "Tackle" Wellington McIntire

Ralph Wellington McIntire was the second in the family to serve as burgess of Vandergrift. He was full of pride and passion for his community.

Early in his high school days, McIntire earned his nickname, "Tackle," from being quite a football player. "Tackle" was interested in many sports; he hunted, fished, and boxed in an amateur boxing league. He practiced his boxing skills in a back room of Vandergrift's Box Factory. During his amateur boxing career he suffered a few knockdowns, but was never knocked out.

Young Ralph McIntire served in the Navy during both World Wars I and II. It was during his service in W.W. II that "Tackle" received several citations and medals of heroism. He served aboard 3 different destroyers. Just outside the New Jersey harbor, his ship suffered an internal explosion. Jack was top-side waiting in the chow line when the explosion occurred. Although suffering from a foot injury due to shrapnel, he carried a number of his shipmates to safety and then tried to save the ship as well. After his medical release from the Navy, he returned to his hometown of Vandergrift.

McIntire served on the Vandergrift Police Motorcycle Squad for 21 years. 4 of those years he served as Chief of Police. He was elected burgess of Vandergrift for 4 terms.

During his fourth term, he died at his Hamilton Avenue home, typing a letter to the businessmen asking for support for the children's Halloween party. The apparent cause of death was due to a heart attack. His terms of office of burgess ran from 1946 to 1962. "Tackle" was loved and admired by all, but most especially by the young people in the town.

Agnes Elizabeth (Long) McIntire

Agnes McIntire was the only woman to serve as burgess of Vandergrift. It was upon her husband's death in 1962, that the town council encouraged her to finish his term of office. She continued the same spirit of warmth and kindness that her husband Jack had started. After finishing the 2 years of her husband's term, she was again encouraged to run for burgess on her own merit. She did so and was narrowly defeated by Richard Hunger.

dergrift to be cold-rolled, heat-treated, temper-rolled to restore hardness, and flattened, trimmed and put into narrow and wide coils. Vandergrift, the Workingman's Paradise, was no longer a steel-making town.

Plans made by U. S. Steel to modernize the Vandergrift plant's finishing facilities seemed to ensure that the mill would continue as one of the most modern and competitive plants in the nation. In 1957 U. S. S. installed a Sendzimir mill capable of reducing 48-inch wide sheets at a rate of 713 feet per minute. The mill also installed a new water treatment plant capable of treating 12 million gallons of water per day for use in their manufacturing process. In his 1958 year-end summary, reported in the *Vandergrift News,* A. T. Reichenbach, division superintendent said,

> *We are continuing our intensified program as one of the highest quality producers of stainless and silicon steel in the industry. Vandergrift plant's safety record makes it one of the safest plants in the steel industry.*

Not to be left behind in the modernization trend, the United Engineering and

Foundry Company planned to spend $1.75 million in the Vandergrift Plant to install a new roll casting pit in a new extension on the molding area. With this, they could produce the largest rolls ever produced in the Vandergrift Plant. A new finishing building with heat-treating furnaces, 4 roll lathes, and a large duplex milling machine would round out the improvements. At this time, the foundry had 900 employees.

In 1964, a giant new piece of technology, a lathe controlled by an electronic brain, was installed. It was the largest in the world of this type. Rolls 5 feet in diameter and 23 feet long could be turned on this lathe.

The foundry was near the end of a 10-year improvement program. A worker who had retired 10 years before would not have recognized the plant if he paid a visit. Technology had arrived, life was changing.

Modernization was exciting for the community, but unfortunately the new automated equipment required substantially fewer workers. This would be a blow to the town's economy. It was a frightening and discouraging time to many. But the foundation of McMurtry's fortitude would again prove true even in the face of dramatic changes to the town's industrial origins.

Paradise Preserved

Mass steel production would never return, but Vandergrift itself would undergo a flurry of positive change. While the mill and foundry were offering limited opportunities economically, the ideal of "something better than the best" was alive and well in the hearts of Vandergrift's citizens. Dr. Joseph O'Brien reflects on this time of change:

> *After being limited by an austere budget with no appropriation for capital improvements for many years, Vandergrift started to show the proverbial "run down at the heels" look. A planning committee of council members was set up to prepare a plan for major improvements to local facilities. The underlying hope was that the projects would have a spin-off effect and stimulate property owners to upgrade their properties....*
>
> *The ripple effect hoped for was dramatic as the town took on a new look and rekindled a sense of pride. People got involved and were competitive in upgrading their properties.*
>
> *The legacy left by this activity is not that it attained the stated objective or overcame all the obstacles, but rather, the lesson that "leadership by*

Courtesy of Bill Fontana

Grant Avenue in the Late 1950s

The Sound of Thunder

In founding Vandergrift, George McMurtry had set the standard for being "something better than the best." The George G. McMurtry Thunderers Drum and Bugle Corps exemplified this idea in the 1950s. Award-winning champions, they were one of the finest musical organizations in Vandergrift history.

The Thunderers were organized by the George G. McMurtry Fire Department in 1950. This group of 40 to 50 talented and dedicated volunteers from all walks of life won 4 Western Pennsylvania Firemen's Association and 2 Pennsylvania State Firemen's Association drum and bugle corps championships.

The success of the Corps can be attributed in part to the director Dr. Joseph C. O'Brien, who trained them and arranged their music, and to the discipline and conformity demanded by Bill Bell, the primary drum major. He developed an espirit de corps and instilled a sense of pride in them and in the town they represented. During its 10 years, the corps regularly thundered down Grant Avenue in their double V formation, shaking the buildings with the greatest sound ever heard in Vandergrift.

example" is a progressive, viable method of governing and that the benefits received by all residents far exceeded the cost of the project.

But these things would have been impossible without people in the community who chose to work together and get something done. These people held a passion for the good of the town.

Together in the face of great economic loss, they hashed and rehashed subjects, pulled strings behind the scenes, fought bitterly, and worked tirelessly. The end result enabled the town to not only survive losses that had crippled other steel towns, but also opened new opportunities that would bring future growth.

It Only Takes A Spark

Everything in life seems to run in cycles of ups and downs, of high activity and low activity, of periods of great achievements and those of little or none. The history of Vandergrift fits this pattern very well. Very often, certain events spark us to new directions which become historically noteworthy, thus the title for this section.

The first lines of the modern hymn "Pass It On" (*Kurt Kaiser; 1969 Communique Music*), are *"It only takes a spark to get a fire going, and soon all those around can warm up in its glowing."* These words express exactly what happened during the 1950s and 1960s, when a small group of

Vandergrift citizens organized the Community Development Council.

At the conclusion of both World War II and the Korean War, the infrastructure of Vandergrift had taken a definite downturn. The town's tax revenues were down as the buildings fell into obsolescence and disrepair. Many of the streets had degenerated into interconnecting potholes, and the once beautiful parks and parklettes had become little more than weed patches. The previous wartime economic boom had reverted to a serious decline. Orders to the mill and foundry dropped. The loss of jobs with the closing of the mill's open hearth was a further economic blow to the town. An effort would be needed to keep the present plant in operation and to draw new business to the area. The depressed appearance of the town was not a good selling point to achieve these goals.

The spark of improvement began in 1955, with three ladies, all members of the Vandergrift Woman's Club. The three had just made a $100 profit on a flower show. With the council's approval, they decided to use the profit to clean up one of the town's parklettes and to plant flowers.

This small improvement led to a request from the president of the Chamber of Commerce for the group to do a town wide beautification project. At a meeting between the Woman's Club and local civic leaders, the Community Development Council (CDC) of Vandergrift was created. The leaders of this group were Justine Condo, Virginia Spiher, and a third person whose name has been lost. The newly formed CDC consisted of representatives from 28 civic, service, business, union, social, religious, veteran, fraternal, and high school groups.

The CDC immediately undertook specific improvement tasks, initially conducting surveys and inspections, from which recommendations and suggestions

When Pirates Roamed Our Streets

Dr. Joesph O'Brien tells about a spark that helped bring business to Vandergrift:

In 1955, the Merchants Division of the Vandergrift Chamber of Commerce was aware of the impending changes and developed a program (which turned out to be an annual event for 14 years) that would promote Vandergrift and appeal to a wide cross section of people and give them a reason to come to town. It was Pirate Days. There was a 3-day promotion during which the stores held special dales, and sponsored a variety of other activities and attractions.

The highlight event was the Saturday evening parade which featured Bob Prince (the Voice of the Pittsburgh Pirates) and 3 Pirate players. Their appearance was augmented with bands, floats, fire apparatus, marching units, mounted units, antique cars and more. Fran Aiello was promotion manager of the Merchant's Division and Dr. Joseph O'Brien served as parade marshal. The parades were very successful each year and brought approximately 10,000 people into town on parade day and provided a captive audience for showcasing Vandergrift's many features.

The legacy of these promotions is not just the memory of success, but the reality that people must have a reason to come to town and once there, must be pleased and satisfied with their experience. If plans are promoted, publicized and produce a substantive and acceptable event, people will make the trip to be a part of it. The bottom line is not the "why" they came to town, but the fact that they did come and were exposed to the many things Vandergrift had to offer.

were made to the town council and businesses. Beginning with three town parks, they initiated general clean ups and the planting of new shrubs and flowers. These first projects were accomplished with volunteer labor and funds donated by the participating groups. The sight of these improvements fanned the improvement flame throughout the community.

The Spark Becomes a Fire

The Burgess, Ralph W. McIntire, proclaimed June 16-22, 1957, to be "Clean-up, Paint-up, Fix-up Week" in Vandergrift. This idea was picked up by the newspapers and further proclaimed on banners around the town. It was to be a week set aside for Vandergrift to spruce up and show its

Rainbow Control

"Rainbow Control: A New Dimension in Emergency Management and Fire Service Concepts." This was the title of the first national presentation of Vandergrift's unique emergency control system. It was made in 1968 by Dr. Joseph C. O'Brien, Rainbow Control Founder and Coordinator, to a large audience at the International Association of Fire Chiefs Conference in Louisville, Kentucky. From there, Dr. O'Brien went on to bring national recognition to Vandergrift by presenting Rainbow Control concepts at many conferences in major cities across the nation.

It was a complete system to manage all types of emergencies using a common access telephone number terminating in a control center capable of alerting, dispatching, and coordinating the pooled public protection and supplemental services of more than 10 participating municipalities.

After years of dedicated service, the operation of Rainbow Control was discontinued in 1989 when the participating communities joined the county 911 system. The legacy of Rainbow Control lives on with many of its ideas and procedures adopted and in use by 911 emergency systems across the nation.

Courtesy of Dr. Joseph O'Brien

Vandergrift-based Rainbow Emergency Control System Operating Console, 1960

community pride. With this, the spark became a consuming fire.

The CDC and the Veterans organizations received approval to turn the Casino Building front lawn into a veteran's memorial garden. The large stone and plaque honoring veterans and the plantings were part of this project. Other trees and shrubs were planted on the Casino grounds as well.

The areas on both sides of Farragut Avenue at the south side of the bridge were acquired, cleaned up, and landscaped to provide a pleasing first impression for anyone entering the town via the bridge. This project was dedicated to the town's veterans and was sponsored by Dr. Eugene Losasso.

With the support and encouragement of the CDC, the Council approved a $150,000 bond issue for improvements to borough buildings, streets, parking, fire department buildings, and schools. The bonds were purchased by the People's Union Bank and Trust Company (now Integra Bank) and were to be paid off by a modest increase in local taxes.

An editorial in the *Vandergrift News* had this to say, *Betterment of a town is everyone's business. It is one of council's primary concerns, but should concern every civic group and every citizen. The council deserve for their efforts our wholehearted approval and support.*

With the bond money in hand, it was full steam ahead. A new borough garage was built at the site of the now unused garbage incinerator at the west end of Longfellow Street. With that completed, the old covered horse shoe pits beside the McMurtry Fire Department and the borough barn at the foot of Linden Street were torn down.

Property was purchased, and houses and businesses demolished on the west side of Columbia Avenue for downtown busi-

Courtesy of Kenneth Blose

Foundry Row Was Demolished to Make Way for a Parking Lot

Courtesy of Buttermilk Falls Publishing Company

Longfellow School Building Coming Down

ness parking. The mill agreed to develop parking areas inside the plant area to help alleviate business parking problems. Columbia Avenue was widened, which made it safer to park on both sides of the street.

The area adjacent to Fire Department No.1 was made into a large parking lot to reduce dangerous Sunday morning congestion on Franklin Avenue and adjacent streets and alleys created by the 4 churches located in this immediate area.

The park in front of the Casino along Washington Avenue was converted into a parking lot. Longfellow Street was widened in the business district to provide parking on both sides of the street. All of this would relieve what the businessmen considered to be their biggest problem—parking.

The foundry did its share to help the parking problem. The company demolished "Foundry Row", which was a row of 28 connected housing units on Perry Avenue that had been built in 1910 for skilled foundry workers. This provided 75 parking spaces for foundry employees and eased the parking problems on Sherman and Franklin Avenues.

Some streets were resurfaced and some on the Heights were surfaced for the first time (Bryant and Poe Streets). Traffic patterns were modified as were street corners at Washington and Sherman Avenue and at Washington and Grant Avenue to facilitate the flow of traffic. New street lights were installed on Columbia Avenue.

In cooperation with the school board, a safety inspection program of Vandergrift's schools was started. The discovery of unsafe conditions along with the high cost of modernization and other factors led to the demolition of the Custer and Longfellow School Buildings. These areas were turned into playgrounds for use by the students at the remaining adjacent schools. The Adams School was remodeled to meet safety standards and was provided with new windows, roof, and heating system.

It became evident to the school board that the present schools were outdated and major improvements at very high cost would soon be necessary. This led to discussion of a jointure with other school districts as was being done in other areas. On April 29, 1958, after much discussion, research, and study, seven schoolboards agreed to a jointure with the objective of building a new high school. The jointure would include Hyde Park, Vandergrift, East Vandergrift, Parks Township, Avonmore, Bell Township, and Allegheny Township (Washington Township and Leechburg districts declined the invitation to join at this time).

Members of the new district visited new school buildings in Pennsylvania and New York, finally settling on a design found in New York. The Pittsburgh architectural firm of Curry, Martin, and Taylor was selected to plan the new Kiski Area High School. The first commencement of the new school was held in 1963.

The fire departments reached an agreement with the council that would provide a 50/50 sharing of building cost for a new No.1 fire department and the expansion of the No. 2 department building. These much needed improvements would soon benefit the fire safety of the whole town.

A committee of the Community Devel-

Courtesy of Buttermilk Falls Publishing Company

The Old George G. McMurtry Fire Hall

Courtesy of Kenneth Blose

The New George G. McMurtry Fire Hall

opment Council (CDC) worked with the librarian to consider why the library was being used so little. The conclusion was that the conditions needed to be improved and made more attractive. A preschool section was set up and a story-telling hour established on Saturday mornings. The Council recommended that a Friends of the Library Association be formed to support library improvements.

In 1964, Vandergrift's Council developed a long-range plan for the town's. The principle objective of the plan was to correct present shortcomings and set a positive course for future development in Vandergrift. The effort resulted in 3 plans. The Land-Use Plan designated areas in the borough best suited for residential facilities, public services, and schools. The Traffic and Parking Plan presented a system to improve traffic flow and parking. The third plan provided for a Borough Planning and Zoning Commission.

This listing of accomplishments by a town facing desperate times is impressive in itself, but there were also many other improvements during this period too numerous to detail. New roads were dedicated; recreational facilities and parks were created; civic and church organizations expanded; volunteer service groups flourished; and businesses prospered as a result of community's new emphasis on improvement. The spirit of McMurtry's dream, passed through the generations, showed itself again.

The Big Guns

During the later half of the 1950s and early 1960s you could have been "In the army now" right here in Vandergrift. Our town was the home of C Battery, 166th Anti-Aircraft Artillery Battalion of the U.S. Army Reserves from January 1955 till June 1959. The unit was commanded by Lieutenant John Stimer of Leechburg, and the Executive Officer was William Bell of Vandergrift. The First Sergeant of the unit was Master Sergeant Kenneth Stull, who had been a defender of Corregidor in the Philippine Islands during World War II.

When first organized, the unit met on the third floor of the Veterans of Foreign Wars Building. In 1957, they moved to 207 Walnut Street (which later became the *Vandergrift News* office and subsequently burned down.) In this new location, they could be issued their primary weapons; a full tracked twin 40mm anti-aircraft gun and a half-tracked quad 50-caliber machine gun.

During the summers of 1956 through 1958, the unit attended summer camp at Fort Miles, Delaware, where it had firing practice and other military training.

In 1959, the 166th AAA Battalion was converted to the 5th Battalion, 43rd Field Artillery, a 155mm towed-howitzer unit. The Vandergrift unit turned in its anti-aircraft weapons and became the service battery of the new field artillery unit. During the next three years, the unit had its summer training at Camp Perry, Ohio, Indiantown Gap, PA and at Camp Pickett, Virginia. The headquarters of the battalion was in New Kensington, with firing batteries at Erie, Meadville, and Franklin, PA. Vandergrift's Service Battery was comprised of 150 men, 95% of which were residents of the Kiski Valley.

On August 15, 1961, the battalion was alerted for active duty as the Cold War heated up with the Berlin Crisis. The battalion was ordered to Fort Sill, Oklahoma. On September 15, the unit's 100 vehicle convey of trucks, 155mm howitzers and other military equipment made the long trip to Oklahoma. Captain Bill Bell was responsible for planning the route, coordinating all the stops, and general trip logistics.

The unit remained at Fort Sill till August 1962, when it returned to its home station. Subsequently, the Service Battery was reassigned to the New Kensington Reserve Center and the Vandergrift center was closed.

The twin 40mm and quad 50-caliber weapons made several appearances in Vandergrift parades to the delight of observers and to the chagrin of the street commissioner as the vehicles' tracks did some damage to streets and curbs.

Reflections Of The Times

Stories of the Day

Louis Hutcherson
Pennsylvania State Police Trooper

(Note: Louis Hutcherson is one of many Vandergrift African Americans who have gone on to successful careers. Most of the material in this section is in response to a series of questions asked of Trooper Hutcherson in an effort to capture or illustrate what it was like to be of a minority race in Vandergrift and in his career.)

Louis Hutcherson was born on May 19, 1940, at Pine Run in Allegheny Township. His father was Hubert Hutcherson; his mother was Josephine (Josie) Johnson Hutcherson. Hubert Hutcherson was born in Macon, Georgia, and lived in Alabama before moving to Pennsylvania. The family moved to Vandergrift from New Kensington in 1945, when Louis's father found work in the mill.

Louis grew up in Vandergrift and attended Vandergrift public schools. He graduated from Vandergrift High School in 1959 and attended Clarion University, but departed before graduating in need of work to support his wife and first child.

During his early years (1940s-1950s), opportunities in America for minorities, specifically for the African American minority were very limited. But growing up in Vandergrift, Louis was unaware of any limitations. His father, like the fathers of his African American friends, worked in the mines, steel mills, or foundries alongside other races who lived in town. There seemed to be no minority question to him as a youngster. It was not until later that he took note that there were no blacks working in any of Vandergrift's stores, banks, or other businesses; no black school teachers, firemen, or policemen.

Lou's father tried in subtle ways to prepare him for the cultural shock he would encounter as he grew older. His father counseled that being black, he had two strikes against him right off, and to be a success he would have to be better than the best—not equal to the best—but better than the best. In many ways his father instilled in him a desire to strive for perfection. "If you are going to do a job, do it right. There is a right way and a wrong way—no in-between." His father never discouraged him from trying even the things that seemed impossible, advising him that, "Nothing in life beats a failure but a try."

In his mid-teens, Lou observed a state policeman who was investigating an automobile accident in North Vandergrift. He was impressed with the officer and set his heart on becoming a state policeman. Years later, when the economics of his life forced him from college, he thought the dream had died.

But while working in a retail business in Brooklyn, his father sent a newspaper clipping reporting that the Pennsylvania State Police were seeking candidates. The clipping indicated that interested persons could be married and only needed to have graduated from high school. Lou resigned from his New York job and moved back to Vandergrift. He then applied for and was accepted to the Pennsylvania State Police Academy. Little did Lou realize that he was the first African American selected for the State Police in Western Pennsylvania and only the fourth in the state.

At the State Police Academy in Hershey, PA, Lou found himself to be the only African American in a class of over 100. At the Academy, he was treated like everyone else—equally bad, as the training was just like military boot camp. Upon graduating from the academy, he was assigned to the State Police barracks in Washington, PA. As the only black officer operating in Western Pennsylvania, he was surprised to find himself a celebrity.

When he stopped in the Hill District of Pittsburgh, he would draw a crowd because he was the first black state policeman they had ever seen. His presence in the State Police uniform and cruiser was truly unique to the region. Once on patrol near the Pittsburgh Airport, he passed a jitney with a black driver and passenger. The driver looked over at him, took a doubletake, and immediately ran off the road hitting a light pole. When asked what happened, the motorist declared that he just could not believe that he had seen a black state policeman.

Although Hutcherson never encountered any hostility from the public to his being an African American in the State Police, there were some unpleasant memories about his relations with the other troopers. At first, when he would enter a room, they would all stop talking, and some would get up and leave. Some told him directly that they were prejudiced; they had been raised that way and had no intention of changing. Lou just rode it out, relying on the self-confidence that assured him that he was just as good an officer as any of his detractors. This attitude along with his performance of duty has stood him in good stead during his 31 years in the Pennsylvania State Police.

Louis Hutcherson stands out as another example for African American youngsters to look up to. In his career as a state trooper, he advanced through the ranks to the rank of Lieutenant and is now the Station Commander in Indiana, PA. He hopes to be promoted to Captain in the near future. He and his wife Nancy have raised and educated 5 successful children in Vandergrift.

State Representative Joseph Preston, Jr.

Another African American from Vandergrift who met with success in life was Joseph Preston, Jr. Joe Preston lived in Vandergrift for the first 7 years of his life and probably never dreamed that he would one day become an example to young people today of what can be achieved, in spite of life's difficulties. Yet, in his 6 consecutive terms as State Representative, he has proven to be an excellent role model for youth in Vandergrift.

Preston was born in Vandergrift in 1947. His formative years were spent in the 18th St. neighborhood. Representative Preston remembers one of the favorite things he liked about elementary school here was the 2-hour lunches. Students were given a couple of hours to go home and eat between classes.

His dad, Smoky Joe Preston, who was a minor league baseball player in town, moved his family to Pittsburgh in 1954 as baseball took him to other teams. Later he would play for a AA farm club in Virginia, but turned down an opportunity to play for the Yankees, because of the combination of his age and the low pay offered to him.

He saw his son graduate from the University of Pittsburgh with a degree in Political Science and Psychology. And in 1982, Joseph Preston, Jr., became State Representative for the 24th District in Pittsburgh.

In the State House, Preston has served on numerous committees, including the Appropriations and the Business and Economic Development Committees. He has been equally active in the community as a member of the Elks Lodge, school advisory boards, the Urban League, the East Liberty Chamber of Commerce, and other civic organizations. He is currently chair of the Pittsburgh Water and Sewer Authority, as well as having been an active member of Baptist Temple Church for more than 35 years, where he is on the Board of Trustees.

He has fond memories of the days he spent in Vandergrift, and still comes into town often. Of particular enjoyment to him are the early mornings when he slips into Vandergrift and takes walks around town. According to Representative Preston, he is able to talk to his Creator and enjoy the quietness and beauty of the town. He reflects that these times serve as a time of rest and relaxation from the pressures of being a legislator.

Richard J. Hunger
A Man Of Action

Richard (Dick) Hunger was born on February 12, 1921, to Samuel and Alice Hunger. Sam Hunger was a virtual legend in his own time for his service to Vandergrift. He is remembered fondly in every quarter. Dick's grandfather, George A. Hunger, was one of Vandergrift's pioneers who operated a lumber yard and was responsible for many of the first buildings in town; he served as burgess of Vandergrift.

When recalling his early years, Hunger's stories reflect the classic picture of life in Vandergrift in the 1920s and during the Depression years. As a boy, he sold the *Vandergrift News* on the street for 2 cents a paper. He picked elderberries along the railroad tracks and sold them door to door. He recalled the old businesses on Grant Avenue and how proud he was when he was able to buy his first pair of boots, which came with a knife in a pocket on the side.

"A happy valley," was his description of early Vandergrift. The high schools in the local towns competed against one another in all sports. Church, social club, and independent baseball teams kept an active schedule in the valley. Hunger was the equipment boy for Vandergrift's independent team and later became their scorekeeper. He recalled night baseball before the lights were installed on Davis Field. The independent team would rent lights that would be set up on the field.

Hunger's teen years came during the Depression which were bad times for the town. The economy in town was pretty much collapsed from 1933 until WWII started. The mill was down, while some work was still being done in the foundry. During the Depression, his father was voted out of office, and until he was hired as Vandergrift's Street Commissioner, other members of the family, especially some uncles, helped the family through the crisis. Christmases during this time, as Dick recalled, were very slim, but also some of the best and most enjoyable.

As a junior in high school in 1938, he was able to restart a defunct local church basketball league and make it pay.

While in high school, Hunger wrote for the *Hi-Newsette*, the school newspaper. When George Spiher became editor of the *Vandergrift News*, he convinced publisher Herbert Brauff to hire Dick to write the *News'* sport column. He did this after school and on weekends for 5 cents an inch. This was not much pay as it took 40-50 words to make one inch of newsprint. He tried to write enough to fill the whole sports page to make money. He continued as a sports journalist until World War Two.

Hunger graduated from Vandergrift High School in 1939 and went to work in the mill. As most young men in his day he expected this to be his life's career. When WWII called him away for service, everything changed. He served in the Army attaining the rank of staff sergeant. When he returned home from the war, he went down to the mill to get his job back and found the workers were on strike. He told the picketers that he had just come home from the service, and that his wife, who had been a Red Cross worker in a hospital in Boston, was pregnant, and he really needed the work. The picketers amazingly let him pass through. But his time at the mill was coming to a close; he saw opportunities elsewhere and eventually moved on.

In the years after WWII, he founded an American Legion Basketball League that played in high schools in town and around the area. In 1947, he arranged for the Harlem Globe Trotters to appear in the high school gymnasium. The Globe Trotters arrived in a school bus to a packed gym.

The Mayor

In 1955, Dick Hunger ran for and won a seat on the town council, a seat he held for 9 years till he was elected mayor. The office of mayor was very close to being a volunteer position. When Hunger became mayor in 1961 the monthly pay was only $100, requiring him to maintain his regular job as an insurance salesman.

Hunger entered into his new office with the objective of improving Vandergrift, especially in areas that would affect children. He had many great and happy experiences growing up here, and it was his goal to recreate some of those great times for the children then living in town and for those in the future. Improving the parking problems in the business district and providing adequate play areas for the children were 2 of his goals.

During the 1960s, the federal government was offering new programs and grants such as the Urban Renewal Program. This program was designed to aid decaying communities. The money was there, but for a small community such as Vandergrift, it was not easily obtainable. Great vision, leadership and determination were required if the town was to benefit. Hunger proved himself more than capable. Cutting through a tangle of bureaucratic red tape, he traveled to Washington, Philadelphia, Harrisburg, and Greensburg to meet with officials who controlled the various programs' funds. In the end, his determination brought about a miniature renaissance in Vandergrift.

During his years as mayor, Hunger saw the construction of McMurtry Towers, a 100-unit highrise building, the Route 56 Bypass, Kennedy Memorial Park, the Vandergrift Pool and Park, the Columbia Avenue Parking Lot, a town library expansion, increases in state-provided maintenance funds, and a variety of new community-oriented activities.

Upon completion of his mayoral services to the community of Vandergrift, Richard Hunger went on to serve the surrounding county as the Executive Director of Emergency Management (911, HazMat teams, and Dive teams) for Westmoreland County, and as the county's Federal and State Grants Coordinator.

Kennedy Memorial Park

There was once a valley running north and south through Vandergrift adjacent to what is now Jackson Avenue. The property was owned by the Vandergrift mill and was used as a waste site for the disposal of ash and slag. Once filled it was leveled and donated to the town for development and use as a park. The area became Davis Field, a set of tennis courts and a playground.

A remaining portion of this donated land was left undeveloped. For a time it had been planted with wheat and became affectionately known as the "Wheat Field." Youngsters played ball on makeshift ballfields, and bonfires for high school pep rallies took place there. It was also used as the high school football team's practice field at times, as well as the site of carnivals and circus performances. Not much thought

Courtesy of Anthony Ferrante

Aerial View of Kennedy Park and Davis Field—the Old Grove has Changed

was given to further development of the area, and it was often badly neglected. By the early 1960s, many referred to the Wheat Field as the "Dust Bowl."

A dramatic event in 1963, the assassination of President John F. Kennedy, caused the character of the Wheat Field to take a new direction. At the next Vandergrift Council meeting it was agreed to name the park Kennedy Memorial Park in tribute to the fallen president. A council member pointed out that the park was in such bad condition it could hardly be considered a tribute to anyone. Under the leadership of Mayor Richard Hunger, it was resolved to make the park into a showplace of the town.

Over the next few years, lighted basketball courts, softball fields, and a first-class Little League field were added to the area. A gazebo modeled after the one on the Diamond in Ligonier, PA, was built for band concerts and other presentations, and the tennis courts were refurbished.

It was decided to use gas lights to light the area. With the help of Paul Gossert, from People's Natural Gas Company, 47 early "Westmoreland" style lamps were selected.

2 special gas lamps were mounted in front of the gazebo—these gave the impression of a tiara and were mounted on 2 very old, historic poles. The 2 poles were found in a museum in Baltimore, Maryland. They had stood on the streets of Baltimore when George Washington passed through with the Continental Army.

Thanks to those with vision, Vandergrift now has one of Pennsylvania's largest parks dedicated to play areas with the combined Kennedy Memorial Park and Davis Field Areas. Thousands and thousands of people have enjoyed the fruits of their effort.

Photo By Mitch Fryer, Courtesy of Buttermilk Falls Publishing Company

Football Workouts in Kennedy Park are Hard Work—Right, Boys?
The Park Today is used for Football, Baseball, Basketball, Other Sports, and Various Community Events

Dorothy Amundson Lear
A Lady Of Vision

Vandergrift has been truly blessed with a distinct history marked by the lives of many unique individuals. One of these unique persons, Dorothy Amundson Lear claimed no high titles during her lifetime in Vandergrift, even though she touched the lives of everyone around her.

She was a wife, mother, homemaker, hostess, secretary, teacher, author, poet, playwright, stage director, musician, artist, neighborhood leader, political leader, Girl Scout leader, Woman's Club president, jury commissioner, school board member, chairman of the board, church youth leader, church pianist, parade organizer, Demolay Mother, Rainbow Girl's Mother Advisor, fund raiser, and in every effort, a friend to all who knew her. Although no monument can be found in town to honor her achievements, she lives in the hearts of all who knew her. She is variously described as a "A Visionary," "Miss Mission Impossible," "The Great Motivator," and "A Great Lady."

Dorothy Gislhaine Hanna Amundson Lear was born in Punxsutawney to Olie C. and Gislhaine Amundson on July 31, 1914. Her father had immigrated from Norway, her mother was of Belgium descent. She was educated in Punxsutawney's public schools and attended Indiana Normal School (now Indiana University of Pennsylvania) for 2 years, majoring in art.

While visiting in Vandergrift with a school friend in 1936, she met Benjamin Franklin Lear. After a 3-year courtship, they were married in Maryland on August 9, 1939. The newly married couple moved into the family home at 185 Grant Avenue where Dr. Lear began his medical practice in partnership with his father, Dr. Isaac Newton Lear. Because Dr. Lear's office was in a part of their home, Dorothy served his medical practice in various capacities including secretary, accountant, surgical nurse, and clean-up person. All who knew her are quick to point out that the most important thing in Dorothy's life was her husband, who she affectionately referred to as Benjie.

Creative Genius

Dorothy's unique plans for theme birthday parties, holiday events, and entertainment are a legend to the many people involved in the lives of the Lear family. The Lear's home and basement were regularly transformed into some exotic, far-away place like Hawaii, a pirate's cove, or the Wild West, and many youngsters had their first and maybe last experience with the foods, music, and customs of these places at the Lear's birthday parties.

Well-remembered events were the block parties held in the alley behind the Lear home—run mostly by and for the neighborhood children—which brought all the neighbors together in a common effort. Christmas decorations were another neighborhood event. Everyone still talks about the beautiful snowy Christmas eve when all the homes for blocks around the Lear home were lighted with luminaries in a project organized and carried out by Dorothy and her sons with all the neighbor's cooperation.

The neighborhood children's favorite, found in front of the Lear home, was the life-sized Santa looking over a long list of the "good children" which contained the names of the neighborhood children, while Mrs. Claus sat in a rocking chair sewing a doll's dress. All the children would come to see if their names were on the list. April Fool's Day brought many trials to Dorothy's family and friends with tricks like lady locks filled with shaving cream or cookies made with pepper.

This same type of vision, planning, organizing, and getting the willing cooperation of others was carried over into her public activities as well. While president of the Women's Club from 1949 to 1951, Dorothy Lear planned fairs and fashion shows yet to be rivaled. On one occasion a fair included a number of live animals in the high school gym. At the height of the big snow in 1950, Dorothy and some friends had to make their way through deep snow to the school to see that the animals were fed.

Care for her children led Dorothy into many activities. In 1951, she wrote and directed a program for all the young talent in town which resulted in a production in the Casino Theater called "I Hear America Singing."

In 1956, she was the prime mover in organizing the local Rainbow for Girls and became its first Mother Advisor and helped shepherd it to drill team and choir championships. She served as an assistant Girl Scout leader at the Methodist Church. When her sons entered Demolay, she became a Demolay Mother. She served as a Sunday School teacher, department superintendent, and youth leader at the Methodist Church. In every case, she brought her special vision and talent to her tasks.

As an author, she wrote a book about her family entitled *Whadaya Hear From the Mob?* She researched the material and wrote the scripts for and directed 9 Christmas Madrigal dinners, which became the centerpiece of Vandergrift's holiday celebration from 1984 to 1993. Many people felt that their Christmas season started with the Madrigal performance. She scripted 2 musical productions called, "Fun Looking Back," and wrote the material for "This is Your Life" productions for Mayor Richard Hunger and Bill Bell. Along with her friends and students in ceramics, she produced 2 cookbooks that were sold to benefit the Children's Clinic of the Kiski Valley.

Civic Leadership

One of Mrs. Lear's great passions was the Children's Clinic of the Kiski Valley. By her interest and effort, she was instrumental in supporting the facility for treating brain-damaged children in Avonmore. Dorothy served, at various times, on the board of directors and as the chairman of the board. She was involved in having Dr. Doman, a famous Philadelphia physician, come to the Children's Clinic on a regular basis. He had developed a method of patterning arm and leg movements of children to improve their mental condition.

Dorothy Lear was the first woman to be elected to the local school board. In the late 1950s she worked hard to improve Vandergrift's education system and facilities. She was one of the architects and leaders in the creation of the jointure that resulted in the Kiski Area School District and the building of the new high school in Allegheny Township.

In 1967, Mrs. Lear was appointed to fill the position of Jury Commissioner for Westmoreland County. She believed in being active in the political process as she served as Vandergrift's Republican Party Chairman for a time. Dorothy Lear served on various boards and committee to include Westmoreland County Woman's Club, American Cancer Society, Salvation Army, Eidemiller Award Committee, Children's Clinic of the Kiski Valley, Kiski Valley Home Nurses, and the American Red Cross.

The Testimony of Her Life

On October 22, 1977, a suprise testimonial dinner was presented in Vandergrift for Dorothy and Dr. Lear. State Representative Joe Petrarca had the day declared "Dorothy Lear Day." The dinner was held at the Sons of Italy Hall. After a wonderful meal, the master of ceremonies, Richard Macino, *Pittsburgh Press* Public Service Director began a "This is Your Life, Dorothy Lear" program to the delight of all present and to the surprise of Dorothy.

No task was too daunting for Dorothy Amundson Lear. Her special talent was being able to see great possibilities in everything and everyone, then to work to overcome any and all obstacles to see her visions become reality. Once envisioned, she had the great ability to get others to see and work toward seemingly impossible goals. She was a true visionary.

Dorothy Lear left this life on July 9, 1994, after a courageous battle against cancer. Gone, but not forgotten.

Joseph Americo Petrarca
A Bulldog in the House

A bulldog generally brings to mind the picture of a medium-sized canine with huge jaws clamped tightly on the end of a bone, fiercely straining to yank it out of the grasp of whatever was holding the other end. In the hundred-year history of Vandergrift, many such men and women have been the town's "bulldogs." Of such mettle was Joseph A. Petrarca.

Hard times are never fun, yet they often become the very forces that make us who we are. For Joe Petrarca, those days of trouble began even before he was born. His papa, Ercole Petrarca, was a copper miner in Salt Lake City, Utah, struggling in the midst of difficult times to make enough money to support his family back in Italy. One day, he hoped to have enough to bring his wife and children across the Atlantic to be with him.

While in Utah a relative from Pennsylvania sent Ercole a pamphlet that told of a grand place called "Vandergrift" near Pittsburgh. It described the America that so many immigrants crossed the sea for. Vandergrift was a city that had work, and plenty of it. And, there were homes—workers could actually own their own homes! On top of that, it was a relatively new town and was still being settled. It didn't take him long to make his decision and make his move.

The first thing Ercole did after moving here was bring his wife and child over from Italy. When Marie Petrarca arrived here with her daughter in March 1928, they found that Vandergrift was a nice place to settle. Many other Italian families had made their home there, and most had bought houses in 2 sections of town known as Vandergrift Heights and the Park Plan.

It was 9 months later on December 20 in a small 2-bedroom house on Longfellow Street that Marie Petrarca give birth to her first and only son, Joseph Americo.

Joe grew up in Vandergrift, and like other young men, at the age of 20, began a career at the Vandergrift foundry that would span 25 years. One year later, Joe had his first experience with politics when he went to the town Council to try to get the Wheat Field grass cut. The Wheat Field was an open unkept field where local children played sandlot ball. The field was constantly in a state of neglect, prompting young Joe Petrarca to appear before council. But much to his chagrin, Council could or would do nothing. It was right then that a spark was ignited. Joe decided to run for Vandergrift Council and change things.

Joe got his wish when a series of opportunities landed him on the Council. One of the first things he did was to have the grass cut at the Wheat Field. During his 12-year stint on Council, he served on the Street Commission, the Budget Committee and the Library Committee where he brought about the expansion of the town's library.

By the early 1960s, Petrarca began to learn the ins and outs of politics and was a major force in the local Democratic Party. Soon his tenacity and determination, first seen by the cutting of the Wheat Field grass, would be moved to even greater political arenas.

In 1972, Joseph Petrarca was elected to the State House of Representatives. He had served on town council 3 terms (12 years) and never forgot the things he had learned there. Even the political skirmishes he had engaged in taught him to fight and prepared him for standing up for the people in his district. They also taught him that "compromise is the name of the game" when it came to getting things done.

Governor, Let Me Tell You Something...

Representative Joe Petrarca had been a legislator in Harrisburg for 55 minutes when he got a call about the State Police barracks in Washington Township. According to Petrarca, World War Three was about to erupt back home over attempts to move the barracks out of Washington Township. Without the State

Police presence in the area, the several surrounding rural districts would have little or no police protection. Petrarca didn't wait around for things to work themselves out. He got an audience with Governor Shapp and spoke with him about the situation. "Spoke" may be too mild a word; at one point, Petrarca became so animated and passionate that he pounded on the governor's desk and said something to the effect of "Governor, let me tell you something...." Not only did the barracks stay put, but Petrarca walked away having given the governor an invitation to come speak in Vandergrift at a Fourth of July celebration. When the governor came to speak, he retold the story of Petrarca banging on his desk, even though he was just a freshman representative.

The desk-pounding episode was the first of many passionate fights for the people in his district. He soon earned a reputation for being a bulldog. People called him a bulldog because he held on and wouldn't let go. Others referred to him as "Tiger Joe" or a "pit bull" because once he sank his teeth into something, he would keep after it until it got done. And a lot of his bulldog inclinations came back to one basic consideration: the people of his town and his district. He said that was why he ran for State Representative in the first place: people told him "Joe, we need you", and he wanted to do something for the town.

From 1972 to 1994, Joe Petrarca introduced more than 500 pieces of legislation, in addition to spearheading 2 changes in the Pennsylvania Constitution. But the legislative actions he remembers the most are those that helped those people who elected him.

On March 13, 1995, Joseph Americo Petrarca died only weeks after witnessing his son, Joe, take his place in office. The family lost a father, a husband, and a brother, and Vandergrift lost a dear friend. But this is one bulldog who will not be forgotten.

Before his retirement, Petrarca had pushed for a organ donor bill, Act 102, that would provide funding for organ donor awareness. On the night of his farewell speech from the floor of the House, Petrarca received word that the bill had passed the Pennsylvania Senate and was on the way to the governor's office for signing. Pennsylvania became one of the first states with such an act and is soon slated to showcase the program to the nation as an example. A lasting tribute to one of Vandergrift's finest.

Dr. Eugene Losasso
They Called Him 'Doc''

Dr. Eugene Losasso, known affectionately as "Doc," was a colorful man who believed in his convictions and pursued them. He was not afraid to stand up for what he believed, even if he stood alone. He had a military demeanor that earned him respect by his very presence. He walked in a stately manner and with purpose.

Doing service for others was a way of life for him, and during the Depression, he frequently refused to accept money for his services. He told his patients to keep their money, they needed it more than he did.

Born in Vandergrift on January 30, 1902, to Theodora and Frank Losasso. He was one of 9 children. In 1922 he graduated from Vandergrift High School and went on to earn his Bachelor of Science degree from the University of Pittsburgh in 1926 and his Doctor of Medicine degree in 1929.

During all his years at the University of Pittsburgh, he enrolled in the R.O.T.C. and was commissioned First Lieutenant in 1929, remaining an active reservist for the next 10 years. After an internship and residency at South Side Hospital, Pittsburgh, he returned to Vandergrift to begin a general medical practice.

It was during this time, on September 11, 1935, that he married Lottie Suzanna Shaffer.

Three days after Pearl Harbor, he volunteered in the Armed Services. He reported on October 12, 1942, and spent 4 years on active duty in the Pacific. He earned the rank of

Captain, attended Officers' Training School at Carlisle, PA; Flight Surgeons' School at San Antonio, Texas; and Air Evacuation School at Bowman Air Force Base at Louisville, Kentucky, where he was appointed commander of the 812th Aeromedical Air Evacuation Squadron. He established and supervised all air evacuation of injured persons from the Pacific Islands to Honolulu and San Francisco. In 1945 he was appointed Base Surgeon and Commander of General Hospital, Hickam Field, Honolulu, and promoted to Lt. Colonel. Dr. Losasso and his command was recognized by Franklin D. Roosevelt for their efforts.

Upon his return from the war, Dr. Losasso completed ophthalmological postgraduate studies in Pittsburgh and New York and opened an ophthalmology practice in Vandergrift.

When the Korean conflict broke out Dr. Losasso once again volunteered his services, this time as Surgeon of the 136th Fighter Bomber Wing; Commanding Officer of the medical group charged with operating an emergency field hospital. He returned from Korea as a full Colonel, his rank when he retired on his 60th birthday, January 30, 1962. During his long military career he was awarded the Legion of Merit, Bronze Star Medal, Commendation Ribbon, 8 campaign medals, and 4 battle stars.

Dr. Losasso returned to his opthalmology practice in 1952, and while remaining active in the reserves, turned his energies to civic efforts. He was president of the Kiski Area School Board when the jointure with the old Vandergrift and Bell Avon districts led to building the new high school. He headed the Highway Committee that brought $40 million worth of highways to this area and played a role in getting the Route 56 Vandergrift Bypass. One of his great undertakings was the Children's Clinic of the Kiski Valley in Avonmore for brain-damaged children. He served as Medical Director of this Clinic for several years.

Dr. Lossaso died on May 18, 1987. The parklette near the Vandergrift bridge, which he established and maintained, now bears a small sign in his honor, placed there by the American Red Cross.

Vandergrift Telephone Company

Alexander Graham Bell's invention of the telephone started a revolution in communications that continues today, linking communities like Vandergrift to cities everywhere in the world. For Vandergrift, the link was formed when their telephone company was chartered in September of 1895. At that time it included the telegraph company, which was dissolved in January of 1924. The Vandergrift Land Improvement Co. financed the town's utilities, but it is unclear if the telephone company was one of those financed.

The Vandergrift Telephone Company grew steadily. New subscribers included John F. Horne, whose phone was installed in his home in April, 1901. He was the president of the Telephone Company.

John Horne's telephone number was 137. Most numbers had 3 or 4 digits, some ending with A-J-L or R to signify different lines. To place a call, you picked up the receiver and listened to make sure no one else was using the line, then waited for the operator to ask "number, please." Party lines were common. These were lines shared by 3 or 4 residences. Each telephone rang a specific number of times to signal whose home was being called. A short, partial ring was heard when another party's phone was "ringing in." Some folks quietly picked up the receiver to eavesdrop on their neighbor's conversations, although most would not admit it. There were no dial tones and no busy signals. The telephone operator told you if the line was in use.

Courtesy of H. Reynolds Clawson, III
John F. Horne

In 1943, over 100 operators served Vandergrift, Avonmore, and Saltsburg, with 2 women working the night shift. Wages were about $.32 per hour. A watchman from the Vandergrift Foundry called in once each hour, apparently to relate that everything was all right. Like today, holidays were busy, especially Christmas Day and Mother's Day. On D-Day in 1944, lines were jammed and calls couldn't go through. Sharing information helped soothe anxiety about loved ones in the Armed Forces, and was much faster than a letter.

The Con-Survey City Directory, published in conjunction

with the *Vandergrift News* in 1947, listed subscribers to the telephone company as follows: the resident's name; the wife's name in parentheses; number of dependents under 18 years of age; and whether the home was owned or rented. This was followed by the resident's occupation, place of employment, home address and accessible telephone number. The directory also listed householders and residents on each rural route leading out of the city. Possibly incurring the wrath of the feminists of the day, the directory also stated that *married women engaged in some responsible occupation are listed individually, in addition to their regular listing with the husband.*

For Example:

France, Leota /e. (Mrs. G.W.) 1st V-Pres. American Legion Aux. Post, No. 114 r R.D.1 (tel. no.) 144L

General Telephone Company took over from Vandergrift Telephone around 1956. At that time, GTE had nearly 168 employees, including part-time and holiday workers. Lorraine Poleski started working at GTE in 1957 and was trained on the job, earning about $.75 an hour. She sometimes worked a split-shift of 10 AM to 2 PM and 6 PM to 10 PM. When number 920 lit up on Lorraine's switchboard, it was given first priority, as someone was in need of police assistance. Switchboard operators also dispatched fire and ambulance calls. On holidays, boxes of candy and fruit were sent to the operators by local merchants in appreciation of a job well done. Lorraine recently donated her operators "headset" to the Vandergrift Historical Society for display in their forthcoming museum.

When she began at GTE, calls between Vandergrift and Leechburg or Vandergrift and Apollo were automatically cut off after 5 minutes; to continue a conversation the customer had to call back. Few private lines were available, and were limited to those whose ill health required this service or to certain businesses. Toll calls went into Pittsburgh via Bell Telephone lines.

Technological changes were incorporated by GTE in 1961-62 with the erection of a new building and installation of a direct-dialing system. GTE hired some 65 people from other telephone companies on a temporary basis to help update its system. One of these companies was Telephone Electronics Inc. from Erie, PA who sent employees to help with the conversion.

Working in various capacities, the men stayed from one week to several months, most of them boarding at the Penn Grant Hotel at $2 per night, or at the Golden Lounge, Riverview. Their average expense account was $28 for room and board, and arrangements were made with Speer's Restaurant in Vandergrift for packed lunches to take with them on the road.

Installation of new telephone lines and poles was an enormous endeavor and included the communities of Oklahoma, Salina, Washington Twp., Avonmore, and Saltsburg. Other technicians worked on installing the modern dialing equipment in the telephone office building. Employment at the telephone company dropped to 62 persons when these changes were implemented.

More improvements were made in 1988 when the manual office was replaced with digital switching equipment, thus eliminating the need for telephone operators whose last day of work in this office was October 29, 1988. The room that once held switchboards would now contain automatic equipment. This allowed for custom calling, less maintenance and more reliable service.

Stanley Peppler, one of the company's 13 Vandergrift employees, started working for GTE in 1962, when the new building was constructed. His job as a switchman paid $1.57 per hour. Today, he is a communications technician and sits before a console in the room that once held switchboards and operators. He monitors the console, taking calls that come in, to keep phone service operating smoothly.

For today's business consumers, conference calls and cell phones have made it possible to speak with almost anyone anywhere. And today in Vandergrift it is possible to access other computers around the world with a local phone call to the Internet—a far cry from the party lines and the telephone operator's friendly "number please" of the early Vandergrift telephone system.

Courtesy of Phinearea Sidizen

Telephone Operators Helen McGaughey, Helen Hyde, Betty Bailey, Peg Zozola

West Vandergrift

We can not leave this era without relating the history of West Vandergrift because it was in this period of time that West Vandergrift became part of the borough.

In the 1920s, if you had gone out Holland Street to the Serpentine Road, and turned right at the top of "Slaughter House Hill," you would have found yourself in "Rabbit Hill." Following the road through "Rabbit Hill," out past the "Indian Diamonds," you would have eventually come to "Little Canada." Know where you are? It will be revealed in due course.

To tell this story from the beginning, we must go back to the late 1700s where we find some of the town's earliest history.

Hugh Owens, immigrated to America in 1797 from Holyrood, Caernarivonshire, Wales, with his wife Mary. After living in Philadelphia for one year, the family came to Allegheny Township in 1799, where they purchased 400 acres of land in the area of present-day West Vandergrift. They lived in a log cabin until a 2-story log house was completed in 1802. This loghouse is still standing and used as a residence at 204 California Avenue (formerly called Log Cabin Road). Members of the Owens family lived at this location till about 1916, when the house and land were sold to Edward H. Welsh, owner and publisher of the *Vandergrift Citizen*. The cabin was occupied by John Garrett, Vandergrift dentist, and son-in-law of Welsh, and stayed in the Garrett family until 1994 when it was sold.

Mr. Welsh undertook the development of the area during the latter part of the 1920s. He laid out streets and installed a water system from local springs. From this beginning, grew present-day West Vandergrift.

A Town of its Own?

The town experienced most of its growth in the late 1920s and the 1930s. Information from early residents indicate that like the Vandergrift Heights, West Vandergrift was no paradise compared to Vandergrift. The first streets were unpaved. Residents remember having to mow the grass growing in the streets (described by one as just 2 muddy ruts), and of hauling shale in an effort to relieve the muddy conditions. Sewage ran through open ditches to be discharged "over the hill" at the lower end of the development. Mr. Welsh had promised that when enough homes had been built, he would have sewers installed. Before this was done however, Welsh had disposed of all the property and had no further legal interest in it. When reminded of his promise, Welsh offered to buy the sewer pipe if the residents would install it. The offer was accepted, and sewers were laid where open drainage existed

The town never had what could be called a business district. The Micheletto's operated a small grocery store which was sold to the Hepler family. It was a general store-type of facility carrying a little bit of everything and providing a much-needed service to the area. This store was in the path of the new Route 56 bypass and was demolished.

The building now occupied by the YMCA was once known as the Belle View School. It was built in 1936 by the Freilino brothers. It served as the elementary school for West Vandergrift, replacing a school of wood construction on the southwest corner of the Serpentine Road and Community Park Road. Early residents referred to it as the "Country School."

The only industry in the town was a mushroom "factory," which was located in a large concrete block building across the road from the Belle View School. Mushrooms were grown for sale in the Pittsburgh Strip District and to the Heinz and Campbell Soup Companies. It was owned by the Zaccagnini family. This "factory" became unprofitable, went out of business, and was torn down. The only other business in the area were popular restaurants and bars, which are still in operation.

Little Canada, Rabbit Hill, and Parking at the Indian Diamonds

Santo and Pauline Carpentieri were early settlers in West Vandergrift, where they built their home in 1928. In 1929, they built a covered, open-sided dance pavilion on their property. It became a very popular attraction throughout the Kiski Valley. A dance band provided music and food and beverages were sold. It managed to operate despite the Sunday Blue Laws. It was a very popular place for the residents of the Valley. Because of its open operation on Sundays, it became known as "Little Canada." The Little Canada dance pavilion was where Carpentieri's Restaurant is now located.

The area was also called "Rabbit Hill" because of the large number of rabbits that made the area home and often provided food for families during the Great Depression. Across Route 56, the Ferrante home now occupies an area that was known as the "Indian Diamonds." It contained a ballfield where West Vandergrift and Vandergrift teams played baseball and softball. Grand beer parties were held after some of the games. It also became a popular area for the new pastime of parking, which was a development of the new automobile age.

Annexed!

West Vandergrift was part of Allegheny Township. As the area grew in population, the need for public services increased, and it seemed the township was unable or unwilling to provide the needed services. As late as the mid-1950s, the area still had dirt roads that were poorly maintained. In winter when it snowed, the roads were not plowed, and the area was virtually impassable. There were no fire hydrants, sewage, street lights, adequate police support, ash collection (most people heated with coal), or community garbage pick-up. Many people burned their garbage or just "threw it over the hill." The township made many promises to provide services, but no action ever seemed to be taken. As the dissatisfaction increased, John Corcetti chaired a citizen's committee, which met at Carpentieri's West Vandergrift Inn with the purpose of having West Vandergrift area annexed to Vandergrift. The committee was successful in getting 70% of the local homeowners to sign a petition to that end.

On April 8, 1957, the *Vandergrift News* had this announcement:

> *This date will go down in the history of Vandergrift as the date upon which a new era opened for the community. A delegation of citizens from Allegheny Township presented a petition requesting annexation of part of that township to include the hamlet of West Vandergrift. Vandergrift will finally break the old borough boundaries which were choking any possibility of expansion of the community.*

This area would increase the geographical size of Vandergrift by 50% and add 475 residents to its population, bringing the total to 10,056.

After winning a challenge to the annexation by the Allegheny Township supervisors, and other court actions, the annexation was approved by Judge Edward Bauer on August 20, 1957. The residents of West Vandergrift were jubilant. The new area, which would be part of the sixth ward, was officially welcomed into Vandergrift by Burgess Ralph McIntire on August 30 by an announcement made at the American Legion Street Fair.

Courtesy of Ron Ankeny and Allegheny Ludlum

Vandergrift Plant Silicon Expansion, Roller Hearth - furnace entry end

Chapter Twelve

The Dream Lives On

Alarming news from Viet Nam ushered out the 1960s. Demonstration marches and violent war protests were on the rise. Riots marked the murder of Martin Luther King. The 1970s rolled in with the country swimming in turmoil. Vandergrift, true to its previous history, remained very much insulated from the social temperament of the rest of the nation.

While the nation reeled under social change, Vandergrift residents were rejoicing over future prospects being proclaimed by the local steel mill. As it would turn out, the optimism would only serve to hide a 17-year storm building on the town's horizon.

In the late 1960s, U. S. Steel's Vandergrift plant added new facilities to increase production of steel for the electrical machinery and equipment industry. 3 new furnaces were added to anneal grain-oriented silicon steel used by the electric machine equipment industry. Also installed was a roller hearth heat-treating line for production of coils up to 48 inches wide; a side trim, slit, and recoil line; a shearing line; high-temperature box annealing furnaces and accompanying bases, and building extensions.

These improvements were notable as recorded in the *News-Citizen* May 14, 1968,

> *Improvements being made at the foundry will make it one of the most modern in the world, with a capacity of producing rolls up to 84 inches in diameter, weighing over 120 tons. Castings weighing 246 tons have been produced at the plant. The present 3-shift operation employs over 1000 workers.*

These were truly exciting events for a steel town that had suffered dramatic employment drops in recent years. It seemed high-technology improvements to the plants would surely bring steel work in the town back to the level of its glory years.

Unfortunately, no one could foresee the challenge looming over the western horizon. Japan was about to forever change the steel-making industry. As the mid-1970s approached, it became increasingly evident that the industry, locally and nationally, was in for its worst decline ever. The much heralded high tech improvements to the Vandergrift plant of the late 1960s and early 1970s would prove no challenge for the onslaught of cheaply produced foreign steel products.

TORNADO !!

June 4, 1980, began like any other hot summer day for the residents of Vandergrift. Thunderstorms were forecast for later, and the air was heavy with the promise of rain. People were going to lunch when the sky started to darken, and the light took on a greenish cast. An ominous rumble was heard in the distance. "Thunder," everyone said. But it wasn't.

At approximately 12:30 p.m. a tornado hit Vandergrift. It was an event so unexpected that some people thought the whirling cloud of debris was volcanic ash from the Mt. Saint Hèlen's eruption. Vandergrift had never had a tornado before. Tornadoes were something that happened in the Midwest, not Western Pennsylvania.

Several other areas in a 4-county region were also damaged by tornadoes. In view of the big picture, Vandergrift got by easily. Several townspeople were injured, some seriously, but no one was killed. 9 homes were destroyed, and more than a dozen declared unsafe for habitation. There was no power and telephone service for some time. Damage estimates were placed in the $1.5 million range.

As soon as word got out that the tornado had touched down in the Heights, volunteers started pouring in. Firemen and paramedics, nurses, and doctors, the Red Cross, the Salvation Army, PennDOT, the county, churches, neighbors, and family members all pitched in to help. Even the mill sent maintenance employees up to the Heights with large equipment including winches and a cherry picker to help clean up debris. Shelters were set up for those who had lost their homes. Medical personnel provided treatment for those who needed it. Crews started clearing the streets and reestablishing communications as soon as the storm had passed.

Townspeople pitched in to provide food and drinks for the work crews and neighbors who were in need. The disaster brought out the best in almost everyone.

Photos Courtesy of Harold Doutt

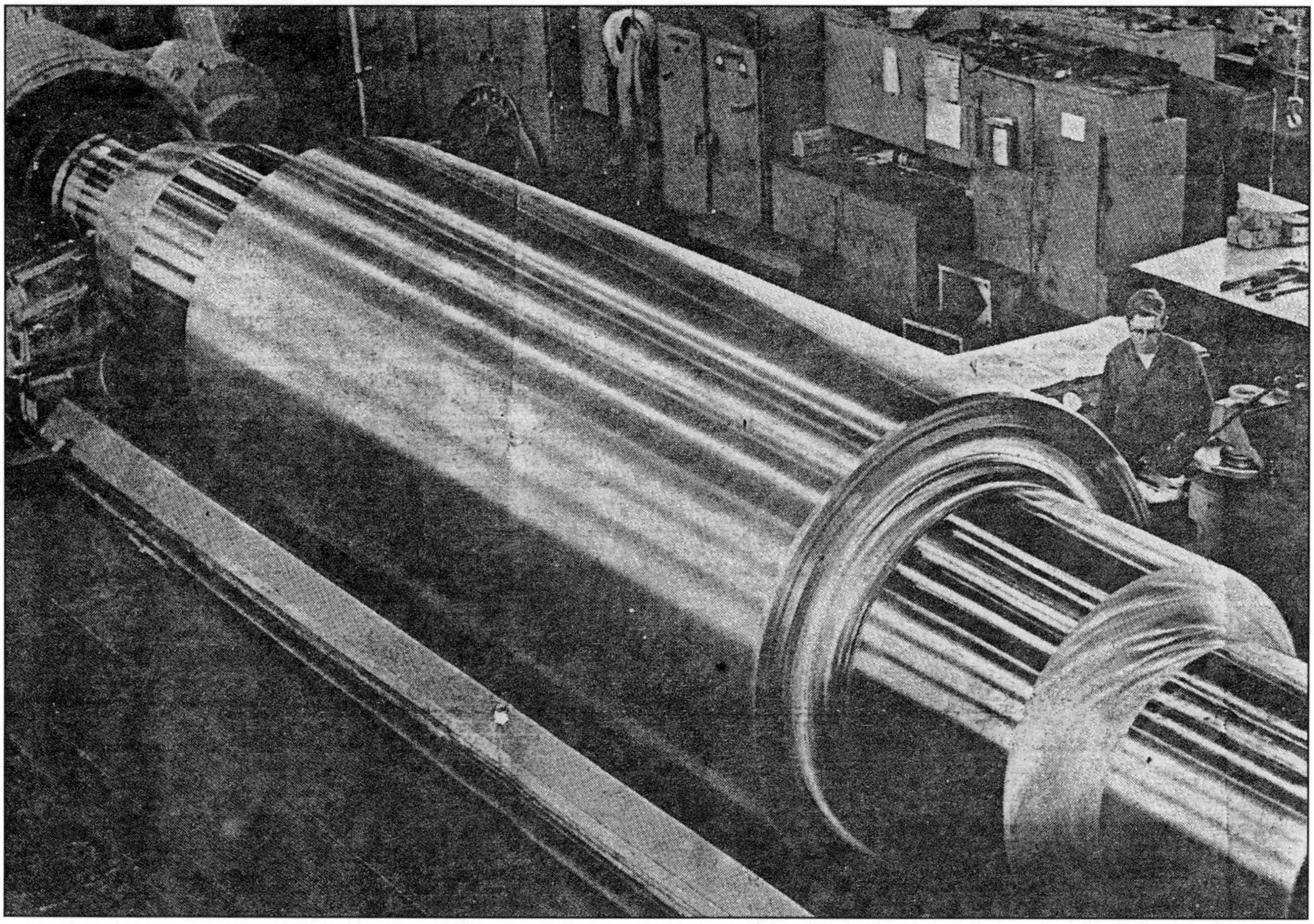

Courtesy of Kenneth Blose

Backup Roll Produced at the Foundry in Vandergrift for the World's Largest Aluminum Plate Rolling Mill. Overall Length of Roll is More Than 42 feet and Finished Weight is 521,000 pounds

For more than a decade through the mid-1970s and 1980s, the Vandergrift plant, management and labor, hung on with tenacious determination. Threats of closure were met time and time again with increased productivity, effectively delaying the company's shutdown plans. Once again the character of McMurtry's men, now resident in their descendants, was shaping destiny.

The year 1986 brought the beginning of the end, and the beginning of the future. On August 1, 1986, local union president Tim Polka found himself and his co-workers officially locked out of the Vandergrift mill. 6 months of intensive negotiations brought an end to the lock out, but it would be only a temporary respite. In the spring of 1988, the mill officially stopped operations.

Resurrection

Nearly a century had passed since McMurtry and his partner, Captain Vandergrift, fired up the first production lines in this workingman's paradise. The familiar sounds of clanging steel, shift change whistles, and humming machinery were gone. An eerie empty silence now settled over the valley bottom where once the heart of Vandergrift's economy pulsed day and night. But then, when the heartbeat seemed forever gone, McMurtry's dream was dramatically rescued.

Unknown to Vandergrift residents, their mayor, James Kerr, had been moving behind the scenes in confidential discussions with the Allegheny Ludlum Steel Corporation. With foresight that would

Aerial View of the Vandergrift Mill. The one-million square-foot plant is located on a 58-acre site.

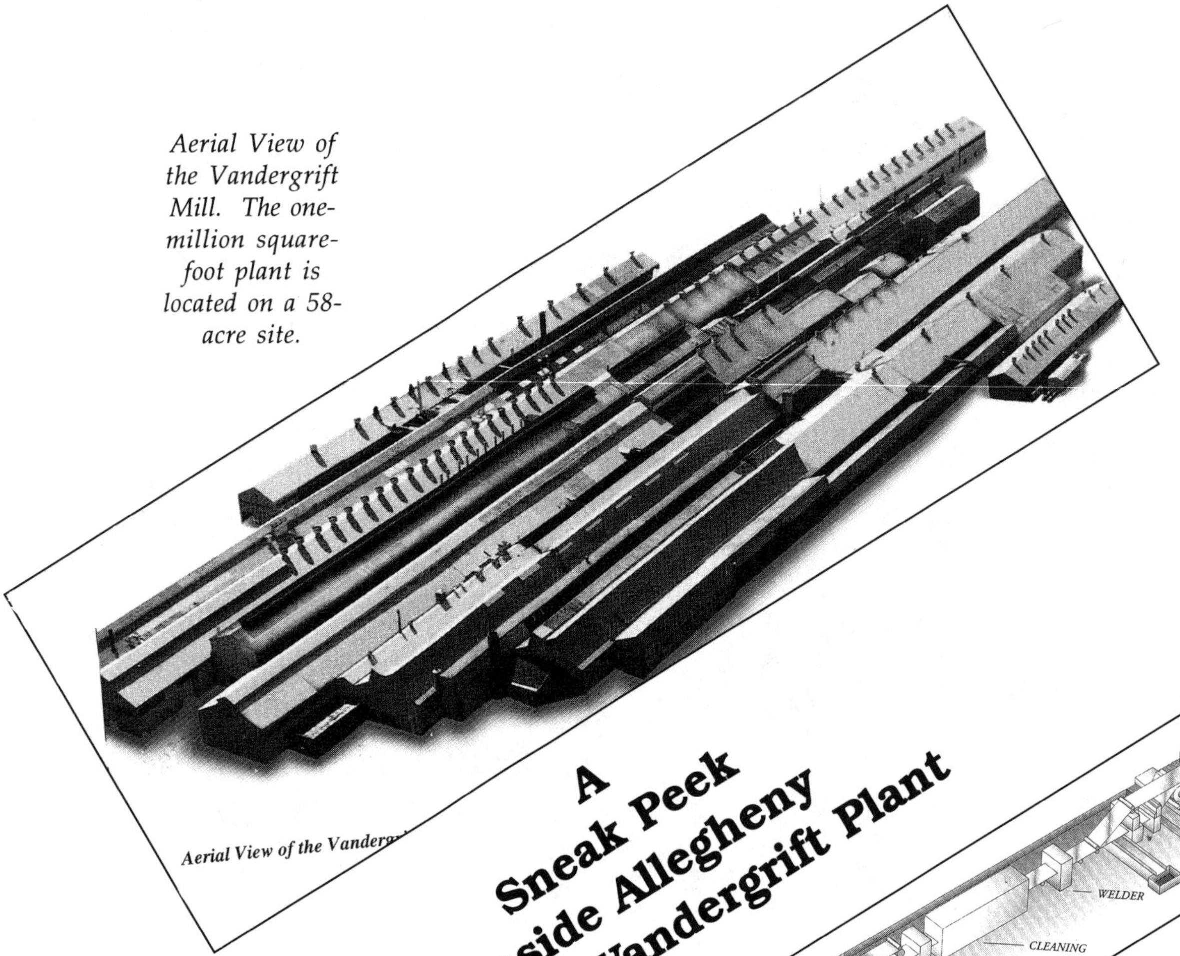

A Sneak Peek inside Allegheny Ludlum's Vandergrift Plant

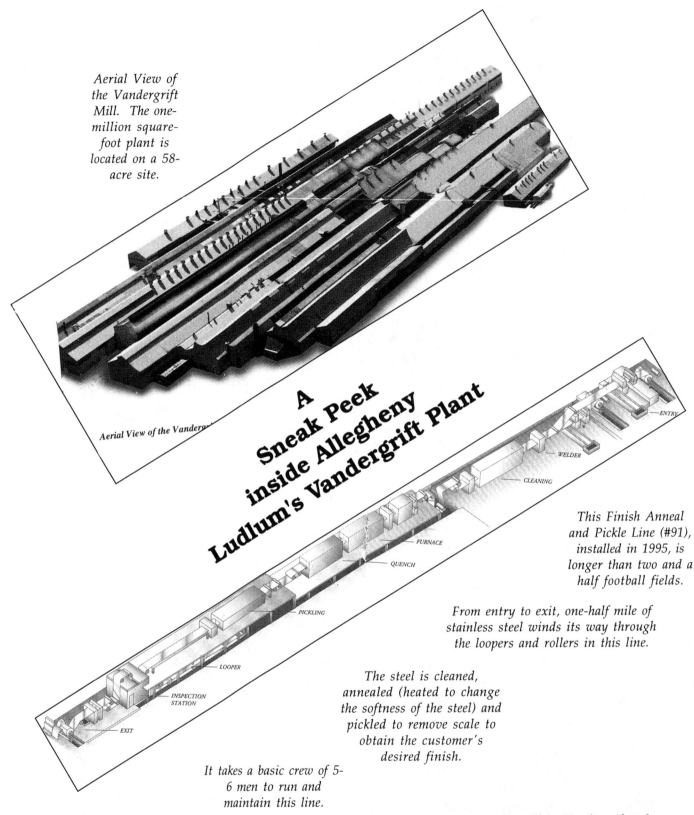

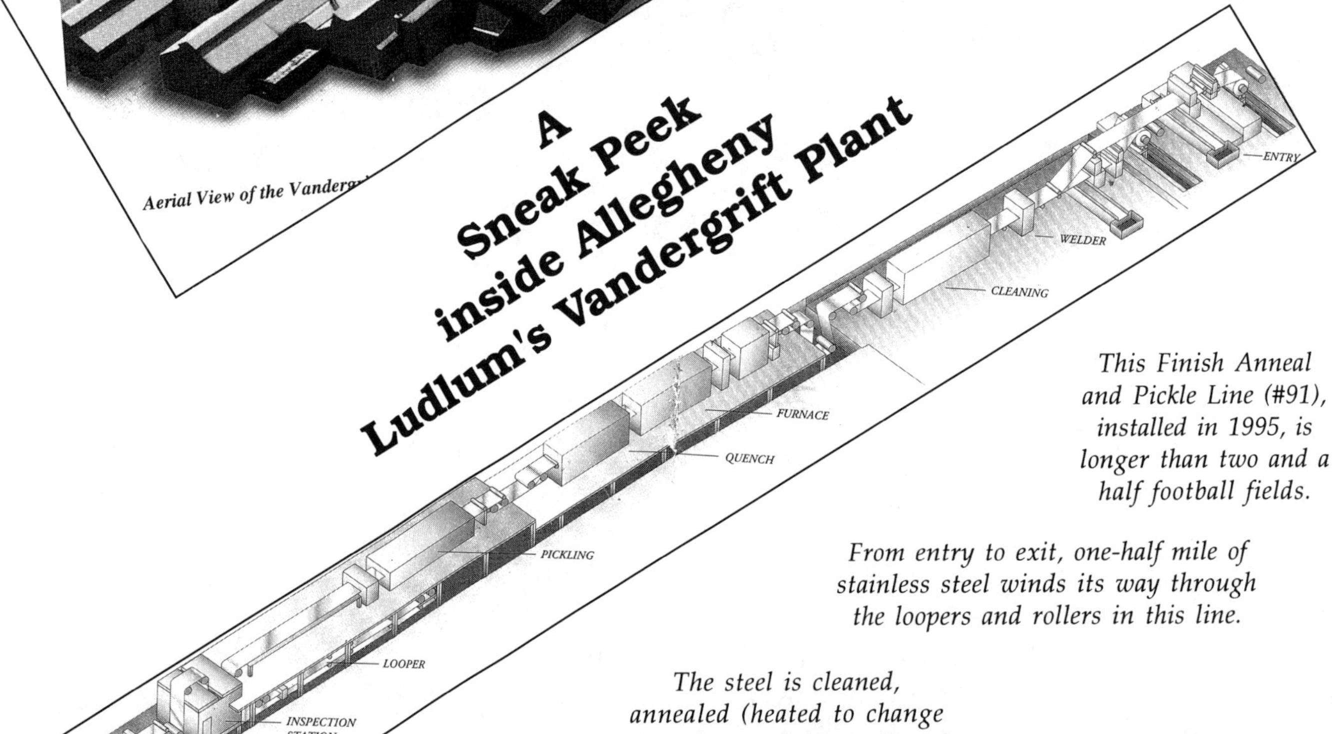

This Finish Anneal and Pickle Line (#91), installed in 1995, is longer than two and a half football fields.

From entry to exit, one-half mile of stainless steel winds its way through the loopers and rollers in this line.

The steel is cleaned, annealed (heated to change the softness of the steel) and pickled to remove scale to obtain the customer's desired finish.

It takes a basic crew of 5-6 men to run and maintain this line.

Allegheny Ludlum's Vandergrift Plant has adopted a motto that exemplifies their work ethic. It is "A Step Above," an echo of McMurtry's desire for Something Better Than The Best.

The mill in Vandergrift today finishes stainless steel that is found in products from computer disks and TV's to double-pane glass windows and refrigerators.

Photo and Diagram courtesy of Allegheny Ludlum

James Kerr

Every ship needs a captain, especially when sailing through rough waters. As mayor, James Kerr was Vandergrift's captain during the often-difficult times of the 1980s. Kerr charted a course during the 1980s that brought it through a storm of unemployment and recession. And so, during a time when things could have been much worse for the town, Vandergrift was kept off the rocks.

Jim Kerr was born in Kittanning, PA, on June 29, 1944. The very early years of his life were spent in Ford City, but he moved to Vandergrift in the second grade. He graduated from the Vandergrift High School in 1962 and attended Indiana University of Pennsylvania and later graduated from mortuary school to became a partner with Raymond W. "Army" Dunmire Funeral Home in Vandergrift. He joined the fire company at an early age and spent 21 years as a fireman. Serving as chief or in some similar capacity for 16 of those years, he also was involved with the Ambulance and Special Services teams.

In 1982, James Kerr was elected mayor of Vandergrift going on to serve a total of 4 terms, not leaving office until he declined to run again in 1994. During his time as mayor, he faced some of the most challenging issues to the survival of McMurtry's town. Through his foresight and planning he became a key player in the Allegheny Ludlum purchase of the closed Vandergrift steel mill. His investment into this issue ensured a solid industrial tax base for the community at a time when other steel towns were falling to ruin.

have impressed even George McMurtry, Mayor Kerr was attempting to build a safety net for his town. In the midst of impossible circumstances, he spurred events that led to the resurrection of the Vandergrift mill.

Only months after the mill shut down, when all seemed hopeless, came the revelation that one of the nation's most notable steel concerns was headed to Vandergrift. After extended negotiations with the local union, and help from State Representative Joseph Petrarca for road improvements, Allegheny Ludlum Steel purchased the now-idle Vandergrift plant. Soon to follow came $200 million in improvements to the facility, including $1 million for its new communications center. The mill is now the showpiece of the Allegheny Ludlum Corporation.

Courtesy of Amy Myers

Entrance to Allegheny Ludlum Steel, Vandergrift

Conclusion

McMurtry's "Better Than the Best" lives on today in a community alive with renewed civic pride. The celebration of a century of excellence has

Parklette Beautification Project

Of all the unique aspects of Vandergrift, one of the most visible is the configuration of the downtown streets. At the curved intersections of some of the streets, small parcels of land were planned to be used as small parks (parklettes).

In 1982, newly elected Mayor James Kerr organized the "Ad Hoc Committee—Direction for the Eighties." From this planning group came the idea for the "Parklette Project." It was an all-volunteer committee, co-chaired by Nancy Kerr and Lois O'Brien, which is still active and self-sustaining.

The goal of the project was to create colorful accents at each parklette and other selected sites that would impress on visitors and those passing through town that Vandergrift was in fact a pleasantly distinctive community. No municipal funds were allocated for this project, so the volunteer committee not only did the planting, weeding, and watering, but raised the funds needed to purchase materials as well.

As an adjunct to this program, Dr. D. Eugene Lossaso purchased the western corner lot at the bridge entrance and had it cleared. He worked with the committee to landscape and beautify that entrance to town and dedicated it to the memory of Vandergrift's Veterans.

spurred a concerted move to historic restorations. The majestic Casino Theater, once neglected and run down, recently reopened its doors to sold-out audiences for live theater presentations. With help from the Victorian Vandergrift Museum and Historical Society, the original town of Vandergrift became part of the National Register of Historic Places in 1995. The organization also operates the new Vandergrift Museum located in the Casino Theater.

Many modern-day men, women, and organizations have worked passionately to maintain McMurtry's ideals. Space would not permit the inclusion of them all. A wise man once said, "The important thing is to make history, not write it." For those true heroes who carry on McMurtry's vision, this is a continuing work. It will be for some future generation to decide which of today's history-makers deserve consideration. Those who truly care about today's challenges seldom care about tomorrow's recognitions. For today, it is enough to note that the idea of "something better than the best" is alive and well in the people of this community.

Photo By Mitch Fryer; Courtesy of Buttermilk Falls Publishing Company

Volunteers Unload Seats for Installation in the Historic Casino Theater

Gazing back through history, it is easy to see how the dreams and ideals of certain men and women are passed down through generations. Dreams and ideals that are founded in integrity and excellence have a way of persevering and growing. Such was the dream and the ideals of George G. McMurtry. Though he claimed his motives were based strictly on profitability, they followed the same ideals of life, liberty, and the pursuit of happiness passed on to this nation by its founding fathers.

One ideal, more than others, the ideal of freedom, perpetuated by McMurtry, left a legacy upon his town that would endure through a century of trials and tests. The opportunity to own one's own house, opportunity to govern one's own town, opportunity to advance by one's own efforts, and freedom of worship were all built into McMurtry's dream. It was from such opportunities and ideals that the character of this community was forged and by which it has continued as "something better than the best." What greater gift can a man leave future generations than quality of character.

> *All hail a prince among men. All hail to the kindly, unselfish, genial friend who was a friend of man. Many men were the beneficiaries of his bounty. We shall not look on his like again. He has gone out of our lives forever, leaving them better for his having lived and planned and toiled. But he has left a heritage which we the living must guard and keep as he would have it kept.*
>
> Printed in the *Vandergrift News,* In Memorial of the Passing of George G. McMurtry, 1915

Courtesy of Ron Ankeny and Allegheny Ludlum

Silver Bowl Given to George McMurtry by the Workers of the Vandergrift Mill. The bowl, today in the possession of the Western Pennsylvania Historical Society, is priceless, but the silver in it is worth more than $60,000.

Reflections Of The Times

Stories of the Day

Vandergrift: A Description

The following is a partial description of Vandergrift as found in the National Register of Historic Places Registration Form, July 25, 1994 by Terry A. Necciai, R. A. (Original area only)

Vandergrift consists of a core of masonry commercial buildings, most of which are two to three stories, surrounded by a few churches and hundreds of two story frame houses, located along tree-lined curvilinear streets. The commercial buildings of the town (primarily along Grant Avenue) consist of a lively variety of architectural types and styles. The most prominent style however, is a brick variation on Romanesque Revival, often intermingled with elements of the Colonial and Classical Revivals. The commercial area, concentrated in the core of the district, is also unusual in the number of row buildings with curved facades following the curvilinear lines of the main intersections. Surrounding the commercial area are streets lined with evenly-spaced frame houses, most of which are stylistically plain, occasionally graced by prominent details of the Queen Anne, Romanesque, Colonial Revival, Classical Revival, American Foursquare, and other styles.

Vandergrift's buildings display a wide variety of colors as well as styles. The earliest buildings in the commercial district were built in a variety of brick colors, including red, orange, yellow, ivory, and brown. A few buildings added in the 1950s are in green glazed tile. A few structures have carrara glass storefronts, a few have modern style marble facings, and several have been altered with scored plywood imitating barn siding. One distinctive feature in Vandergrift is the storefront transom arch, with stained and/or leaded glass, in a sweeping, Art Nouveau-influenced curve over the storefront. The upper stories of storefront buildings often have round-arched window openings, with layers of brick voussoirs, in the Romanesque Revival style.

The residential structures are nearly all frame. Most have porches. The houses vary from repeated, utilitarian styles, resembling company-built housing, particularly in the Hamilton Avenue area, to multi-family houses and some more sophisticated repeated houses along Sherman Avenue, to some almost high-style larger homes along Washington Avenue. The most typical house form has a plan that is essentially American Foursquare, with a facade that is vaguely Queen Anne/Colonial Revival.

Perhaps the most unique architectural feature of the community was the construction of so many corner buildings with curved facades. This arrangement allowed a very unusual architectural effect, where Romanesque and/or Colonial Revival features were repeated across multi-bay facades, with numerous pilasteers and windows. The street intersections, as a result, are surrounded by surrealistically curved walls with an overwhelming presence of the 1890s vernacular architectural details. Vandergrift's architecture, though not its primary source of significance, is important. The town is in many ways a frozen example of the architectural trends of the 1890s, and of the fabric that can be woven from ordinary buildings when assembled with carefully detailed landscape architecture. The architecture of the individual buildings was unusual for industrial towns in the region in this era.

The Vandergrift Churches
Beginnings and Endings

The late 1960s were birth years for what many have called a "new move of God." Much of the teaching of the new move was pentecostal, but with a new title, the Charismatic Renewal. It was named this because of the emphasis on "gifts" or "charismata" that were often displayed among followers. Prayer and Bible study groups sprang up at several places at once throughout the Valley, as in the early days of Vandergrift.

The Vandergrift Ministerium sponsored a local chapter of a nationwide group called Key '73. Rev. Randall of First Baptist Church, Rev. Murray of First Presbyterian, Rev. Hess of First Methodist, and several other pastors were active in forming this group composed of Catholics and Protestants with the purpose of evangelism, worship and Bible study. The group prayed and worked together and placed a portion of scripture in every household in town. They also established a telephone prayer chain, which began in April 1974 and continued until January 1985. Members of this group also helped begin a coffee house ministry for young people.

The group became Key '74, then Key '75 and '76 and took the name "Christian Action Group" in 1977. The Christian Action Group sponsored a Bible study that met in First Presbyterian's social hall for most of its existence. The primary teacher was Rev. Glenn McIlwain, a 700 Club associate. The group frequently held large meetings in local churches and halls and featured nationally known teachers and entertainers. In addition, they held monthly worship services at a local nursing home and sent visitation teams to local hospitals. This group continued until the mid-1980s.

A Catholic prayer group started at St. Gertrude's in 1976. The Rev. Marion Gallo led them in Bible study, worship, and prayer. Dr. Donald Virostek often served as lay leader.

New Beginnings

In 1982, a local group of Christians who had been meeting in a Vandergrift home brought an evangelist to town for regular weekly meetings. These meetings began in No. 1 Fire Hall and resulted in many people coming to faith in Christ and spiritual renewal. The meetings quickly outgrew the fire hall, were moved to North Apollo, and later to the Casino Theatre in Vandergrift. From these meetings 2 churches evolved—Bethel Family Church of Vandergrift and Kiski Valley Full Gospel Fellowship of East Vandergrift.

Bethel Family Church of Vandergrift was founded in January 1983 and serves the Vandergrift community and the Kiski Valley today from its new home at 305 Emerson Street. Pastor Jim Laero and the members of Bethel Family Church developed a community-oriented ministry with an emphasis on building up families and God's people to fullness of life.

The Kiski Valley Full Gospel Fellowship began services in Apollo and called a pastor to serve them. In December 1989, they bought the elementary school building in East Vandergrift. They are remodeling to meet the needs of the congregation and the community. The present pastor is Robert F. Schultz, Jr.

Endings

While the Charismatic renewal was going on, some people were moving on, away from Vandergrift. By the 1980s, so many members of the Greek Orthodox Church on Lincoln Avenue had gone that the church could no longer support a priest. Now, in 1995, the sanctuary is used only for special occasions when a priest from New Kensington or Pittsburgh comes to lead the rituals. The basement of the church is used by the local Meals on Wheels organization for food storage and preparation.

The Vandergrift Free Methodist Church had also suffered from dwindling membership. They voted to merge with the Leechburg congregation to form Kiski Unity Free Methodist Church in 1982. The combined group met in Leechburg until their new building was built in Allegheny Township in 1987.

Another building was lost when in early 1985 All Saints Church in East Vandergrift was severely damaged by fire. The Greensburg diocese did not permit rebuilding, but merged this congregation with the other two Catholic churches, Holy Trinity and St. Casimir's.

Falling population was also cited when this merger was quickly followed in June 1985 by the merger of Holy Trinity and St. Casimir's into one new parish. Holy Trinity's building was torn down in November 1992, and St. Casimir's building was enlarged and remodeled. The new Our Lady, Queen of Peace sanctuary was rededicated on December 6, 1992. Later a new parish hall was built and the former site of Holy Trinity became a parking lot.

History Marked

In 1983, St. Gertrude Church began preparing for their 85th anniversary event. In September, the congregation and all the valley residents received news of a gift everyone was proud of. On September 23, 1983, St. Gertrude Church was officially placed on the National Register of Historic Places, because of its architectural and historic significance. Now flood-lit at night, the tall Romanesque towers and the lovely rose window shine like a beacon over the Valley.

In 1995, as the town of Vandergrift and many churches celebrated 100 years, there was opportunity to view a town filled with unique religious heritage and still rich in the fruit this heritage has given to new generations.

Index of Names

I

J

K

L

Q

no entries

R

S

Index of Topics

N

O

P

Q

no entries

R

S

T

U

no entries

V

W

X

no entries

Y

no entries

Z

no entries

Bibliography

Allen, Frederick Lewis. *The Big Change.* (Harper & Row, 1952)

Blose, Ken. *The End Of The Sixties.* (Information from : 1967 News-Citizen Oct 2, 9, 13, 14, Nov 1, 2, 4, 7, 10, 16, 17, 21, 22 Dec 2, 8, 20, 21, 22, 23, 30; 1968 April 1, 2, 8, 10, 20 May 8, 14, 23, 25, 29 June 3, 4, 14. Comprehensive Plan, Borough of Vandergrift, early 1960s.) (an unpublished short story)

Blose, Ken. *A Man Of Action: Richard Hunger.* (From a taped interview with Dick Hunger with Jeff Garrett, in November 1994.) (an unpublished short story)

Blose, Ken. *It Only Takes A Spark.* (From scrapbooks in the holdings of the Vandergrift Public Library, originators unknown but believed to be Justine Condo and/or Phyllis Murphy Gumbert.) (an unpublished short story)

Buck, Solon J. and Buck, Elizabeth H. *The Planting of Civilization in Western Pennsylvania.* (Pittsburgh: University of Pittsburgh Press, 1939)

Freedman, Russell. *Franklin Delano Roosevelt.* (New York: Clarion Books Houghton Mifflin Co., 1990)

Garrett, Jeff. *A Bulldog In The House: Joseph A. Petrarca.* (From an interview with Joseph Petrarca, Nov. 18, 1994 @ Joe Petrarca's with Jeff Garrett, with Mary Jane Slicker on the camera. Also present: His wife, Madeline Petrarca, and his son, Joseph Petrarca. Also from articles in the *Valley News Dispatch* and the *Vandergrift News*, the third week of March, 1995) (an unpublished short story)

Gumbert, Phyllis Murphy. (1960s?) *History of the Townsend Family.* Paper presented to the Apollo Memorial Library. Courtesy of the family of Mr. H. Clawson, Vandergrift, PA, 15690.

Harpster, John W. *Crossroads - Descriptions Of Western Pennsylvania 1720 - 1829.* (Pittsburgh: University of Pittsburgh Press)

Ivey, Mark; Miles, Gregory; Prokesch, Steven and Symonds, William C. *The toughest job in the business: How they're remaking U. S. Steel.* Business Week, February 25, 1985. pp 51 -53.

Kunstler, James Howard. *The Geography of Nowhere: the rise and decline of America's man-made landscape.* (New York: Simon and Schuster, 1993.)

Lear, Dorothy. *General Practioner.* Edited by Ken Blose. (an unpublished short story)

Nichols, H. W. *Beautiful Grove.* From Fallen Leaves column in *The Vandergrift News,* (196-). Courtesy of *The Vandergrift News* and Buttermilk Falls Publishing Company, Vandergrift, PA 15690.

Nichols, H.W. *First House on Van Site Short on Conveniences.* From Fallen Leaves column in *The Vandergrift News,* (196-). Courtesy of *The Vandergrift News* and Buttermilk Falls Publishing Company, Vandergrift, PA 15690.

Nichols, H.W. *Only Few Still Alive Who Can Recall Farm.* From Fallen Leaves column in *The Vandergrift News,* (196-). Courtesy of *The Vandergrift News* and Buttermilk Falls Publishing Company, Vandergrift, PA 15690.

Nichols, H.W. *Townsend Farm Remembered.* From Fallen Leaves column in *The Vandergrift News,* (196-). Courtesy of *The Vandergrift News* and Buttermilk Falls Publishing Company, Vandergrift, PA 15690.

Nichols, H.W. *Villages Were Numerous Along Old Kiskiminetas.* From Fallen Leaves column in *The Vandergrift News,* (196-). Courtesy of *The Vandergrift News* and Buttermilk Falls Publishing Company, Vandergrift, PA 15690.

Nichols, Henry and Adams, John Adams. *Post Office Opened 20 Years Ago.* Edited by Ken Blose. *The Vandergrift News* Aquaintance Edition, 1918, (No month or day given)

O'Brien, Dr. Joseph. *Rainbow Control.* (Edited by Ken Blose.) (an unpublished short story)

Owens, John. *First 75 Years: A history of Vandergrift.* (Vandergrift, PA: *The Vandergrift News-Citizen,* 1972)

Owens, John. *Levi Gilmer Stitt.* Interview with Levi Stitt in 1948; interview with Mrs. Willavene Mumaw, niece of Levi Stitt. History of Vandergrift Plant, U.S.X. files, no writer, no date. Family history notes of Rosalind Schall Gibson, niece of Levi Stitt. (an unpublished short story)

Rau, Margaret. *The Kiskiminetas River And The Apollo Bridges.* (Apollo, PA: Apollo Historical Society, 1992)

Rau, Margaret. *Rock Furnace.* (Apollo, PA: Apollo Historical Society, 19—)

Shuster, Sandy. *The Closing of the Open Hearth...* (From an interview with John Jenks and John Milberger, former Vandergrift Mill Superintendents, in September 1995) (an unpublished short story)

Stephenson, Clarence D. *The Pennsylvania Canal Indiana and Westmoreland Counties.* (Marion Center, PA: Indiana County Historical Series No. One, self-published by author, 1961)

Tarbell, Ida. *The Golden Rule of Business.* Series of articles from American Magazine, 1915. Later published as a book, *New Ideals in Business (1916).*

Townsend, N.E. (1908). *Recollections of Yesterday at the Old Home. The Vandergrift Citizen,* Vandergrift, PA. Courtesy of the Library and Archives Division, Historical Society of Western Pennsylvania. 4338 Bigelow Boulevard, Pittsburgh, PA 15213.

Wallace, Paul A.W. *Indians In Pennsylvania.* (___________: Pennsylvania Historical and Museum Commission, 1993)

Wallace, Paul A.W. *Indian Paths of Pennsylvania.* (______: Pennsylvania Historical and Museum Commission, 1965, 1993)

___________. *The History of Armstrong County,* Pennsylvania (Pre-1900)

___________. *The Pennsylvania Canal. Greensburg Tribune-Review: Focus Magazine* (June 13, 1993)

___________. *Pennsylvania Canal.* Roaring Run Watershed Association, Apollo, PA, ND

___________. *This Fabulous Century.* Time Life Books (Vol. 3, 1920-1930, 1969)

___________. *The Enclopedia Americana,* The Americana Corporation, New York

___________. *Vandergrift, A Working Man's Paradise.* Iron Age Magazine, Nov. 21, 1901.

___________. *The Vandergrift Citizen.* (Vandergrift, PA: 19—)

Articles:
Basket-Ball Tournament, (1925)
Bear Act at Casino, (April 2, 1925)
Borough Manager's Office Busy, (April 9, 1925)
Borough Manager Opens Office, (March 19, 1925)
Casino Improvement Bonds, (August 2, 1926) {Chapter 3}
George G. McMurtry Fire Dept. Purchases Ladder Truck, (March 12, 1925)
New Fire Truck Driver Appointed, (March 26, 1925)
New Pumper Arrived Saturday, (March 26, 1925)
Open Hearth Banquet Planned For Big Time, (March 26, 1925)
Publisher's Announcement, (March 12, 1925)
Scottdale Wins Co Tournament, (1925)
Shrine Holds Annual Banquet and Dance, (March 12, 1925)
Vandergrift Gets Fine Fire Fighting Equipment, (March 26, 1925)
Vandergrift Transportation Company Bus Schedule, (March 26, 1925)
W.T. Smith Elected Borough Manager, (March 12, 1925)

____________. *The Vandergrift News.* (Vandergrift, PA: Buttermilk Falls Publishing Company, 19—)
Articles:
All Milk Must Be Inspected By The State, (July 19, 1924)
All Ready For The Big Spooks' Revel, (October 30, 1924)
An Opportunity to Get Rid of Rats, (February 14, 1924)
Another Garage Nearly Completed, (October 9, 1924)
Atwater Kent Radio, Advert. (December 15, 1928)
Big Tournament in Tennis Planned, (June 7, 1923)
Boxing Show Attracted Many, (November 2, 1922)
Cannon Dedication Planned, (May 5, 1921)
Casino Theater Awarded to Elliot, (November 1924)
Council Favors—Fill 9th Alley, Steam Utility, Playground Plans, (June 5, 1924)
Council Raises—Cannon Will be Placed in Washington Avenue Park, (February 10, 1921)
Cows in Garden, Owners Fined, (October 2, 1924)
Dead Fish Strew Banks of River, (August 11, 1921)
Deer Reappear in Nearby Country, (August 18, 1921)
Fine New Home for the Sons of Italy, (November 10, 1921)
Foundry Company Will Fill Old Cut, (July 15, 1920)
Glove Company Never Shuts Down, (February 17, 1921)

Golden Jubilee Edition, (December 31, 1956)
Grant Avenue Parking Fight Starts Today, (March 15, 1923)
Green Cab Buys Yellow Cab Co., (October 2, 1924)
Gun Received From War Department, (January 20, 1921)
Home Radio, (June 15, 1922)
Klan Visits Local Church, (November 20, 1924)
Land Company Will Deed Cut to Boro, (June 9, 1921)
Liberty Theater Destroyed by Fire, (January 19, 1922)
Local Musicians Please Radio Fans, (December 11, 1924)
Local Radio Fans Reach Across Sea, (December 4, 1924)
Many Attend Klan Meeting, (October 9, 1924)
Mystery Shrouds Mardolenio Deaths, (March 1, 1923)
New Casino Modern Theater, (December 11, 1924)
New County (Editorial), (April 21, 1921)
No Tenants Thrown Out, (February 23, 1922)
Noted Singer on Lyceum Course, (October 16, 1924)
Oklahoma Boy in Pictures, (November 2, 1922)
Patriotic Society Being Organized, (October 16, 1924)
Plan Opening For New Auditorium, (February 21, 1924)
Popular and Growing Bank, (January 18, 1923)
Radio Hints, (June 19, 1924)
Radio News, (January 25, 1923)
Red Cross Day, (November 1924)
Scrap Shell Cuts Loose at Foundry, (December 22, 1921)
Scrap War Shell Wrecks Furnace, (March 1, 1923)
Seal Sale is Doubled, (January 18, 1923)
Shoplifting is Becoming a Habit, (December 22, 1921)
Six Arrested in East Vandergrift Raid, (November 27, 1924)
Something New In Vandergrift, Credit Plan, Adv. (July 27, 1922)
Speak-easy Raided at North Vandergrift, (January 25, 1924)
Sports - Baseball, (April 19, 1923)
Sports - Baseball, (May 3, 1923)
State Police Raid Many Booze Dens, (March 1, 1923)
Stoughton Building Changes Hands, (February 14, 1924)
Street Car Line Up to the People, (March 10, 1921)
Street Repaired, (October 9, 1924)
Tennis Courts Ready, (July 19, 1924)
Town Purchases Casino Property, (February 21, 1924)

Valley Fair Open Next Wednesday, (July 28, 1924)
Valley Ku Klux Hold Pow-wows, (September 28, 1922)
Van Woman Admitted to Cambria Bar, (January 19, 1922)
Vandergrift to Have Kennel Show, (January 25, 1924)
Will Make Park of Old Railroad Cut, (April 7, 1921)
William J Bryan To Speak Here..., (October 30, 1924)
Wireless Contest, Advert. (April 27, 1922) {Chapter 3}

Other Miscellaneous Issues, Including:
July 22, 1909
June 6, 1910
April 25, 1912
May 2, 1912
May 9, 1912
May 20, 1912
July 25, 1912, to January 16, 1913
August 10, 1915
July 20, 1916
August 31, 1916
July 3, 1919
October 18, 1928
October 29, 1928
January 4, 1929
January 7, 1929
September 30th, 1930
November 17, 1930
August ?, 1932
September ?, 1932

__________. *The Vandergrift News-Citizen.* (Vandergrift, PA: Buttermilk Falls Publishing Company, 19—)
Other Miscellaneous Issues, Including:
Diamond Jubilee Edition , 1972
March 17, 1976
December 4, 1991

The World Book Encyclopedia. Volume 18, Field Enterprises Educational Corporation, Chicago, Ill., 1952.